The National **Literacy** *Strategy*

Grammar for writing

**Department for
Education and Employment**

Department for Education and Employment
Sanctuary Buildings
Great Smith Street
London SW1P 3BT

ISBN 0 19 312401 7

Acknowledgements

- Professor Richard Hudson and Dr Catherine Walters for advice on grammatical content
- Macmillan Press Ltd for permission to reprint, in Teaching Unit 41, an extract from Dennis
  Freeborn, with Peter French and David Langford, *Varieties of English: An Introduction to the
  Study of Language* (Macmillan Education, 1986)

Contents

This book has a two-fold purpose:

- to provide lively whole class activities for teaching the Key Stage 2 sentence level objectives in the National Literacy Strategy *Framework for teaching;*

- to explain and illustrate the varied forms which shared writing can take as a powerful medium for teaching writing.

Part 1

Introduction and rationale

We all use language to think and communicate. Language is systematically organised by its grammar which is inextricably linked to meaning and communication – we cannot make sense without shaping grammatical and linguistic structures. All pupils have extensive grammatical knowledge. Much of this is implicit, but they are able to generalise and improvise from this knowledge. Teaching which focuses on grammar helps to make this knowledge explicit, extend children's range and develop more confident and versatile language use.

This guidance is designed to help teachers teach writing. It focuses on the teaching of the sentence level objectives in the National Literacy Strategy *Framework for teaching*. We have called it 'Grammar for writing' to emphasise the centrality of grammar in the teaching of writing. In the video accompanying Module 3 of the NLS 1998 training materials, Professor David Crystal explains the importance of grammar:

> 'Grammar is what gives sense to language … Sentences make words yield up their meanings. Sentences actively create sense in language and the business of the study of sentences is the study of grammar.'

Some would argue that the study of grammar is worth teaching in its own right because it is intrinsically interesting – and so it is. This is not the primary aim here; our aim is to improve children's writing. Grammar is fundamental to this, as a means to an end, but a means which involves investigation, problem-solving, language play and a growing awareness of and interest in how language works. This book focuses on the teaching of sentence level objectives in the Literacy Hour but, throughout, the emphasis is on how children's growing understanding and use of grammar helps them to write more effectively.

It should be clear from this that the purpose of teaching grammar is not simply the naming of parts of speech, nor is it to provide arbitrary rules for 'correct' English. It is about making children aware of key grammatical principles and their effects, to increase the range of choices open to them when they write.

Children learn grammar as an integral part of learning to speak from the earliest stages. The development of oral language is vitally important in its own right as well as being essential to success in literacy. In the course of development, children will use grammar in a wide variety of ways, often with considerable complexity. Very young children will imply meanings using single words in a variety of grammatical ways. For example, a one-year-old saying 'Milk' could mean: *Look! There's some milk*; *Can I have more milk?*; *Is that one milk?* etc., showing what they mean by tone of voice and/or gesture. Older children often use very complex grammatical constructions in speech which may not be appropriate as written forms. Children frequently encounter very sophisticated grammar in the speech and writing of others which they understand without difficulty.

The National Literacy Strategy sentence level teaching objectives are not intended to provide developmental descriptions of this kind. They focus on a limited but important range of skills that children need for writing. They are about extending and making explicit aspects of children's intuitive knowledge of grammar, focusing on aspects of grammar which tend to distinguish written from spoken texts. The grammatical characteristics of spoken language are different in significant ways from those of written language. These differences are related to the permanence of the written form, and the need to be concise and explicit, and because often the intended reader is separated from the writer by time and space. Whereas speakers often rely on context, facial expression, intonation, pauses, etc. to convey meaning and create effect, writers often use more explicit grammatical structures as well as other organisational features, such as paragraphs, headings and sometimes diagrams, to communicate ideas. The following two texts illustrate some of the differences:

A Today we learnt about taste and Miss Ward put some things out on the table and we had to taste them and what we had to do is they all had numbers by them and we had to taste them and it had a different taste to them and we had to taste them and see if it was sweet, salt, and bitter and sour and I did not taste any sour.

B Taste experiment
We had to taste foods which had different numbers to see if they tasted sweet, salt, bitter or sour. I thought the best taste was cheese and the worst was pickle. I did not find anything sour.

In these two examples, the intentions are similar: to explain the experiment. Text A recounts the events but backtracks and repeats. When written down, these repetitions stand out but, when spoken, they make sense. The speaker joins all the thoughts together with 'and' and uses intonation, gesture and stress to keep the listener on track. Text B is more clearly a written recount. It contains far fewer clauses than A and joins them in more complex ways, ie by subordination rather than the continuous use of the conjunction 'and'. The effect is a more focused and free-standing account which can be read by any reader.

The growth of competence in writing also contributes importantly to the broader development of children's thinking. The more context-free and explicit nature of writing helps children become increasingly reflective about language. By structuring and restructuring ideas in writing, children extend their powers of imagination, learn to express increasingly complex, abstract and logical relationships, develop skills of reasoning and critical evaluation. This, in turn, feeds back into their competence as thinkers and speakers.

It is instructive to look at the key messages about children's writing from the national tests derived from analysis of a sample of scripts. These give a very clear indication of the writing skills that children need to succeed in as they move through to their secondary education (*Standards at Key Stage 2 English, Mathematics and Science. Report on the 1999 National Curriculum Assessments for 11-year-olds*, QCA, 2000).

Key messages about writing from the National Curriculum tests

To reach a secure level 2A by the end of Key Stage 1, children should be able to:

- write with legible and accurate handwriting;
- discriminate and spell phonemes accurately – especially long vowels;
- understand spellings of simple word roots and inflectional endings: 'ed', 'ing', etc.;
- write and punctuate simple sentences;
- sequence them coherently in a text;
- select from an increasing range of vocabulary to enhance meaning, create effects and add precision to their writing.

To reach a secure level 4 by the end of Key Stage 2, children should be able to:

- apply spelling rules and conventions, eg consonant doubling, pluralisation, affixes;
- apply strategies to choose correct vowel formation;
- modify the meanings of words by adding words or phrases for effect and precision;
- develop more varied and complex sentences;
- use commas to mark clauses in complex sentences;
- pay more attention to the ending and thus the direction of the narrative;
- use formal, impersonal styles, eg consistent use of third person or the passive voice;
- review and edit work for clarity and interest, organisation and purpose;
- connect ideas at both text and sentence levels;
- organise texts in other ways than by order of event;
- adapt their writing to the purposes and characteristics of non-fiction text types.

Some of these expectations refer to phonics and spelling which are addressed in other guidance (National Literacy Strategy, *Progression in Phonics* and *Spelling Bank*, DfEE, 1999). Nevertheless, it is striking how many of them are directly or indirectly about grammar – about children's ability to manipulate words in sentences and to link sentences together. Some are specifically grammatical, eg the ability to form and punctuate simple sentences at Key Stage 1 or to develop more complex sentences at Key Stage 2. Others, like the use of formal styles, the purposes and characteristics of non-fiction text types and the direction of narrative also depend on the writer's awareness and control of grammar.

Across the primary years, there are three key features of grammar which need to be addressed. All of these are covered in the National Literacy Strategy *Framework for teaching*. They are particularly important because they mark key differences between the ways in which grammar is used in spoken and written English.

Text cohesion

Throughout the primary years children should learn how to link sentences:

- at Key Stage 1, they should be able to create a coherent sequence of ideas;

- through Key Stage 2, they should learn to select from a wide range of connecting words and phrases, and to use verbs and pronouns consistently to create cohesive chronological and non-chronological texts to suit a variety of audiences and purposes.

Sentence construction and punctuation

- at Key Stage 1: the representation of ideas in sentences is a characteristic of written text which children need to be made aware of through reading and learn to control in writing. Written sentences are differently structured from spoken utterances which can rely on gesture, intonation and stress to fill out the speaker's meaning;

- at Key Stage 2: the ability to link ideas within sentences by combining and sequencing clauses enables children to structure and connect ideas in a wide variety of ways, which create interest for readers and make children's writing more precise, varied, engaging and fit for purpose.

Word choice and modification

- at Key Stage 1, children should draw from their reading an increasingly rich vocabulary, and learn to select words and phrases that add colour and precision to their writing and refine its meaning and are appropriate to its audience and purpose;

- through Key Stage 2 children should learn how to enhance their meaning through the choice of words and through modifying nouns and verbs to add focus, variety and interest for the reader.

The teaching of writing

Evidence from the early stages of the National Literacy Strategy (*The National Literacy Strategy. An evaluation of the first year of the National Literacy Strategy*, OFSTED, 1999) shows that, in most classrooms, while both reading and writing have been emphasised, the teaching of reading, particularly shared reading, has been more systematic and better structured. It is most likely that this was a major factor in the substantial rise in reading scores in 1999. Yet, despite frequent opportunities for writing, repeated encouragement and careful marking, many children still find writing difficult and do their best to avoid it.

The National Curriculum English Order
provides a model of the writing process.
Children should learn to *plan*, *draft*, *revise*,
edit, *present* and *evaluate* their writing. Each
of the elements is important in the production
of a finished piece of writing. Effective
teaching will often focus on particular aspects
of this process, eg planning a story, an
explanation, an argument, or revising a draft to
change or improve it. At regular intervals, all
children should have experience of developing
a piece of writing through the whole process.

However, it is easy to misinterpret this model by treating it as a simple linear process or omitting
essential elements altogether. Consider the following illustration.

Daniel is 10. He has class writing time once or twice a week. This week he has written a story about
a journey, linked to a book read in shared reading time and done some imaginative writing linked to
the history topic on Romans. Mostly, the lessons begin with discussion about the topic. His teacher
helps the class think it through, provides ideas about what to write and builds up a bank of useful
vocabulary on a flipchart. After that, they all begin to write. In the course of writing, Daniel is
expected to help himself but can go to his teacher if he gets stuck. His teacher, meanwhile,
supervises and encourages children as they work. At the end of the lesson, the work is handed in
and Daniel usually receives it back the next day or the day after. His teacher will have identified
some spellings and made helpful and encouraging comments on his work. However, looking back
over his work through the year, a number of things become clear:

- Most of the writing is narrative.
- There is a high proportion of unfinished or poorly finished work.
- The teacher's corrections and comments seem to have had very little effect.
- His writing does not seem to have improved very much.

There is an implicit sequence to this teaching:

> The teacher prepares and stimulates ideas for writing with the class.

> The children write independently.

> The teacher responds, eg discusses, marks, etc.

Setting the sequence out in this simplified way is revealing. It shows how the teaching of writing can
easily be reduced to teaching by correction – teaching after the event – instead of teaching *at the
point of writing*. Thus, most of Daniel's direct teaching is focused on stimulating ideas and preparing
him to write, while he is left to compose, ie to draft and revise, his work on his own, after which the

teacher proofreads and corrects it for him. It should go without saying that responding to and marking children's work remain very important and should be effective (see Module 3, page 51 in the National Literacy Strategy training materials on 'constructive marking'). Nevertheless, set against the National Curriculum model of writing above, this process simply misses out on key areas of essential teaching.

A useful way to think about writing is to turn the National Literacy Strategy 'searchlights' model of reading inside out. Successful readers need to orchestrate a range of cues (phonic, graphic, grammatical and information drawn from the wider context of the text – its organisation and meaning). But, while a reader has to decode, understand and interpret a text, a writer has to invent it. For a writer each 'searchlight' represents a range of *decisions*, rather than cues, that have to be orchestrated to create a text. Many children find independent writing a struggle because they are faced with too many hard things to do at once. They have to plan what they will write, think of which words and sentences to write, work out the spellings and transcribe it all on to the page. Often, most of their attention is taken up by spelling and scribing, leaving little mental space to think about the compositional aspects of their writing. Repeated experiences of this kind are likely to reinforce, rather than overcome, children's problems, making them increasingly reluctant writers in the process.

Teaching at the point of writing, in contrast, focuses on demonstrating and exploring the decisions that writers make in the process of composition. Once embarked on, it soon becomes clear that the writing process model is not linear at all but iterative. Drafting, revising and sometimes the presentation of the text are all aspects of a common process involving constant rereading and improvement. Writers rarely draft without rereading and revising as they go. It is with this kind of process in mind, that shared writing has such a prominent place in the Literacy Hour.

Shared, independent and guided writing

The goal of shared and guided writing is independent writing but, as we saw with Daniel above, the range of decisions facing a writer at the point of writing can seem formidable. Shared and guided writing enable teachers to support children by 'scaffolding' some of these decisions in order to pay attention to others. This is particularly important for teaching composition which, for slower writers, can be obscured because so much of their attention is taken up with spelling and handwriting, which slows them down and deflects attention from what they are writing about. Teaching compositional skills must go hand-in-hand with teaching handwriting and spelling, and children should be learning to compose text from the earliest stages. Handwriting and spelling need to be developed to a level of automaticity where they 'go underground' and cease to dominate children's attention as they try to write. But they must not stand in the way of teaching compositional skills which are even more fundamental to effective writing.

These compositional skills are stated in the National Curriculum and reflected in the sentence and text level objectives in the National Literacy Strategy *Framework for teaching*:

Children should be taught to:

- choose form and content to suit a particular purpose;
- broaden their vocabulary and use it in inventive ways;
- use language and style appropriate to the reader;
- use and adapt features of a form of writing drawing on their reading;
- use features of layout, presentation and organisation effectively.

Understanding and using these compositional skills must be grounded in a rich experience of reading and reflecting on quality written texts, and on the use of these texts as models for writing. The ability to control and manipulate texts for audience and purpose depends on an ability to understand and control the sentences of which they are composed. Reading is not merely a vehicle for writing and has important priority in its own right. However, the assumption that children will simply bring their reading experience to bear in their writing is mistaken. Some children will do this easily but, for the majority, teachers will need to structure these links explicitly.

Shared writing

Shared writing is a powerful teaching strategy and the principal means of teaching writing in the Literacy Hour. It is much more than merely scribing for pupils, writing down their ideas like an enthusiastic secretary. It has an essential place in the Literacy Hour because it enables teachers to:

- work with the whole class, to model, explore and discuss the choices writers make at the point of writing (rather than by correction), demonstrating and sharing the compositional process directly;

- make the links between reading and writing explicit by reading and investigating how writers have used language to achieve particular effects, and using written texts as models for writing, eg through imitation and innovation in the early stages to understanding and using underlying structures and principles towards the end of Key Stage 2;

- scaffold some aspects of writing, eg the spelling and transcribing, to enable children to concentrate on how to compose their writing, eg through the choice of words or phrases and ways of constructing sentences to achieve particular purposes or effects;

- focus on particular aspects of the writing process:
  - planning
  - composing
  - revising, editing and redrafting;

- introduce children to appropriate concepts and technical language as a means of discussing what writers do and internalising principles to apply in their own work;

- provide an essential step towards independent writing by helping children to understand and apply specific skills and strategies.

Key features of shared writing

During shared writing it is important to:

- agree how **the audience and purpose** of the writing task will determine the structure, grammatical features and content;

- **use the specific objectives** from the text, sentence or word level work;

- **rehearse sentences** before writing them down. (In this way pupils are more likely to learn how to compose in sentences. This habit can also help pupils to 'get it right' first time as sentences are orally revised before being committed to the page.);

- encourage the **automatic** use of basic punctuation;

- **constantly and cumulatively reread** to gain a flow from one sentence into another – as well as checking for possible improvements or errors;

- **discuss and explain** why one decision might be preferable to another;

- pause during the writing to focus discussion upon the specific objective but, otherwise, move the rest of the composition on quickly so that pupils' attention is not lost;

- take suggestions from pupils who will make effective contributions, but also ask pupils who may struggle, in order **to check misconceptions** and provide further opportunities for explanation. These pupils should be specifically checked up on when they are using dry-wipe boards to assure the quality of their writing. Where a small group remains uncertain they may be targeted as a guided group;

- make the occasional **deliberate error** to hold pupils' attention and focus on common errors or an error related to the specific objective being taught.

A shared writing session should be clearly focused upon one or two specific teaching objectives at sentence and text level. There are three broad teaching techniques which can be used during a shared writing session to help children move towards greater independence.

TEACHER DEMONSTRATION

Most shared writing sessions begin with demonstration or modelling by the teacher. The teacher demonstrates how to write a text – how to use a particular feature, or compose a text type – maintaining a clear focus on the objective(s). She or he thinks the process through aloud, rehearsing the sentence before writing, making changes to its construction or word choice and explaining why one form or word is preferable to another. The teacher writes the sentence, rereads it and changes it again if necessary. She or he demonstrates at least two sentences. The teacher does not take contributions from the children at this point but will expect the children to offer opinions on her or his choice of words or construction of sentences. Every so often shared writing is used to orchestrate a number of different objectives, calling upon all that has been learned so far. The length of time spent on demonstration will depend on the type of writing, the objective and the attention span of the children. It is important not to try to pack in too much teaching in these sessions but to move on to the children having a go themselves.

TEACHER SCRIBING

The pupils now make contributions building upon the teacher's initial demonstration. The teacher focuses and limits the pupils' contributions to the objective(s), eg previous sentence level work, reading of similar texts, word level work, prompt sheets, writing frameworks, or planning sheets. The teacher challenges pupils' contributions in order to refine their understanding and compositional skills.

The children can offer their contributions by raising their hands, but more considered contributions and fuller class participation can be achieved by asking the children, individually or in pairs, to note down their idea, eg word, clause, sentence. When the teacher receives a contribution from the children, she or he will explain its merits or ask the children to do so. The teacher may ask for a number of contributions before making and explaining her choice. If the children use dry-wipe boards and thick-nibbed pens, they can hold their contributions up for the teacher to read. The teacher can then decide either to choose a contribution that will move the lesson on quickly or a contribution which will stimulate discussion and offer the opportunity to make a teaching point.

SUPPORTED COMPOSITION

The focus here is on the children's composition. Children might use dry-wipe boards or notebooks to write in pairs, or individually, a limited amount of text, sharply focused upon a specific objective. This needs to be swift, and once sentences are complete they should be held up so that the teacher can make an immediate assessment. Successful examples can be reviewed with the class, whilst misconceptions are identified and corrected. The aim is to practise a number of times until the large majority, if not all, of the class have mastered the objective to the point where they can apply it when they write. Progress should be visible and swift.

From time to time, perhaps fortnightly, supported composition should be allowed a longer time than 15 minutes in order to orchestrate recent work on language effects, sentence construction or organisation of a particular text type. How to plan, using a range of different strategies, how to translate a plan into a fluent first draft, how to revise for improvements and how to check for errors will all be considered in different 15-minute shared writing sessions over the year. However, it is essential to bring these elements together to serve a specific composition in which the writer is also required to consider effective use of language and sentence construction in a supported context. During an extended supported composition period of 50 minutes (using the 30 minutes whole class teaching time and the 20 minutes independent working time), the teacher directs the organisation of the composition in two or three mid-plenaries and the children construct their own text, individually or in pairs.

Independent writing

Because of the constraints of time, guided writing cannot always be used as a stepping stone into independent writing. However, most children should be able to manage the transition from shared to independent writing so long as the shared writing is carefully planned to provide the necessary support. The points above on:

- teacher demonstration,
- teacher scribing and
- supported composition

have been made with this in mind and teachers should plan to move through this sequence towards supported composition as a preparation for independent writing. The focus of the work in shared writing should be continued into purposeful writing tasks through which children apply their new learning.

Shared writing sessions can be used to scaffold independent writing in a number of ways, for example by providing:

- a worked out plan for children to write to. This might be a story but could be a non-fiction plan linked to one of the six main text types and related to work in other subjects;

- writing tasks for children to complete or 'infill' in a partially worked text;

- an outline in note form or as a flow chart for children to expand in full prose;

- a clear narrative ending or punch line, with known steps towards it, to be retold to create tension or surprise;

- a basic text to be elaborated by vocabulary changes and the addition of appropriate phrases, eg to create anticipation and interest for a reader;

- a series of statements or sentences to be joined into a cohesive whole text;

- a text to change, by altering its purpose or audience, eg changing a recount to a procedure or altering a first person diary to a third person narrative.

Independent writing of this kind can be focused and challenging. It can flow readily from whole class work in shared writing and be scaffolded at different levels according to children's needs. Tasks like these fit comfortably into the Literacy Hour structure, where the teacher's time can be divided between guided group work and general supervision of work by others. The more focused and structured nature of this kind of writing gives children more control and success in writing and enables the teacher to monitor and support more effectively. The plenary session at the end of the Literacy Hour is an opportunity to reflect on what has been learned over a whole cycle of work from shared through to independent working.

Using this general pattern of support, teachers can plan to move children towards increasing autonomy in their writing. As they become more familiar and successful in these relatively scaffolded independent tasks, the props can be removed. The rate and sequence of this process must be judged by the teacher. Certainly, children should always have plenty of opportunity in all aspects of their work to write independently and teachers must be careful not to allow structure of this kind to lower expectations.

Guided writing

In most classes, the arithmetic of time means that children will receive substantially less time in group teaching than they will in whole class teaching. For this reason, as well as those outlined above, shared writing is likely to be the most significant and influential teaching strategy in the Literacy Hour. Group teaching has important and obvious advantages over working with a whole class and, because it is in relatively short supply in most classes, needs to be carefully targeted to make the most of it. Much of the guidance on shared writing above applies equally to guided writing. The main difference is that guided writing, like guided reading, is an additional supported step towards independent writing, where the onus is on the children to make decisions, compose and revise their own texts. Guided writing should be planned with three major purposes in mind:

- to support children in planning and drafting their own work
  Teachers should support children working on their own independent writing. The work should normally be drawn from previous shared text work with the whole class. As in guided reading, the teacher's task is to help children orchestrate all the decisions needed to draft their own text. But, as in shared writing, the work can be carefully scaffolded so that children can focus on particular aspects, eg:

- retelling a known story in a sequence of complete sentences;
- planning a piece of explanatory writing drawn from a model discussed in earlier shared text work;
- writing the next paragraph in an explanation begun with the whole class;
- writing in a formal style linked to a particular text type using the third person or the passive voice.

- to revise and edit work in progress
  Children who have been working independently should bring their work to a group discussion from time to time. These times should be used to acknowledge and praise, to revise and improve writing:
  - rereading it for clarity and purpose;
  - use of punctuation to enhance meaning;
  - choosing vocabulary;
  - how words and phrases can be strengthened or given greater precision;
  - where and why more complex sentences might be appropriate;
  - cohesion: use of connectives; consistency of tense, time, person; consistent use of pronouns.

- to provide differentiated support for particular groups:
  - to rerun a shared writing session with more support and focus for less secure writers;
  - to prepare a group of children who are learning English as an additional language in advance of a shared writing session;
  - to work intensively with able writers on composing or editing a draft;
  - to work intensively on supported independent writing with less able writers.

Teaching writing in the Literacy Hour

Because we are treating grammar as a means to an end and not as an end in itself, the teaching of grammar must be strongly embedded in the teaching of shared reading and writing at both Key Stages. Nevertheless, teachers need to use these contexts to focus attention explicitly on grammatical features. It is easy to miss this out by taking it for granted in reading and by over-scaffolding the work in shared writing, ie doing the work for the children. Many children develop an intuitive awareness of grammatical forms and features through reading, but do not learn how to articulate and apply these when they write. This is a major reason why so many seem to progress in reading while their writing still lags behind.

Most teaching of writing should follow a similar sequence:

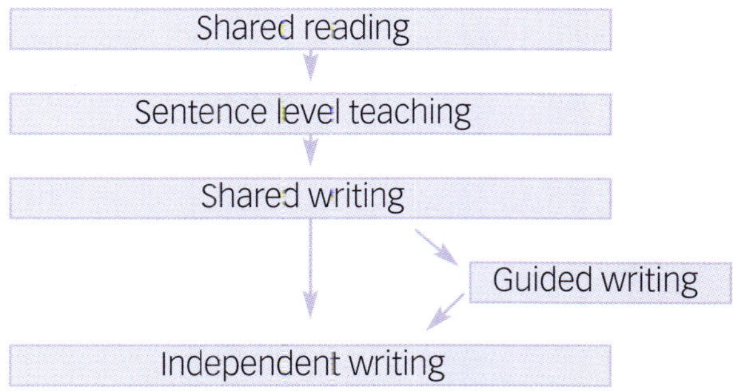

This process fits the structure of the Literacy Hour and allows children to investigate the effects of vocabulary and grammatical choices, within a context of connected and purposeful reading and writing.

The teaching of writing should start from:

- exploration of written texts to identify some important grammatical choices writers have made to achieve their purpose, eg choice of verbs, use of pronouns, sentence structure;
- active investigation of these grammatical features to explore their effects;
- application of these features through teacher-led shared writing;
- use of shared writing as a framework for independent writing supported through group guided writing, where possible.

Teaching text level objectives

This book focuses on practical support for the teaching of sentence level objectives from the National Literacy Strategy *Framework for teaching*. However, these activities are a means to an end, not an end in themselves. The point of teaching them is to improve children's writing. This book also emphasises the role of shared writing as another tool for improving children's writing, but it should not be viewed as a 'programme' for teaching writing. The content for children's writing is derived from the text level objectives which are not covered in this book. However, each teaching unit suggests possible text level objectives through which the sentence level objectives may be practised.

Planning to write starts with establishing a purpose. The purpose (and the audience) determines the text type, which in turn determines the structure, organisation and coherence of the writing. It also determines the types of sentences, their structure and the language features used in the text. To help link text and sentence level objectives, Sections 1 and 2 in Part 3 summarise the main features and some characteristic writing points associated with each text type.

Sentence level teaching can only improve children's writing if it genuinely and continually connects with real, purposeful writing. At every stage, therefore, you should ensure that children:

- consider the effects of the grammatical choices being investigated on meaning, the kinds of text they might be appropriate for and how different options may impact on readers;

- have sufficient understanding to be able to apply this learning in their own writing, and ensure that they do so.

Balancing the teaching time

The National Literacy Strategy *Framework for teaching* gives some guidance on the balance of time to be spent on teaching the various aspects of literacy. Since it was written, some teachers have found that there are several different ways of rearranging the component parts of the Literacy Hour, while still maintaining the overall balance and adhering to the key principles. Many have found that teaching the word level work in the first part of the lesson has been helpful. In other classes, teachers plan for separate or additional phonics sessions or additional guided reading and writing sessions for particular groups.

The summary below offers a guide to the balance of time for the first 30 minutes of whole class work at Key Stage 2 with a view to securing time for the teaching of writing. It is not a rigid prescription but should be used as a baseline for evaluating variations against the need to maintain the overall balance of teaching across the week.

Guide to balance of class work in the Literacy Hour

KEY STAGE 2			
2/3 days per week		2/3 days per week	
Shared reading	15 minutes per day	Shared writing to cover sentence and text level objectives	30 minutes per day
Spelling and other word level objectives	15 minutes per day		

Key Stage 2 principles

- Many teachers have re-ordered parts 1 and 2 of the Literacy Hour to get more continuity between shared reading and the group and independent work that follows.

- Sentence level work should be a specific teaching focus for two to three days per week drawing on high quality written texts but integral to the teaching of shared writing.

- It makes sense to treat the first 30 minutes of the Literacy Hour as a continuous teaching sequence with focused attention to particular grammatical features as an integral part. In the course of this time, children should:
  - work from examples of written texts to explore the effects of particular grammatical choices;
  - investigate these features through activities such as cloze activities, transforming sentences, collecting and classifying words and phrases to understand principles and conventions;
  - apply this knowledge in composing real texts through shared writing.

- This sequence may need to be planned over several days for continuity and extension work, and to develop shared writing into sustained, independent writing.

- What children learn about grammar should help them to make appropriate choices when they write, not just to write complicated sentences for the sake of it.

- This work will need to be revisited and revised at regular intervals.

- Use guided writing times to teach children to compose, edit and revise their writing independently.

- Independent work (which may also be scaffolded) should be used to:
  - continue grammatical investigations from class work;
  - write more sustained text independently.

Pupil targets and assessment

This guidance has also been designed to help teachers set clear writing targets for children. Children's confidence in writing will grow from aiming for and achieving success. Teachers should use the objectives as targets: to explain to children what they are expected to learn about writing, and to involve them in evaluating their own progress towards these targets. Setting pupil targets does not mean setting a different one for each child. For most children, group or whole class targets will suffice, linked to the work planned for shared writing. These may then be adjusted to suit individual needs with more specific individual targets, where necessary.

Pupil targets can be phrased effectively in the form of 'We can …' statements. Teachers can use these statements as a focus for class discussion, particularly in Literacy Hour plenary sessions, and for marking children's work. Such statements enable children to gain control, aim for specific improvements in their own work and, above all, earn praise, encouragement and recognition for success. Targets also provide a focus for discussion with parents and records of achievement as the child moves through the term and the year. Examples of such statements might include the following.

- We can use a capital letter and full stop to punctuate a sentence. (Year 1)

- We can plan our writing carefully by thinking up and collecting ideas and using charts and story boards. (Year 3)

- We can write complex sentences using a wide range of subordinates, such as *because*, *although*, *while* and *since*. (Year 5)

Part 2

The teaching units

How to use the teaching units

This book connects teaching sentence level objectives with teaching writing. There are activities for teaching all the sentence level objectives in the National Literacy *Framework for teaching* and suggestions for applying the sentence level skills and understanding to writing. These have been clustered to comprise teaching units. The table on page 31 shows how the objectives are covered by the teaching units. For each teaching unit there is a similar format:

NLS objective

Principles and explanation

This section defines principles, rules or conventions, as appropriate. Full definitions for all grammatical terminology used in the National Literacy Strategy *Framework for teaching* can be found in the revised version of the Glossary in Section 7 of Part 3 of this book and also on the DfEE Standards Site: http://www.standards.dfee.gov.uk/literacy/glossary/. There may also be teaching points about aspects of the objective children tend to find difficult and an explanation of the importance of the objective to writing.

Sentence level activities

This section contains a number of activities which will further children's understanding of the content of the objective, eg verbs, complex sentences, commas. Some of these activities are described in full. Others are only given a name (eg Function, Collect and classify) because the generic instructions for these are given in Section 3 of Part 3 in this book.

Punctuation fans are required for this activity. Templates for these are contained in the accompanying disk.

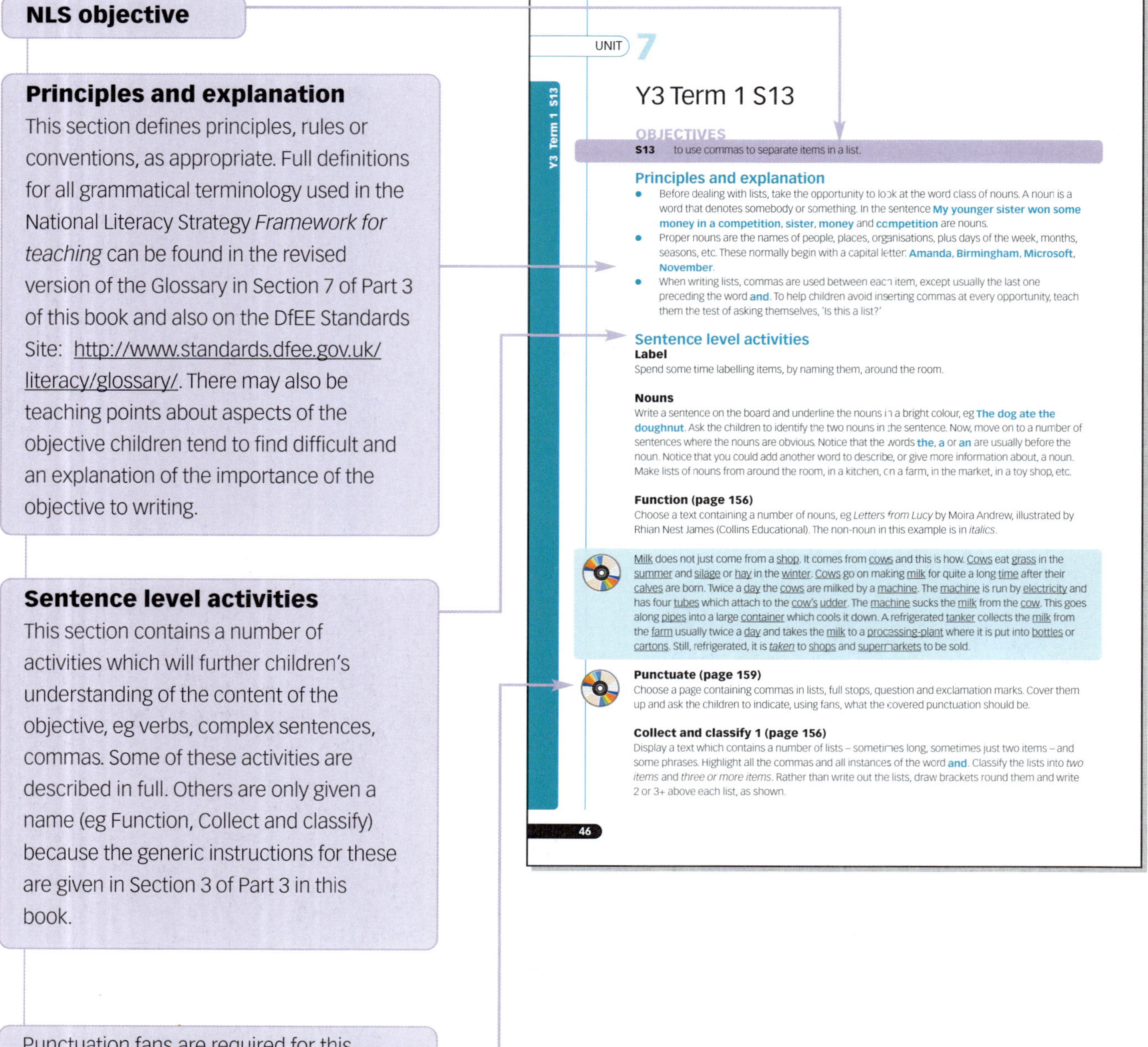

Generic activity and page number for instructions. Many of the activities are repeated each year so general instructions are included in Section 3 of Part 3 in this book. Specific material and variations for carrying out the activity are included here.

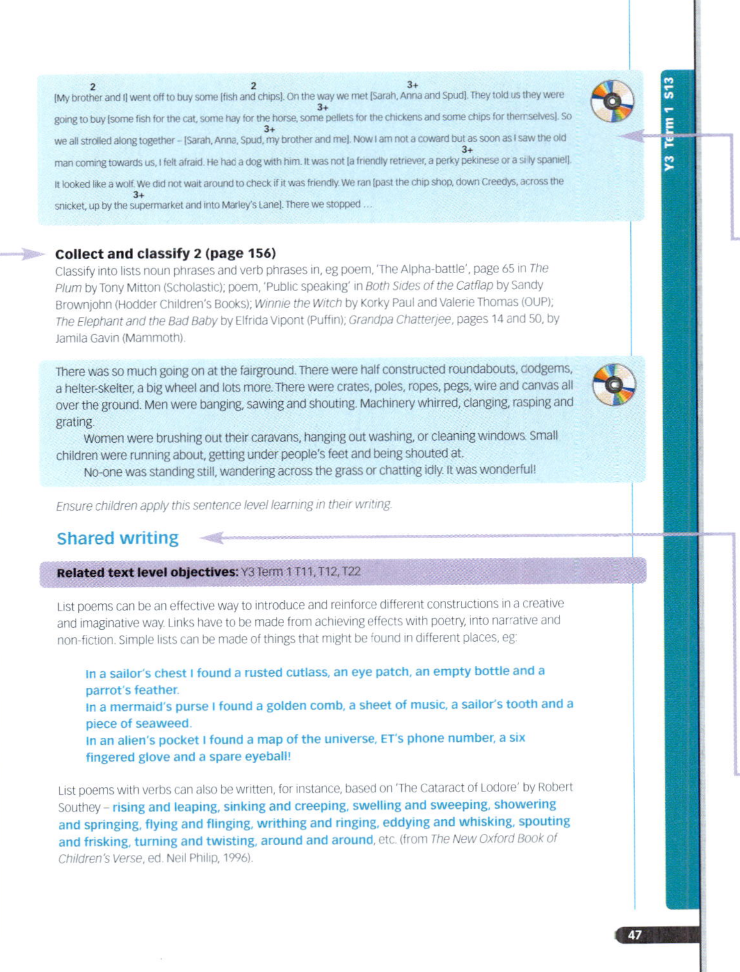

Text for activity

The text features required for the activity are stated and illustrated in the given text. However, it is anticipated that you will mostly use texts from shared reading for these activities. If required, the given texts are contained in the accompanying disk where they are enlarged to A4 format. These may be enlarged further to A2 for use with a class or copied onto an overhead transparency.

Shared writing

Related text level objectives are listed and suggestions for demonstrating the application of the sentence level objective in a particular form of writing are given. This may lead into suggestions for interactive writing and supported composition in which the children take over the composition closely guided or scaffolded by the teacher.

Planning

The activities are intended to be carried out in the 15-minute sentence level time in the Literacy Hour. You may well find that you can do two of the sentence level activities in the 15 minutes. Alternatively, you may do one and start another, leaving the children to complete it in the independent session, and then return to it in the plenary. None of these activities is complete without the children articulating what they have learned both about the principles of the language feature or the sentence structure they have been considering, and the implications of this knowledge for their own writing. You may wish to put the sentence level activity straight into practice in shared writing during the following 15 minutes.

A choice of sentence level activities is included in each teaching unit. You may need to carry out just one activity with your classes, whereas other classes may need to do all the activities and more to give the children adequate practice. But the aim is to move into applying the sentence level skills and knowledge in writing, not to get stuck on activities.

Teaching sentence level activities

- Each teaching unit provides a number of different possible activities to help deepen children's understanding of the sentence level objectives. These activities provide the basis for investigation and discussion about how language is constructed and used effectively in written forms.

- These activities involve the whole class and require the active, brisk participation of the children.

- Children will be motivated by the investigative nature of these activities, but they will need help in articulating their deductions from the investigations.

- There is a **choice** of activity in each unit. The number of activities you choose to do will depend on the previous experience of the children. However, it is important not to spend longer than necessary on these activities, as it is the application of the principles in shared and independent writing which is the ultimate object of sentence level work.

- Some activities are used repeatedly in different teaching units. To save space, the generic instructions for these activities are provided in Section 3 of Part 3 in this book; the page number is indicated after the activity title. Additional instructions and the text, sentences or words for the activity are included in the teaching unit.

- Many of the activities use texts. An example of a suitable text is often included in the teaching unit, but it is expected that you will wish to use a page of text from a book you are using in shared reading, or one the children have already read. Usually the text needs to be marked either before or during the activity. It is possible to mark text by covering the page in the book with a sheet of acetate and using a water soluble pen or using removable highlighting tape. (See the Resources section on the DfEE Standards Site: http://www.standards.dfee.gov.uk/literacy/).

- Many of the activities suggest that children use hand-held dry-wipe boards (see the Resources section on the DfEE Standards Site). The purpose is to involve all members of the class. Usually it is adequate to have one between two children. They take turns in writing. They both discuss what to write. While one writes, the other checks for accuracy. At a cue from the teacher, the children hold up their dry-wipe boards. The teacher scans them quickly, assessing the level of response and deciding on the next teaching move. Sometimes it will be appropriate to take a correct answer and move on. At other times, the teacher may wish to choose an answer which indicates a misperception which is shared by a number of the children and take the opportunity to do some corrective teaching.

- During the activities, help the children to see the relationship between different examples of the focused grammatical feature (eg verbs, commas, complex sentences) and draw out from them the underlying principles governing its use and effect in writing. Avoid telling the children the principles at the outset, but ensure they have all grasped them by the end of the activity.

- At the end of the activity, ask the children to summarise what they have learned about the particular focus element they have been investigating. Sometimes, this can be done first in pairs or threes, using dry-wipe boards to ensure maximum involvement, before entering a class discussion.

- The principles, generalisations or explanation which they have, with your guidance, extracted from the activity should be written on a poster as a reminder for when they use this element in their own writing.

- You should also plan to include references to this element in future teaching.

- Expect children to use what they have learned from these activities in their writing, not only in any immediate follow-up independent writing, but in all their subsequent writing where appropriate.

Teaching writing

Sample sequence: Year 3, Term 1, S9: to notice and investigate a range of other devices for presenting texts, eg speech bubbles, enlarged or italicised print, captions and headings, inset text. Explore purposes and collect examples.

1 Sentence level teaching focus – putting the spotlight on the objective and introducing it to the class.

2 Sentence level activities – interactive whole class activities for maximum involvement using 'show me' and 'get up and go' techniques. Activities include collecting and categorising, transforming, substituting, deleting and predicting, constructing rules and explanations.

3 Define principles – working with the children to define their understanding of the objective. Ask children to articulate what they have learned. They should be able to:

- provide a definition (eg of an adjective) and also

- say something about how it is used.

4 Teacher demonstration and scribing – demonstrating writing in front of the children, talking them through the process, and showing how to employ the objective within the course of a fluent piece of writing. Children may be involved in helping you compose – but always keep up the explanatory commentary and maintain the focus upon the objective in use.

As well as focusing on the day's objective, continually demonstrate how to:
- *rehearse sentences in speech before committing them to paper;*
- *frequently reread the text during writing to maintain fluency and spot any errors;*
- *reread at the end to check for coherence and accuracy.*

5 Support composition – helping children focus on the objective as they try their hand at a short piece of writing. This may involve sentence-makers for young children, working on a whiteboard or collaborative writing.

6 Independent writing – the children write a text, focusing upon the objective.

7 Review – marking and response are carefully focused by the objective. You can now use examples from children's work to make further teaching points. It may be worth asking several children to work straight onto an overhead transparency, so that in the plenary several examples can be reviewed to see what has worked and where improvements might be made.

How the objectives are covered by the teaching units

Objective	Teaching unit	Objective	Teaching unit	Objective	Teaching unit	Objective	Teaching unit
Y3 Term 1		**Y4 Term 1**		**Y5 Term 1**		**Y6 Term 1**	
S3	1	S1	20	S1	28, 30, 31	S1	44
S4	2	S2	21	S2	33	S2	45
S5	1, 2	S3	22	S3	34	S3	45
S6	3	S4	23	S4	35	S4	46
S7	4	S5	24	S5	36	S5	47
S8	4	T15	25	S6	34	S6	47
S9	5	**Y4 Term 2**		S7	36	**Y6 Term 2**	
S10	6	S2	26	S8	37	S1	48
S11	6	S2	27	S9	37	S2	49
S12	6	S3	28	T14	38	S3	47
S13	7	S4	28	**Y5 Term 2**		S4	50
T16	8	T19	29	S1	28, 30, 31	S5	51
T23	9	**Y4 Term 3**		S2	33	T2	52
Y3 Term 2		S1	30	S3	35	**Y6 Term 3**	
S2	10	S3	31	S4	39	S1	53
S3	10	S4	32	S5	40	S2	54
S4	11			S6	41	S3	48, 49
S5	11			S7	40	S4	47
S8	12			S8	40		
S9	13			S9	40		
S10	14			S10	39		
S11	14			**Y5 Term 3**			
Y3 Term 3				S1	33		
S2	15			S2	35		
S3	15			S3	42		
S4	16			S4	43		
S5	17			S5	27		
S6	18			S6	43		
S7	19			S7	43		

Year 3

Teaching units 1–19

Before working from these teaching units, please read the following sections:

- Introduction and rationale (page 7);
- How to use the teaching units (page 24).

A few reminders:

- Instructions for activities displaying page numbers are to be found in Section 3 of Part 3.
- For work on any grammatical feature in a previous or subsequent year or term, please refer to the grammatical subject index Section 8 of Part 3.
- These units do **not** include the teaching for text level objectives.
- The activities in the units can be used, reused and elaborated.
- Sentence level learning should be applied in shared, guided and independent writing.

Y3 Term 1 S3 and S5

OBJECTIVES

S3 the function of verbs in sentences through: noticing that sentences cannot make sense without them; collecting and classifying examples of verbs from reading and own knowledge, eg *run, chase, sprint; eat, consume, gobble; said, whispered, shrieked;* experimenting with changing simple verbs in sentences and discussing their impact on meaning;

S5 to use the term 'verb' appropriately;

Principles and explanation

- A verb is a word (or words) that expresses an action, a happening, a process or a state. It can be thought of as a 'doing' word, eg **shouts**, **has played**, **is skating**, **gives**, or a 'being' word, eg **am**, **is**, **were**, **will be**, **has been**, **liked living**, **knows**, **will feel**.
- Verbs often occur in chains, eg **was living**; **were playing**; **have been working**.
- Every sentence needs a verb.
- There are often many verbs connected with a particular action or state of being, and it is important to choose the right one for meaning and impact.

Sentence level activities

Function (page 156)

Choose a page of a text, eg *The Hodgeheg*, pages 9 or 10 by Dick King Smith (Puffin) or use the example below. The non-verb in the example is in *italics*.

Tim <u>ran</u>. He <u>ran</u> so fast that his feet <u>seemed</u> disconnected to the rest of him. But it <u>would be</u> no good – not with Mitch Morgan behind him. Mitch Morgan <u>was</u> taller and faster than everyone else in their class. Tim <u>hurtled</u> down the alley, the sound of feet <u>pounding</u> after him. His lungs <u>ached</u> and his feet <u>jarred</u> against the ground.

"You'<u>ve</u> <u>had</u> it, Huntley," a voice <u>yelled</u>.

Tim <u>raced</u> round the corner at the end of the alley. Someone's back gate <u>was</u> open so he <u>darted</u> in, <u>pulling</u> the gate shut behind him. He <u>leaned</u> against the wooden fence <u>trying</u> hard not to <u>pant</u> too loudly. His heart <u>banged</u>. His lungs <u>heaved</u>. Down the alley <u>came</u> the sound of Mitch, his feet <u>thudding</u> on the tarmac. Tim <u>squeezed</u> his eyes shut tight. He <u>dared</u> not <u>breathe</u>. Mitch <u>shot</u> past. Soon the sound of his feet <u>faded</u>. Tim <u>opened</u> his eyes – and <u>saw</u> that someone <u>was</u> <u>staring</u> at him out of their kitchen window. The *back* door of the house <u>flew</u> open and a huge dog <u>bounded</u> out.

Action verbs

Suggest an action, eg **Go across the room**, and let pupils try different ways of performing it, providing appropriate verbs to define their actions.

Cloze (page 157)

Try inserting alternative verbs – the simplest you can think of (core vocabulary) and the most unusual (expanding vocabulary). Reread the text to see whether the meaning has been changed or whether the altered verbs really do add impact.

Look up

Provide a list of basic verbs and use thesaurus to find alternative, more powerful possibilities.

Quickmake (page 158)

Starting sentence: **It swirled and fluttered to the floor.**

More cloze (page 157)

Cover the verb chains in any text.

At playtime it **was raining** so they **stayed** in. Mrs Johnson **sat** at her desk, frowning. She **sipped** her mug of coffee slowly, **taking** each sip into her mouth and **swilling** it round, then **sucking** it back through her teeth with a sharp intake. Chris **stared** at his teacher.

"It **is** rude to **stare**," **snapped** Mrs Johnson.

Everyone **looked** up and Chris **did** a cherry. It **felt** as if his face **was** on fire. It **felt** as if the roots of his hair **were** on fire. I **could win** prizes for **blushing**, he **thought**. He **stared** down at the pattern on his desk and **waited**. He **willed** the colour away. When he **looked** back up, no-one **was looking** at him any longer. They **were reading** their comics or **playing** games. Outside the rain **thudded** down.

Ensure children apply this sentence level learning in their writing.

Shared writing

Related text level objectives: Y3 Term 1 T6, T12

Children should be encouraged to think of appropriate verbs as they are writing, rather than just leaving it to the redrafting stage.

Model the beginning of a poem based on the senses, where it is so quiet that you can hear many things that normally cannot be heard, such as an ant walking. Use a repeating pattern to provide a structure, eg:

> **It was so quiet that I heard**
> **an ant march across the lawn.**
> **It was so quiet that I heard**
> **a leaf uncurl like a green tongue.**
> **It was so quiet that I heard**
> **a raindrop skid down the window pane …**

The children's choice of verbs may be somewhat lacklustre. Help them select unusual and specific verbs. Pause at each verb, giving children a moment to write their suggestion on their dry-wipe boards. They should hold up their suggestions and you choose, giving reasons for your choice.

Y3 Term 1 S4 and S5

OBJECTIVES

S4 to use verb tenses with increasing accuracy in speaking and writing, eg *catch/caught, see/saw, go/went*, etc. Use past tense consistently for narration;

S5 to use the term 'verb' appropriately;

Principles and explanations

- The tense of a verb indicates when the action happened. In English the regular past tense ending is **-ed**, but there are many irregular past tenses, eg **caught**, **found**, **crept**.
- Certain text types are usually in the past (narrative/recount); some are in the present (instructions, explanations, reports).
- Some dialects have a number of non-standard verb forms, which can be particularly difficult for children to notice, eg **He was frit**; **I seen her**. Note any local dialect forms and their standard English equivalents and help pupils recognise where the standard English version is appropriate.

Sentence level activities

Compare (page 157)

Display a text and another version written in a different tense, eg:

Frogs live in water and are found throughout the world. Some frogs in other parts of the world are brightly coloured. In Great Britain they are a dark green colour. In South America there is a tree frog that exudes a poisonous substance onto its skin.	Frogs lived in water and were found throughout the world. Some frogs in other parts of the world were brightly coloured. In Great Britain they were a dark green colour. In South America there was a tree frog that exuded a poisonous substance onto its skin.
They eat insects. They catch the insects with their tongue. A frog's tongue has a sticky substance on it and this helps them to catch insects. The tongue is quite long and they flick it out suddenly. This takes the insect by surprise.	They ate insects. They caught the insects with their tongue. A frog's tongue had a sticky substance on it and this helped them to catch insects. The tongue was quite long and they flicked it out suddenly. This took the insect by surprise.

Discuss the effect of using the present and past tense in non-chronological reports such as this. Point out how inappropriate it is to use the past tense here. This is not history, but what is happening now.

Collect and classify (page 156)

Classify the verbs in the Compare activity above into those which end in **-ed** and those which do not. Continue to collect verbs in reading to add to each list. Introduce the word 'tense'.

Change

Say some verbs, eg **catch**, **go**, **see**, **ask**, **play**, **sleep**, **read,** and ask the children to write the past tense version on their dry-wipe boards.

Replace (page 160)

Write a recount of a text in the present tense, eg *Goal* by Colin McNaughton (Collins).

Non-standard

Build a list directly from pupils' work (do not reveal sources) of non-standard forms of verbs in past tense, eg **He goed away**. Provide standard versions. Use the list for pupils to check own work. The children can take it in turns during shared writing to spot either inconsistent use of tense or non-standard forms.

Oral

Ask the children to relate briefly an incident that happened to them. Ask the class to listen out for the past tense verbs and write as many as they can on their dry-wipe boards. Check that the narrator does not veer away from the past tense.

Improve (page 161)

Write a text which slips between tenses and ask the children to make it consistent, eg:

Jo crept along to Grandma's room. She edged the door open and peeped inside. On the bedside table stood the package. Jo held her breath and walked to the table. The package was like a magnet. It seemed to draw her in. She had to know what was inside. She picks it up and feels the shape. In her mind she sees a thin necklace of pink cowrie shells. She knows it is wrong but it is too tempting. The paper at the edge of the package is loose. Her fingers itch.

Ensure children apply this sentence level learning in their writing.

Shared writing

Related text level objectives: Y3 Term 1 T9, T10, T15

Encourage children to rehearse their sentence in their heads before writing, to read it after they have written it and to reread paragraphs to ensure they have not strayed out of the tense.

Write narratives with the children. Develop a feel for the characteristic voice of narrative by using interesting verbs rather than only the mundane **went**, **got** and **came**. Use speech verbs to describe how a character speaks, eg **shrieked**, **murmured**. Start a new line for each new speaker. Remind pupils of the need not to shift tense.

- For those children who have not yet internalised some of the irregular past tense verb forms, make opportunities in shared writing to model use of verbs in the past tense: **slid** instead of **slided**, **made** instead of **maked**.
- In guided writing, look out for children straying into the present tense in the middle of writing a narrative and take the opportunity to put them back on track.

Y3 Term 1 S6

OBJECTIVES

S6 to secure knowledge of question marks and exclamation marks in reading, understand their purpose and use appropriately in own writing;

Principles and explanation

- Questions are sentences that are usually meant to gain a response. They may be asked to seek information, ask permission or help or as a polite demand, eg **Could you be quiet?**
- Some questions begin with question words such as **who? what? why? where? when?**
- Some questions are statements with the words re-ordered, eg **Has he got a pair of scissors? Is she better? Can you play the piano?**
- Polite commands and questions asking for permission or help often start: **Please may … ?, Could … ?, Would it be possible … ?**
- An exclamation is an utterance expressing emphasis, eg emotion (joy, wonder, anger, surprise, etc.), irony or facetiousness. It is usually followed in writing by an exclamation mark (!).
- Exclamations such as **Oh dear! Ow! What a beautiful day!** are examples of sentences without verbs.

Sentence level activities

Investigating questions 1

Make a statement sentence, eg **Paul jumped off his bike.**, on a sentence maker, washing line or computer screen, or even hand the children word cards to make a human sentence. Ask the children, 'If this is the answer, what would the question be?' **Did Paul jump off his bike?** Ask the children to re-order the sentence to create the question and ask what else is required. Write the question on the board. Think of other questions this statement might be the answer to, eg **Who jumped off his bike? What did Paul do? What did Paul jump off? Whose bike did he jump off?**

Investigating questions 2

What questions would prompt the following answers?

- Paul jumped off his bike because he saw a monster. (**Why did … ?**)
- Paul jumped off his bike just before lunch. (**When did … ?**)
- Paul jumped off his bike awkwardly. (**How did … ?**)

Notice the construction of all these questions in relation to each other and the answer. Look at the question words: **who? where? when? what? why?** These are all questions of information. Give the children another statement to write questions for in independent time.

To generate information on a non-fiction topic, or to plan a recount or narrative, questions of information are needed.

- Use a 'question hand' (on each finger there is a different 'wh' word – who? where? when? what? why?) to generate questions in other subject areas, eg science investigations.
- Use the 'question hand' to plan recounts and narrative: who? – characters; where? – setting; when – did this occur?; what – happened?, why? – underlying theme.

Different sorts of questions

List the sorts of questions children ask in the classroom, eg **Can we go out to play?** and typical questions asked at home, eg **Have you tidied your room?** Collect questions into two sorts: information or permission/help/demand. Draw the children's attention to your own questions – and theirs. Discuss which type of question they are.

Collect and classify (page 156)

Search through books for exclamation marks. Discuss how they are used and think up some categories: surprise and fear, amusement, loudness, etc. Practise using the intonation of the voice to express what the exclamation mark is indicating – avoid simply shouting.

Ensure children apply this sentence level learning in their writing.

Shared writing

Related text level objectives: Y3 Term 3 T14

- Use work from across the curriculum to generate a list of statements: **What we know** or **What we have found out**. Alongside this, list questions under the title, **What we would like to know**.
- When discussing poetry/narrative, encourage children to ask questions about the text – both the content and the way it is written.
- After reading a poem/picture book, discuss what the children liked/did not like, and what puzzled them – frame the puzzles as questions to ask the author.
- List what the children know about a character and the questions they'd ask him or her.
- Use questions in stories to draw the reader in, eg **What sound was it?**
- Compose question poems. Read the opening of Blake's 'Tyger'. Notice how the poet asks the tiger a series of questions, eg 'In what distant deeps or skies/burnt the fire of thine eyes?'. List possible questions to ask different creatures. Use the idea from Sandy Brownjohn's book, *Does It Have To Rhyme?* (Hodder & Stoughton) for writing a poem based on questions and answers.

> Now what could I ask a tiger – perhaps where his stripes came from, so I'm going to write **Tiger where did you find those dark stripes?** There I have used a question mark. Now for the reply. Let's make it really magical – **I found them in the shadows on the moon.** What might I ask an eagle? Who could help me with a question. In pairs decide on a question. Let's see who is ready. Sally? Yes, **Why do you live in the clouds?** That is a good one. Quick, work in pairs to write an answer. Hold up your boards.

- List a series of questions to ask different creatures. Beside each, invent magical and poetic answers. Pupils can work next in pairs, setting each other questions about creatures, plants or other aspects of nature such as a mountain, a river, a snow flake.
- When revising writing, check that full stops, capital letters, question and exclamation marks are all in place.

Y3 Term 1 S7 and S8

OBJECTIVES

S7 the basic conventions of speech punctuation through: identifying speech marks in reading; beginning to use in own writing; using capital letters to mark the start of direct speech;

S8 to use the term 'speech marks';

Principles and explanation

- All fiction uses a new line for each speaker.
- All spoken words are enclosed in speech marks.
- All non-spoken words are outside the speech marks.
- The break between speech and 'non-spoken words' is normally signalled by a comma, eg
  'Come in here,' said dad. 'We've found it.'
- A capital letter signals the start of direct speech.
- Emphasise the importance of starting each *different* speaker on a new line (a convention shared with play scripts). For less able writers this is more important than punctuation in making their dialogue intelligible, and provides a good basis for adding punctuation at a later stage.

Sentence level activities

Collect and classify (page 156)

Mark all the speech marks in a page of text, eg *Hmm* by Colin McNaughton (Anderson Press). Check that they are all enclosing the words actually spoken. Look at the words outside speech marks and classify their function.

"What's your baby called then?" asked Sam.

"Teddy," muttered Mum, pausing for a moment.

"That's a silly name, I reckon," said Sam.

"Why's that?" demanded Mum, tidying up the dishes and giving the table a quick wipe.

"Well, he'll get teased, I reckon." Sam stared at the baby. It was fast asleep. He could see that it was breathing as the nostrils flared ever so slightly with each breath.

"My Mum reckons I looked like a treacle pudding when I was born," whispered Sam.

"Come along now," snapped Mum, wiping the table again with a sudden flourish. "There's a lot of tidying left to be done in your room."

Sam looked at the baby's cheeks. Fat as a hamster, he thought to himself. The cheeks were so podgy that he wanted to poke them, to feel them sink in. But he didn't dare.

"All right, I reckon I'd best get it done," mumbled Sam, as he headed for the stairs.

- Spot speech marks in texts. Ask **Who spoke this? What did they say? How did they say it?** Read aloud with expression.
- When gathering opinions or questions by class members, use speech bubbles to capture different children's views.
- Mask out what a character says. Given what we know about the character, decide what they might say.
- When reading aloud, adopt voices or use children to read different characters. Highlight text to indicate different speakers' lines.
- Two children role-play a brief conversation. Use this to write down what has been said, writing the spoken words in a different colour.
- Convert speech bubbles to speech using speech marks.

- Convert a section of the dialogue into a play, showing how this text type doesn't use speech marks and how the characters' identification is placed in the margin.
- Convert a section of a play into narrative and direct speech.

Ensure children apply this sentence level learning in their writing.

Shared writing

Related text level objectives: Y3 Term 1 T2, T10, T15

Choose two characters from a story being used in shared reading. Write an opening paragraph of about four sentences which tells a little bit about the two characters with contributions from the children. Now ask children to imagine a brief conversation between them. Begin the next paragraph with one of the characters asking the other a question. Draw attention to the new paragraph, the capital letter, question mark and speech marks and comma. Ask the children to contribute the answer and write it, indicating the start of a new paragraph. Continue the conversation with some background narrative, sometimes demonstrating and sometimes asking the children to have a go on dry-wipe boards.

Abdi is going to speak next. In that case we need a new line, because he's a new speaker. And we need to leave a little a space before the new line, and to open the speech marks. Right. What might it say now, think about the sort of character he is, would he just give the key away? **'I know where the key can be found but why should I help?'** OK, is that all he might say for now? I'll close speech marks to show he has finished speaking. **"** And of course I need to show who has been speaking so I'll add this: **said Abdi**. Actually, I think I'll show how he said it because I want to show the reader the sort of person he is: **said Abdi with a thin smile**. What do we need to separate the direct speech from the 'said' bit? Fine, a comma. So I'll put one in here. I've written a thin smile because I want to show the reader that he is not generous, he is rather mean so his smile would be thin and mean too …

Y3 Term 1 S9

OBJECTIVES

S9 to notice and investigate a range of other devices for presenting texts, eg speech bubbles, enlarged or italicised print, captions and headings, inset text. Explore purposes and collect examples;

Principles and explanation

- There are many different ways to present and organise texts to help the reader.
- A range of different devices is used by writers with the intention of helping the reader, eg by drawing attention to certain key aspects of a text or presenting information in an easily accessible way. It is easy for adults to take presentational devices and text conventions for granted. Help children notice not just the meaning of texts, but also the ways authors, designers and publishers draw attention to that meaning.

Sentence level activities

- Show the children a page(s) in which certain devices such as bold, capitalisation, italic have been used. Discuss why the author has chosen to use them.
- Give out a number of texts for the children to look through in groups to find more. They should consider why particular devices are used and be prepared to tell the class.
- Under headings: Bold, All caps, Italic, Underlined, Enlarged, Other, classify the examples to see whether authors follow similar conventions.
- Examine some non-fiction texts to ascertain how authors use headings, subheadings, captions.
- Children survey different texts, including magazines, newspapers, comics. Cut out different features.
- Investigate the use of different typefaces in a non-fiction book, eg for headings, captions, index, glossary.
- Return to a book you have just read with the class, and 'read' it again for organisational and presentational devices: How did the author (and designer) help us to read this the way they wanted us to read it?
- Look at dictionaries and glossaries to see different ways to present information.
- Look at flow charts and diagrams as examples of different ways to present information. Discuss whether flow charts and diagrams can put messages across more clearly than prose.

Ensure children apply this sentence level learning to their writing.

Shared writing

Related text level objectives: Y3 Term 1 T19, T21, T22

In shared writing use such devices as bold, enlarged and italicised print sparingly, otherwise children may overuse them. Speech bubbles can be used in other curriculum areas to capture key questions for investigations or key comments and observations made by different children, eg writing up observations in science. Headings and subheadings are increasingly useful in non-fiction as they help children separate and organise information into distinctive paragraphs.

If possible, conduct shared writing sessions using ICT facilities, demonstrating the use of italic and bold print, etc.

UNIT **6**

Y3 Term 1 S10, S11 and S12

OBJECTIVES

S10 to identify the boundaries between separate sentences in reading and in their own writing;
S11 to write in complete sentences;
S12 to demarcate the end of a sentence with a full-stop and the start of a new one with a capital letter;

Principles and explanation

A simple sentence consists of one clause (including just one verb or verb phrase). At the heart of many simple sentences is an actor, eg **John/the dog**, and an action, eg **ate/barked** – these should be identifiable no matter how much extra information or detail is added, eg *The* **brave** *lady* **with the big red umbrella** *fed* **the small hungry lion.**

Sentence level activities

Challenge

Challenge the children to produce examples of the shortest possible sentence with a subject and a verb (an actor and an action), eg **John ate., Hermione kicked.**

Expansion

Choose one short sentence and show how you can gradually expand it.

SUBJECT	VERB + ENDING
John	ate.
The boy	ate lunch.
The unhappy boy	ate his meagre lunch.
The unhappy boy with no shoes	ate his meagre lunch on the doorstep.

Complete

Emphasise the sense of completeness which comes from having these two elements in place. **The brave lady with the big red umbrella** is not complete – she needs a verb, an action, eg *fed* **the small hungry lion**; *was* **sad**. On strips, provide sentence + conjunction and pronoun, eg **Liam picked up the key but he ….** The children have to complete the sentences.

Cloze (page 157)

Provide a passage with no full stops. Ask the children to read the passage aloud and decide where the stops go.

Consequences

Play a Consequences-type game in pairs. Each child writes the first half of a sentence (the subject) and folds the paper over left to right so that the last letter is showing and the other person knows where to continue writing. They exchange papers and then write a verb and the remainder of the sentence. They exchange papers again and open them up to have a look at what sentence has resulted.

Construct (page 158)

SUBJECT (BLUE)	VERB + ENDING (RED)
The old dog	was in the attic.
The teacher	tried to get in through the window.
A secret mirror	barked at the postman.
The old lady in the teashop	shouted loudly.
Mary, Mary, quite contrary	wore a yellow dress.
The fly in the ointment	slid down the banisters.
Simple Simon	fried herb sausages for tea.
My friend Samuel	wanted a ride in a balloon.
Mr Smith	met a pieman.
The oldest magician in the world	grew silver bells.
The grand old Duke of York	cried.
	grew roses in a boot.
	made delicious pies.
	wore green slippers.
	danced the hornpipe.
	sledged all the way down the hill.
	couldn't get down.
	fell in the pond.
	tripped over the bucket.

Variation on construct

Give out equal numbers of subject and *and* cards and double the number of ending cards (eg seven subject cards, seven *and* cards and fourteen ending cards). The children should make sentences using one subject, *and*, and two endings.

Ensure children apply this sentence level learning in their writing.

Shared writing

Related text level objectives: Y3 Term 1 T11, T22

Write a simple non-chronological report on a subject derived from another curriculum area.
- Plan the content of the report using a planning frame. Agree the content of each paragraph.
- Write the opening paragraph, thinking aloud, and explaining why you are choosing specific words and particular constructions. Reread and make alterations as necessary. Demonstrate how to take the planning sheet and turn the notes made into sentences.
- Ask the children to contribute the next two sentences of the next paragraph. Check they are keeping to the subject matter agreed for the paragraph and that they have constructed two complete sentences and can tell you where they are demarcated.
- Complete the paragraph and reread both paragraphs.
- Invite the children in pairs to construct the two or three sentences of the next paragraph, correctly punctuated on dry-wipe boards. Review some of these.
- Let children take turns to compose and demarcate sentences. Partners should check each other's writing.
- These reports can be completed in independent or guided time.

Correctly punctuated sentences should be expected at point of writing – not as an afterthought in revision – as they are helpful to the writer to make sense as she or he composes and rereads.

Y3 Term 1 S13

OBJECTIVES

S13   to use commas to separate items in a list.

Principles and explanation

- Before dealing with lists, take the opportunity to look at the word class of nouns. A noun is a word that denotes somebody or something. In the sentence **My younger sister won some money in a competition**, **sister**, **money** and **competition** are nouns.
- Proper nouns are the names of people, places, organisations, plus days of the week, months, seasons, etc. These normally begin with a capital letter: **Amanda**, **Birmingham**, **Microsoft**, **November**.
- When writing lists, commas are used between each item, except usually the last one preceding the word **and**. To help children avoid inserting commas at every opportunity, teach them the test of asking themselves, 'Is this a list?'

Sentence level activities

Label

Spend some time labelling items, by naming them, around the room.

Nouns

Write a sentence on the board and underline the nouns in a bright colour, eg **The dog ate the doughnut**. Ask the children to identify the two nouns in the sentence. Now, move on to a number of sentences where the nouns are obvious. Notice that the words **the**, **a** or **an** are usually before the noun. Notice that you could add another word to describe, or give more information about, a noun. Make lists of nouns from around the room, in a kitchen, on a farm, in the market, in a toy shop, etc.

Function (page 156)

Choose a text containing a number of nouns, eg *Letters from Lucy* by Moira Andrew, illustrated by Rhian Nest James (Collins Educational). The non-noun in this example is in *italics*.

Milk does not just come from a shop. It comes from cows and this is how. Cows eat grass in the summer and silage or hay in the winter. Cows go on making milk for quite a long time after their calves are born. Twice a day the cows are milked by a machine. The machine is run by electricity and has four tubes which attach to the cow's udder. The machine sucks the milk from the cow. This goes along pipes into a large container which cools it down. A refrigerated tanker collects the milk from the farm usually twice a day and takes the milk to a processing-plant where it is put into bottles or cartons. Still, refrigerated, it is *taken* to shops and supermarkets to be sold.

Punctuate (page 159)

Choose a page containing commas in lists, full stops, question and exclamation marks. Cover them up and ask the children to indicate, using fans, what the covered punctuation should be.

Collect and classify 1 (page 156)

Display a text which contains a number of lists – sometimes long, sometimes just two items – and some phrases. Highlight all the commas and all instances of the word **and**. Classify the lists into *two items* and *three or more items*. Rather than write out the lists, draw brackets round them and write 2 or 3+ above each list, as shown.

[My brother and I]² went off to buy some [fish and chips]². On the way we met [Sarah, Anna and Spud]³⁺. They told us they were going to buy [some fish for the cat, some hay for the horse, some pellets for the chickens and some chips for themselves]³⁺. So we all strolled along together – [Sarah, Anna, Spud, my brother and me]³⁺. Now I am not a coward but as soon as I saw the old man coming towards us, I felt afraid. He had a dog with him. It was not [a friendly retriever, a perky pekinese or a silly spaniel]³⁺. It looked like a wolf. We did not wait around to check if it was friendly. We ran [past the chip shop, down Creedys, across the snicket, up by the supermarket and into Marley's Lane]³⁺. There we stopped …

Collect and classify 2 (page 156)

Classify into lists noun phrases and verb phrases in, eg poem, 'The Alpha-battle', page 65 in *The Plum* by Tony Mitton (Scholastic); poem, 'Public speaking' in *Both Sides of the Catflap* by Sandy Brownjohn (Hodder Children's Books); *Winnie the Witch* by Korky Paul and Valerie Thomas (OUP); *The Elephant and the Bad Baby* by Elfrida Vipont (Puffin); *Grandpa Chatterjee*, pages 14 and 50, by Jamila Gavin (Mammoth).

There was so much going on at the fairground. There were half constructed roundabouts, dodgems, a helter-skelter, a big wheel and lots more. There were crates, poles, ropes, pegs, wire and canvas all over the ground. Men were banging, sawing and shouting. Machinery whirred, clanging, rasping and grating.

Women were brushing out their caravans, hanging out washing, or cleaning windows. Small children were running about, getting under people's feet and being shouted at.

No-one was standing still, wandering across the grass or chatting idly. It was wonderful!

Ensure children apply this sentence level learning in their writing.

Shared writing

Related text level objectives: Y3 Term 1 T11, T12, T22

List poems can be an effective way to introduce and reinforce different constructions in a creative and imaginative way. Links have to be made from achieving effects with poetry, into narrative and non-fiction. Simple lists can be made of things that might be found in different places, eg:

In a sailor's chest I found a rusted cutlass, an eye patch, an empty bottle and a parrot's feather.
In a mermaid's purse I found a golden comb, a sheet of music, a sailor's tooth and a piece of seaweed.
In an alien's pocket I found a map of the universe, ET's phone number, a six fingered glove and a spare eyeball!

List poems with verbs can also be written, for instance, based on 'The Cataract of Lodore' by Robert Southey – **rising and leaping, sinking and creeping, swelling and sweeping, showering and springing, flying and flinging, writhing and ringing, eddying and whisking, spouting and frisking, turning and twisting, around and around**, etc. (from *The New Oxford Book of Children's Verse*, ed. Neil Philip, 1996).

Y3 Term 1 T16

OBJECTIVES

T16 to begin to organise stories into paragraphs; to begin to use paragraphing in presentation of dialogue in stories;

Principles and explanation

- There are no hard and fast 'rules' for how many sentences will constitute a paragraph. It is something the writer decides, as an aspect of organising and structuring the writing. However, if this structuring is to be effective, decisions about paragraphs cannot be simply arbitrary.

- Paragraphs clarify the organisation of a piece of writing, making it easier to read and understand. The basis of paragraph organisation is semantic. In constructing paragraphs a writer assists the reader by 'chunking' related thoughts or ideas.

- In starting another paragraph the writer often signals a shift to something 'new' – for example, a different stage of the narrative, a different time or a different location.

- A basic awareness of paragraphs and the way they are demarcated will come from reading. However, the paragraphing of many reading texts, even those aimed at fairly young readers, is often very sophisticated. It is probably easier to approach an initial *understanding* of paragraphing through writing rather than through reading

- The paragraphing of direct speech tends, from a pupil perspective, to confuse other aspects of paragraphing in many narrative texts. It is probably better to separate these out as learning issues in the early stages.

- Year 3 pupils need to begin to understand how to organise simple narratives into basic paragraph units which relate to story structure (eg Para. 1: 'It began when …'; Para. 2: 'What happened next was …'; Para. 3: 'In the end …').

Shared writing

Paragraphing is helped substantially by thinking in 'boxes' when analysing the structure of stories or when planning to write them. Introduce the idea of 'boxing' stories.

- Take any simple, known story (eg 'Humpty Dumpty') and, through discussion/interactivity, segment it into three boxes, representing the main stages of the narrative:

1	Humpty sits on wall.

2	Humpty falls off wall.

3	Soldiers can't repair Humpty.

These could well be represented pictorially.

- Through teacher demonstration show how a simple story can be written, based on the above and organised on the principle of **one paragraph per box**.

BOX 1

The sun was hot, very hot. Humpty Dumpty sat on the wall. For hours he gazed proudly at his uniformed troops as they stood in rigid ranks before him. He felt on top of the world. Life was great. He was great. He was top egg. Sheer power welled up inside him. He leant forward and punched the air with his clenched fist. "Yes!"

BOX 2

Suddenly his rounded body began to rock. He felt giddy and his world began to spin. He wobbled. He toppled. He fell. Splat! His shell shattered and its contents oozed onto the hot concrete, a yellow yolk glistening in the middle.

BOX 3

Cautiously the exhausted soldiers broke rank and approached the wall. They huddled around the rapidly frying egg. They looked at each other in shocked silence. Then they laughed. There was no way now that they could put their leader back together again. What is more, they would not have done so, even if they could.

Let me show you how I would write this story. I'll try to explain what I'm thinking as I do it. Remember, I'm going to write one paragraph for each box. So what's my first paragraph going to be about? Yes, Humpty sitting on the wall. I want to make him seem really full of himself … cocky … so that it will be funnier when he falls off. I also want it to be very hot. You'll see why in a minute. I've got to get the soldiers in there somehow as well, so that they are in my story ready for when I need them later on. So this is how I'm going to start. Does he sound cocky enough? Right, I haven't quite finished this paragraph yet.

In the next paragraph he's going to fall off, so I need to put in something which leads up to that. Can you see what's going to happen yet? Let's read it back together.

Now I'm ready to start the next bit … the bit where he falls off. That's my second box isn't it? So I'm going to finish my first paragraph now and start the second one. How do I show the reader what I'm doing?

- Extend this into whole class and/or supported composition, following the model and keeping to the **one paragraph per box** rule. In the earlier stages this task can be broken down into writing and discussing one paragraph at a time. Either retell the same story (in which case hide the teacher's version to prevent straight copying – although it doesn't matter if pupils 'borrow' ideas, words, etc.) or for more originality try different ones. Amongst innumerable other possibilities are 'Jack and Jill', 'Little Miss Muffet', 'Incey Wincey Spider'.

The idea of **boxing** story segments in this way potentially provides the basis for both a **plan** and a **writing frame** for any piece of narrative writing.

Y3 Term 1 T23

OBJECTIVES

T23 to write simple non-chronological reports from known information, eg from own experience or from texts read, using notes made to organise and present ideas. Write for a known audience, eg other pupils in class, teacher, parent.

Principles and explanation

- See Teaching Unit 8.
- Year 3 pupils need to begin to understand how to organise non-chronological texts into a simple structure of paragraphs based on the grouping of information (eg writing about a bird: Para. 1: What it looks like; Para. 2: Where it lives; Para. 3: How it brings up its young).

Shared writing

- Write a simple non-chronological report about **Indian elephants** based on the information provided.

The Indian elephant is smaller than the African elephant.
A newborn elephant weighs about 110 kg.
An adult eats lots of leaves and grass.
Adults look hairless.
A baby elephant is called a calf.
It could live to be eighty.
Its trunk is really a nose.
Its trunk can break branches.
Its habitat is being destroyed.
It is the second largest land animal.
A newborn calf is covered in fuzzy hair.
It uses its trunk to drink.
It breathes through its trunk.
The baby stays in the group until it is about ten years old.
The tip of its trunk can pick up a single berry.
Adults feed in the morning and evening.
Its trunk sucks up water and squirts it into its mouth.

Divide up the separate sentences (cut into strips or write on cards) and get pupils to sort them into three boxes. Do not predetermine what these will be. Allow the pupils to rationalise the sorting and discuss this.

After sorting, give each box a summative 'title'.

The boxes might emerge as follows, but alternative organisations are possible, and perfectly valid if they can be justified. At this level, however, do not allow too many different boxes.

1 Adult elephants

2 Baby elephants

3 The elephant's trunk

Write up the report about Indian elephants using the **one paragraph per box** principle.

- Establish a writing purpose and audience. Ask pupils to generate pieces of information at random on some topic about which they already have a lot of knowledge. Just write down anything you can think of about … (This could, for example, be information about themselves for a letter to a friend, or information about being in Class Y3 to send down to the Infants who are moving up in September.)

  Next, sort the information into a small number of boxes. This may, incidentally, help provoke discussion about which information is relevant and which isn't.

  Title the boxes and proceed as above, reinforcing the **one paragraph per box** principle.

  This approach can equally well be used with information which is gathered from one or more text sources rather than generated from prior knowledge. Remember to ensure that any information texts supplied for this purpose are appropriately accessible for this age group.

- In other areas of the curriculum, collate and organise information in a diagrammatic form and use this as a basis for organising paragraphs for writing, eg:

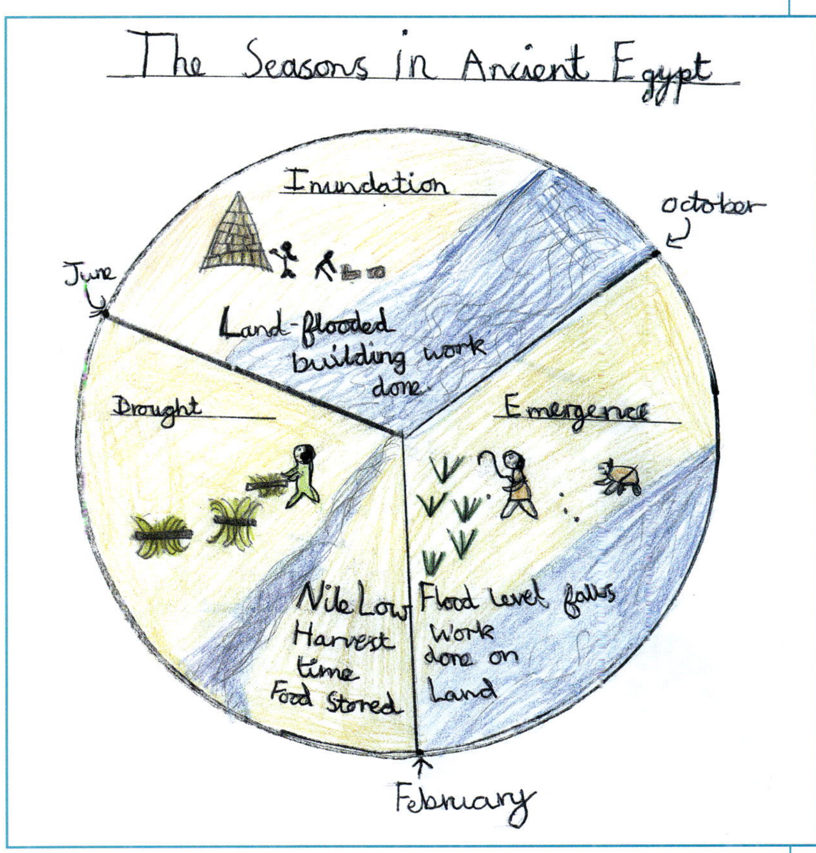

- When information gathering, try a reverse approach to the above. Having established a subject, purpose and audience for a particular piece of non-chronological report writing, define (title) the three boxes first. **What are the three most important things we want to know about …?**

  Locate/research information to fill the three predefined boxes, and then proceed as above.

The idea of **boxing** information in this way potentially provides the basis for both a **plan** and a **writing frame** for any piece of non-fiction writing

UNIT **10**

Y3 Term 2 S2 and S3

OBJECTIVES

S2 the function of adjectives within sentences, through: identifying adjectives in shared reading; discussing and defining what they have in common, eg words which qualify nouns; experimenting with deleting and substituting adjectives and noting effects on meaning; collecting and classifying adjectives, eg for colours, sizes, moods; experimenting with the impact of different adjectives through shared writing;

S3 to use the term 'adjective' appropriately;

Principles and explanation

- An adjective is a word that describes somebody or something, eg **old**, **white**, **busy**, **careful**. Adjectives either come before a noun, eg **the *old* man**, or after verbs such as **be**, **get**, **seem**, **feel**, **look**, eg **the man feels old**.
- Adjectives are effective if used sparingly. Sometimes, it may be more effective to use a precise noun rather than use an adjective. Avoid repeating adjectives, unless to gain a specific effect. Adjectives should add new information to the noun which the reader needs to know.

Sentence level activities

Function (page 156)

The non-adjective in this example is in *italics*.

He rode on till at last he came to a <u>deep</u> forest. Here the <u>poor</u> prince paused. The trees were <u>tall</u> and the forest was <u>dark</u>. He nudged his <u>faithful</u> horse forwards. Almost immediately they moved from the warmth of the <u>open</u> landscape into a <u>strange</u> world. It was quite <u>still</u>. <u>Cool</u> shadows hid <u>secret</u> rustlings. The <u>poor</u> prince gripped the <u>leather</u> reins. He thought of home – <u>warm</u> blankets, <u>hot</u> drinks, <u>sweet</u> cakes, steam on the *window* – anything other than the <u>vague</u> shadows that seemed to move on the edge of his vision.

Follow up by finding adjectives in texts and the nouns they modify.

Cloze (page 157)

He tugged his **heavy**, **black** coat closer but even so the **cold** air seemed to sneak in. As they moved further into the forest the darkness moved closer. He could no longer see the **silver** buttons on his coat. His hands became **odd** shapes in front of him. So it was that he did not see the horse's **sharp** ears stick upright as she picked up on a **distant** sound, too **soft** for a human to hear. It was a sound that she knew only too well – the sound of **sharp** claws, the **soft** padding of **swift** feet. It was the sound of a wolf. A **lean**, **grey** wolf with **sharp** eyes and an **empty** belly padded towards them …

Improve (page 161)

Write a text containing some weak nouns and some adjectives which are superfluous to requirement or stylistically clumsy. The children should consider the use of adjectives and also whether a stronger, more precise noun might be better in some instances, eg **fruit** and **bird**. The text below provides an example. Read these sentences aloud to the children:

The youngest son took the basket and made his way to the end of the garden. He stopped at the tree and picked not one, not two, but three fruit. He placed them in the basket and covered them with a cloth so they would neither ruin nor spoil.

Enlarge for sharing.

That afternoon he set off on his journey. He climbed the huge, great enormous mountain and he paused on the top to watch the great birds circle overhead. He climbed down into the valley where the great river flowed. There he paused to watch the silver, bright, colourful fish leap in the flowing water, fresh from the melting cold snow on the mountains. He saw the great, grizzly bears scoop the fish and crunch them between pointed, jagged, sharp, white teeth. He forded the moving river and strode into the forest.

Continue as independent work.

On the third day of walking through the forest he met an ancient, old woman. She was so old that her wrinkly skin was wrinkled like a dried, shrunken peach. Her hair hung limply and her eyes had lost all spark of life. Her back was crooked, bent and thoroughly odd and her hands were like an ancient, old claw. From cracked, cut, dry lips she spoke, "I'm nearly starving. Have you got something a poor old woman could eat?"

The youngest son did not hesitate. "Here, old Mother you may have a taste of this bit of fruit." No sooner had the old woman touched the fruit than her skin began to change …

Quickmake (page 158)

Cards: noun, verb, adjective.
Sentence starter: **The man is hot.**

Ensure children apply this sentence level learning in their writing.

Shared writing

Related text level objectives: T6, T7 and T17 (texts where adjectives are inappropriate); T12–T16 (instructional texts in which adjectives have limited function: colour, size, number); T8–T10 (characterisation and setting)

- The use of effective nouns and adjectives should be considered at the point of writing. Children should be encouraged to have a couple of attempts at a sentence before committing it to paper, and then to consider it again after it has been written.

- In fiction writing, encourage children to consider the best use of descriptive words. Discourage the use of more than two adjectives to modify a noun as a basic rule of thumb. Ask them to consider strengthening the noun before considering adding any adjectives. Demonstrate this when you are writing a setting for a story.

- Before writing a non-fiction text, ask children whether adjectives would be appropriate and, if so, in which circumstances.

Y3 Term 2 S4 and S5

OBJECTIVES

S4 to extend knowledge and understanding of pluralisation through: recognising the use of singular and plural forms in speech and through shared reading; transforming sentences from singular to plural and vice versa, noting which words have to change and which do not; understanding the term 'collective noun' and collecting examples – experiment with inventing other collective nouns; noticing which nouns can be pluralised and which cannot, eg *trousers*, *rain*; recognising pluralisation as one test of a noun;

S5 to use the terms 'singular' and 'plural' appropriately;

Principles and explanation

- Nouns can be singular (just one) or plural (more than one), and are usually pluralised by the addition of **-s** or **-es**. There are some exceptions, eg **mouse**, **mice**, and some nouns are the same in singular and plural, eg **sheep**. There are also collective nouns, eg **team**, and some words which only exist in the plural, eg **trousers**.
- Pronouns referring to the noun are affected by pluralisation, eg **he**/**they**, as are verb-endings, eg **The man sings.**/**The men sing**.

Sentence level activities

Replace (page 160)

With the class's help, use Post-it® notes to substitute plural nouns for singular nouns in a text. Read the text, and consider which other words need to be changed as a result of the pluralisation of nouns.

Collect and classify (page 156)

Collect plurals from shared and individual reading. Classify under the following headings:

- collective nouns
- nouns always expressed in the plural
- nouns which are the same in both singular and plural
- **-s** and **-es** endings
- irregular forms.

Singular and plural race

Each pupil draws columns labelled Singular and Plural. Give a limited time and a defined environment, eg **the classroom**. Pupils list, in the correct columns, as many nouns as they can spot, eg **one teacher**, **lots of pupils**. At the end they count up and you check to see who is the Singular Winner and the Plural Winner.

Plural nouns

Search for plural nouns and their related verbs and pronouns in text.

Convert

Convert a prepared and varied list of singular nouns into the plural, eg **man**, **child**, **person**, **dog**, **sheep**, **horse**, **flower**.

Ensure children apply this sentence level learning in their writing.

Shared writing

Related objectives: Y3 Term 2 S10–S11 (noun–verb agreement); Y3 Term 2 W9 (spelling); Y3 Term 2 T6, T7, T16 (lists) and Y3 Term 2 S6, S7 (commas)

- When revising a piece of writing, check agreement between nouns and verbs.
- Invite pupils to set captions to a cartoon strip or describe the steps in a familiar operation so that composition can proceed with suitable stopping points for discussion of the plurals.
- Compose a passage recounting, for example, the animals seen during a visit to a farm or market, thus providing opportunities for pupils to suggest, explain and discuss choices such as **cow, cows, cattle, herd**.

Now I am going to write the next part of the story. I'm going to take care with the singular and plural nouns, as this is where we need to list what they saw at the fair. I think I'll start by listing what they saw, with some use of adjectives to help the reader picture the creatures.

The twins watched as a man in a leather apron led out some of the strangest creatures imaginable. First there were two black and white cows, with very long horns. Their calves ambled beside them, brown-eyed and gentle. You'll have noticed that I turned calfs into calves **They were followed by a man carrying a cage of bright yellow birds, and two dappled donkeys.**

Now I'm going to bring on some sheep so I could say a 'flock of sheep' because you cannot write sheeps! **A young girl led in a flock of sheep, and the twins were astonished to see a bright ginger fox scurrying round like a sheepdog.**

I want to bring in the wolves – wolf is the same as calf so I need to write wolves, not wolfs. **Next a man walked by with a string of wolves, held on a chain.** I want to add that the wolves looked hungry. So, They was or were hungry? Which should it be? Let's check our reminder sheet.

Yes, **The wolves were hungry, their bodies quite lean. Above the man's head danced a swarm of bees.** There, that is another way of saying lots of bees, when you say 'a swarm of bees'. Do you remember that is called a collective noun? Who can suggest what might appear next?

12

Y3 Term 2 S8

OBJECTIVES

S8 other uses of capitalisation from reading, eg names, headings, special emphasis, new lines in poetry;

Principles and explanation

- Capital letters are used for the first letter of a sentence; for 'I'; for special names such as people, places, titles, headings, days of the week, months, planets, organisations; for people's initials; for abbreviations; for emphasis; for important words in the titles of books, films, etc.; sometimes for the first line in a poem, etc.
- Link this closely to writing in sentences. It is an objective to return to on many occasions, formally and informally, so that over time starting a sentence with a capital letter becomes a habit.
- Instructional and explanatory texts, in particular, employ devices such as arrows, lines, boxes, etc., for clarity and often brevity.

Sentence level objectives

Collect and classify (page 156)

Look for capital letters on a page from three or four different sorts of books. Classify them according to their function – beginning of a sentence, names (people, places, days, months), personal pronoun 'I', first lines of poems, titles, initials, other. Add to the list in subsequent days as more examples are found. Make a poster as a reminder when writing.

Spot the capital

Read a paragraph from a book or other text such as a travel brochure in which there are quite a few names, names of places, days of the week, months. The children should not be able to see it. When you read a word which starts with a capital, children should raise their hands and say 'capital'. When you finish a sentence, say 'full stop'. Display the text afterwards.

Sally Bucket lived in Busky Lane near to the Spa shop. She knew that she also lived in Liverpool but that was a big place. She lived in a row of houses like a giant loaf of bread. Each house was joined to the next one. Sally thought that if the end house got pushed too hard by the wind they might all fall over. She had seen her uncle Ned do that with cards.

In Busky Lane lived Sally's friends. There was her best friend Sita. There were Kylie and Jason. They lived at number 28. They were twins and had their birthday on the same day in June. Sally's birthday was in April. Sita's birthday was in December. It was like having two Christmases at once. Sally also had a brother who was a bit of a bother. His name was Billy Bucket.

Today was Wednesday. Sally was very excited. On Monday Sita's mum had promised to take both the girls out on Wednesday. Today was Wednesday so Sally waited at the window looking out for Sita.

Ensure children apply this sentence level learning in their writing.

Shared writing

Related text level objective: Y3 Term 2 T16

- Describe how to get from the school to a nearby point which requires using names of streets, towns, etc. as appropriate. Use connectives, eg **To Medwell station. Walk out of the front gate. Next, turn left down Angel Rd. Then cross the street at the lights at Waller's chemist.**

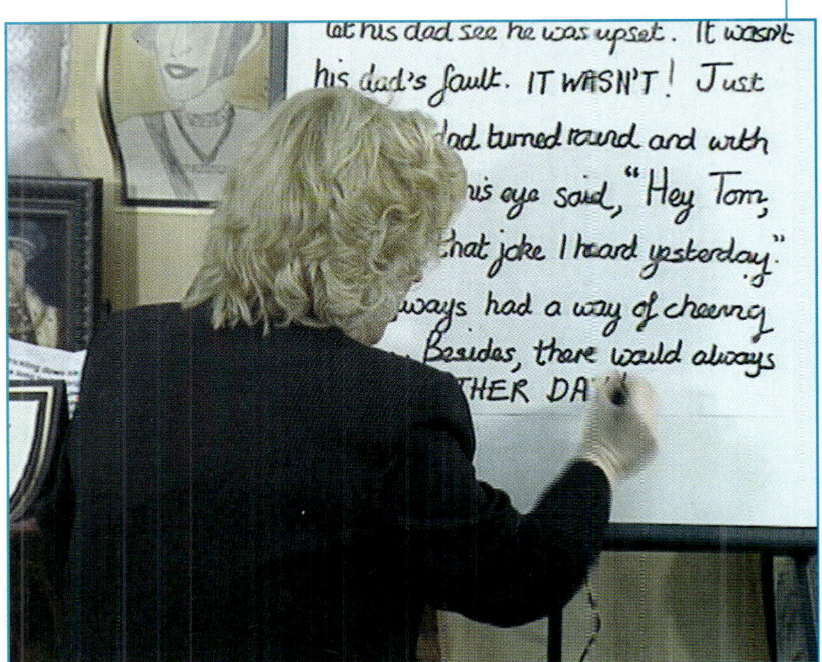

After writing the title and the two opening instructions, ask the children where to go after that. Consider a suitable connective and where the capital letters belong. Notice the direct language: **walk**, **turn**, **cross** – no unnecessary words.

If the destination is not reached before the end of the lesson, this activity can be concluded in independent time. Discuss the merits of instructions as opposed to a map. The children could draw a map in independent time putting in street names with capital letters (including Rd, St, Ave, Close, etc.).

- During all shared writing, emphasise and talk aloud about the need to use and check for capital letters for names and headings, especially at the start of sentences. This needs to become an automatic habit, especially for beginning sentences, so it must be emphasised. Sometimes, make purposeful errors by missing out a capital and encourage children to spot when you make an omission.

- Construct and label a flow chart or set of diagrams to perform a classroom task such as washing the paint equipment, feeding an animal, watering plants, turning on the computer.

13

Y3 Term 2 S9

OBJECTIVE

S9 to experiment with deleting words in sentences to see which are essential to retain meaning and which are not;

Principles and explanation

- On the whole, the essential words are key nouns and verbs. Descriptive words and phrases can usually be removed.
- When determiners **the** or **a/an** are removed the text sounds telegraphed when read aloud.
- Prepositions, eg **with**, **on**, can be removed only if the whole phrase (**with no shoes**) goes.

Sentence level activities

Reduce

Make a sentence with plenty of adjectives and other descriptive words and phrases on a sentence maker, washing line or computer screen, eg **Slowly and silently, the unhappy boy with no shoes ate his meagre lunch on the back doorstep.** Using masking tape or Post-its®, and starting with the first word, try removing one word at a time, asking children to assess the resultant sentence as follows:

- still makes complete sense;
- makes sense but sounds like notes (not complete);
- makes sense but meaning has changed;
- not possible.

Discuss how many words you could remove while still retaining the absolute core of the sense (**boy ate**) and remove them. On this evidence, discuss which classes of words can be deleted without destroying the sense, and which can't. Take other opportunities for quick-fire practice in trimming sentences to the bare bones.

Long and short

Look at texts in which short sentences are occasionally interspersed with longer ones to create effect, eg 'In my opinion, parents should always be consulted before children are given presents which parents may not want. We have had animals similar to these in the past. They bred. We don't want them again …', page 45, from *The Battle of Bubble and Squeak* by Philippa Pearce (Puffin).

Ensure children apply this sentence level learning in their writing.

Shared writing

Related text level objective: Y3 Term 2 T17

Teacher demonstration

- Use the rules you devise to inform your note-taking procedures, helping pupils see that in notes, elaboration is unnecessary.
- Watch a video relevant to current study, then watch it again with the purpose of taking notes, pausing the tape as necessary.

Supported composition

Ask pupils to do the same with this or another video. Pause for around one minute. Ask pupils to note the key point or points on dry-wipe boards and hold these up. Note children who have:

- not noted salient points
- included fewer essential words, eg adjectives, determiners.

Write a paragraph in which one or two short sentences are placed among longer sentences to create an effect of surprise or to build up suspense. Write the sentences in different colours (rainbow sentences) to see the visual effect of length variation.

Y3 Term 2 S10 and S11

OBJECTIVES

S10 to understand the differences between verbs in the 1st, 2nd and 3rd person, eg *I/we do*, *you do*, *he/she/it/they do/does* through: collecting and categorising examples and noting the difference between singular and plural persons; discussing the purposes for which each can be used; relating to different types of text, eg 1st person for diaries, personal letters; 2nd person for instructions, directions; 3rd person for narrative, recounts; experimenting with transforming sentences and noting which words need to be changed;

S11 to understand the need for grammatical agreement in speech and writing, eg *I am*; *we are*.

Principles and explanation

Verbs change depending on their 'person' – the speaker (first), the person spoken to (second), or the person spoken about (third). Different types of text are written in a particular person (see above).

Sentence level activities

Pronouns

Read out the beginnings of a number of texts. Ask whether they contain the words **I/we** or **he/she/they**. Introduce the idea of first and third person. Read the texts again, asking children to note down first or third person for each. Go through and tell them the correct answers. Note whether certain texts are generally written in first or third person (see objective S10 above).

Replace (page 160)

When using a third person text in shared reading, help children identify and highlight the relevant pronouns (**he/she/they**, etc.) and all related verbs.

Rewrite a third person text in the first person. Stop at each highlighted item. Children note down what they think the new version will be each time before suggesting what you should scribe. Read through the complete first person version to check that everything agrees.

Collect and classify (page 156)

Use a recipe, a set of assembly instructions or rules, eg the poem, 'Instructions for Growing Poetry' in *Plum* by Tony Mitton (Scholastic):

In case of fire –
Sound the alarm
Close the door of your room
Do not use the lift
Make your way to the stairs by Room 8
<u>Walk</u> down the stairs
Turn right at the bottom
Leave the building through the blue double doors
Assemble in the car park

Find the verbs. Note that:

- they often occur at the beginning of a sentence;
- they are, therefore, not preceded by a noun or pronoun;
- they are the 'you' or second person form of the verb – in the form of a command – **You do this or you do that** – but with *you* omitted;
- adjectives and adverbs are only used if absolutely necessary to the procedure, eg **blue double doors; *three* tablespoons of flour; fold the flour *gently* into the mixture**.

Examine

Examine another two types of instructional text and check whether the same conventions apply.

Ensure children apply this sentence level learning in their writing.

Shared writing

Related text level objectives: Y3 Term 2 T11, T12, T16 (also Y3 Term 3 T3)

- Write a short third person text, occasionally slipping in the odd **I/we**. Ask the children to put their hands up if they see this happening, eg **He went shopping yesterday. He wanted to buy a suit but we ended up with some chocolates**. Repeat with a first person recount, occasionally putting in **he/she/they**.
- Explain that this can happen when we write, and children should keep an eye open for it when proofreading their work.
- Develop a proofreading poster of things to check for when rereading your own work or proof-reading for a partner. Include agreement of person along with agreement of tense, points about punctuation, spelling, etc.
- Make up a set of instructions for a Martian, eg how to put on a pair of trousers, how to make cheese on toast.

Changing person/changing viewpoint

- Using as a stimulus a book such as Jon Scieszka's *The True Story of the Three Little Pigs*, and/or the traditional version, write a sequel to address the question 'What do you think happened after the official end of this story?' This could possibly be in letter form (see also Allan Ahlberg's *The Jolly Postman*, etc.).
- In the context of the above, deliberately experiment with writing in the first, second and third person, singular and plural. Use this as an opportunity to further consolidate verb use, agreement, etc., but also explore the relationship between the 'person' of the verb and the viewpoint of the character, ie **It is not just a question of changing 'I' to 'he', but of asking, 'How does this change affect the viewpoint of the story?'.** The tale will probably be told quite differently from the perspective of one of the characters than from that of another, and differently again if told by a third party narrator, eg:

First person singular: (The wolf continues the story.)
I feel rotten. Rotting in gaol is really rotten. **I** wish **I**'d never even heard of pigs, let alone pork.

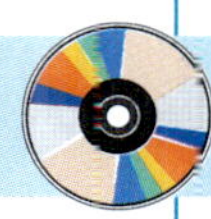

Second person singular: (The wolf writes to the surviving pig.)
You're the clever one aren't **you**? **You** had it sorted from the beginning, building your house out of bricks.

Third person singular (and plural): (Objective narration)
Well, the wolf got what **he** deserved. As for the third little pig, **he** came out with all the glory. It was the other two pigs who had the worst of it. After all **they** were eaten, and there wasn't a lot **they** could do about that.

First person plural: (Two pigs write from 'beyond the grave'.)
What did **we** do to deserve this? **We** went to all that trouble to build **our** houses out of environmentally friendly materials from a sustainable source. What thanks did **we** get?

Second person plural: (Surviving pig writes to his brothers.)
You two needn't feel hard done to. **You** were stupid from an early age. In fact, **you** were both born a few bricks short of a chimney.

NB In many of these, verbs using a different 'person' will occur in the same narrative (giving opportunity for further discussion), but, if focusing on the story viewpoint, it is usually possible to keep the principal emphasis as suggested above. Such an approach could be used in writing a sequel to almost any traditional tale.

15

Y3 Term 3 S2 and S3

OBJECTIVES

S2 to identify pronouns and to understand their functions in sentences through: noticing in speech and reading how they stand in place of nouns; substituting pronouns for common and proper nouns in own writing; distinguishing personal pronouns, eg *I*, *you*, *him*, *it* and possessive pronouns, eg *my*, *your*, *hers*; distinguishing the 1st, 2nd and 3rd person forms of pronouns, eg *I*, *me*, *we*, *you*, *she*, *her*, *them*; investigating the contexts and purposes for using pronouns in different persons, linked to previous term's work on 1st and 3rd person; investigating how pronouns are used to mark gender: *he, she, they*; etc.;

S3 to ensure grammatical agreement in speech and writing of pronouns and verbs, eg *I am*, *we are*, in standard English;

Principles and explanations

- See objective S2 above; for a full definition of pronouns, see the Glossary (in Part 3).
- Pronouns are essential in enabling people to write economically. However, overuse of pronouns confuses the reader, leaving them unsure who the pronouns refer to.

Sentence level activities

Function (page 156)

Choose a text full of pronouns, eg *Dear Daddy* by Philippe Dupasquier (Puffin). The non-pronoun in this example is in *italics*.

I sniffed at my breakfast in disgust. My sister Sali managed to eat hers quickly. She smiled at me.
   "You must eat yours," she begged. But I did not feel like eating.
   In the corner Daisy lay fast asleep. I watched her blanket rise and fall as she slept. Sali crawled across to her and tugged the blanket right up to Daisy's chin.
   "We don't want her getting cold," she whispered to me. We stared at the sleeping form. She seemed so small and helpless. Where was our father? Where was he? It was a question that we would return to many times. I smiled at Sali and *picked* up the bowl. We would all need to be strong.

Pronoun game

Ask a child to start the game off by saying something about him or herself. All children repeat the statement pointing to themselves; they then repeat it pointing to the person sitting next to them and substituting **you**. They continue to repeat the statement using the pronouns, **she**, **he**, **it**, **we**, **you** (plural) and **they** pointing to appropriate people or objects in the room. Have a list of the pronouns on the board. As the children say each statement, write the form of the verb by each pronoun. At the end discuss the list.

That's mine!

Children point to themselves and say **That's mine**, to their neighbour, **That's yours**, to a boy, **That's his**, and so on with **hers**, **yours**, **theirs**. A variation on this game is 'That's my book!'

Collect and classify (page 156)

Make a table with two columns, headed Pronoun and Noun. When the children find a pronoun, write it in the first column and the noun which the pronoun refers to in the second column. Do a *pronoun check*: ask the question 'Are both noun and pronoun the same gender and the same number?' Discuss how the writer occasionally changes back to a noun so that the reader knows exactly who the pronouns refer to. Look at all the **she**s. How do we know whether they refer to Joc or her mother?

Joc tapped **her** foot impatiently while **she** waited for **her** mother to decide. **Her** mother seemed to be taking an age. First **she** had to turn the oven on and then **she** decided the sink needed cleaning. Joc waited patiently, but **she** could not help drumming **her** fingers upon the table. One sharp glance from **her** mother and Joc stopped.

Just when it looked as if **her** mother might decide, Joc's brother Chris wandered in, with **his** friend Taro. The two boys made straight for the fridge. **They** didn't even glance at Mrs Holton. It was as if **they** had not even seen **her**.

"Who said **you** could help **yourselves**?" snapped Mrs Holton. The boys grinned sheepishly.

"But **we** are starving," whined Chris. Taro looked embarrassed. **He** hadn't bargained to mingle with an irate mother on the prowl.

She fixed the children with one of **her** famous looks and, with a sharp intake of breath, launched into what turned out to be a force eight blast of irritation that had brewed over the last few weeks. **They** deserved **it** and **they** knew **it**. Joc stared at **her** shoecaps and toed the carpet.

Ensure children apply this sentence level learning in their writing.

Shared writing

Related text level objectives: Y3 Term 3 T3, T12

Write a first person account of an incident in a story which has been read in shared reading, for instance by taking on the role of Hogarth in the *The Iron Man* by Ted Hughes.

Model how writers have to be careful about pronouns which do not clearly specify who they refer to. Also talk through which pronouns to use. This could be particularly important for children in the class just starting to learn to speak English as an additional language.

After the children have written on to dry-wipe boards, they could exchange work with each other. They could try to identify pronouns (put a list on the board, as above) and then check that they can track back to identify who is the person referred to.

Y3 Term 3 S4

OBJECTIVES

S4 to use speech marks and other dialogue punctuation appropriately in writing and to use the conventions which mark boundaries between spoken words and the rest of the sentence;

Principles and explanation

- In dialogue, give each new speaker a new line.
- Enclose direct speech in speech marks and separate it from the reporting clause with a comma (or ? or !). All punctuation relating to the speech should be inside the speech marks.
- Where a speech is interrupted **in mid-sentence** by the reporting clause, re-open the direct speech in lower case. Otherwise the first letter of direct speech should always be a capital, eg:
  'Don't climb on that wall,' *shouted Mrs Bloggs, as she hung out the washing.* **'It's dangerous'.**
  'Don't climb on that wall,' *shouted Mrs Bloggs, as she hung out the washing,* **'because you might fall off and hurt yourself.'**
  (The reporting clause is in *italics*.)

Sentence level objectives
Comic strip

Enlarge a comic strip on a photocopier or OHT. Ask the children to say which bit indicates the direct speech, and which bit tells you what happens. Make sure children are familiar with conventions, including narrative boxes and think balloons. Convert the comic strip into direct speech, with a narrative thread to substitute for the pictures, ie reporting clause and any necessary background detail. Ensure some reporting clauses are inserted in the middle of speeches, and check with the model text to see if your punctuation matches. Ensure that whatever is spoken reveals character. Use speech verbs or adverbs to describe how things are said.

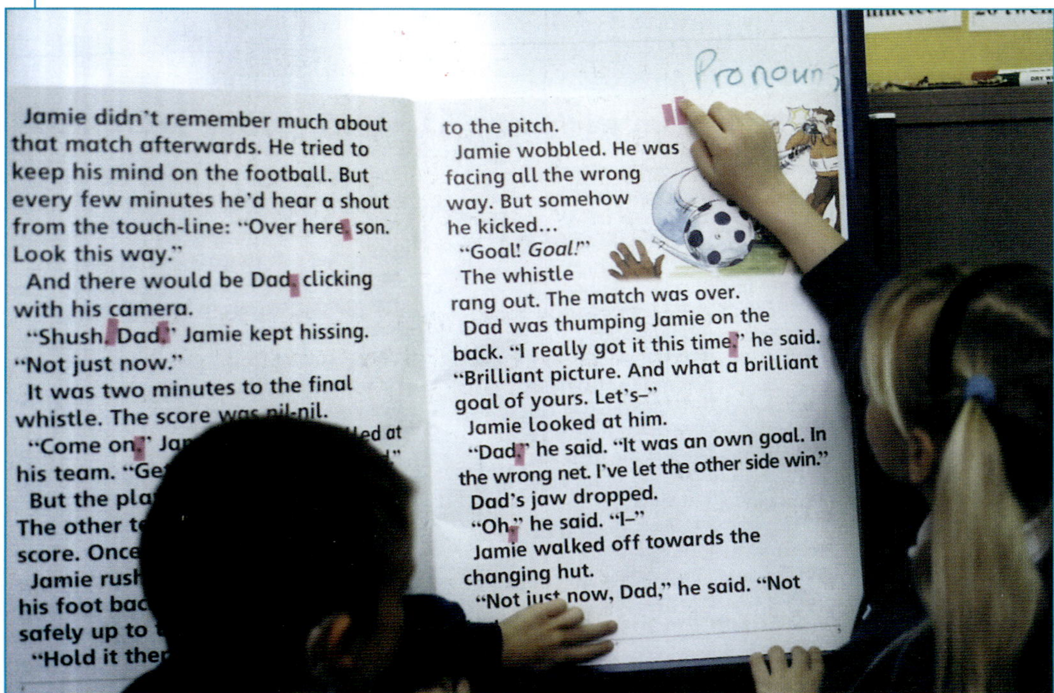

Collect and classify (page 156)

Highlight speech and narrative in different colours. Discuss conventions of punctuation. Ask pupils to devise rules for direct speech punctuation, depending on your findings. (See Teaching Unit 4.) Concentrate particularly on occasions where the reporting clause is inserted in the middle of a speech. Create a model of speech punctuation on a poster.

Ensure children apply this sentence level learning in their writing.

Shared writing

Related text level objectives: Y3 Term 3 T12, T13

Teacher demonstration

- Use a video of a soap opera or similar from TV. Using the pause button, transcribe a scene as dialogue. Involve the children in adding reporting clauses and necessary detail, eg the setting.

- One member of class goes out and comes back in a particular mood. He or she goes up to someone and says something. The accosted person replies. Children write the snippet of dialogue on dry-wipe boards, using correct punctuation and inserting reporting clauses and necessary detail. Explore the use of reporting clauses. They can describe a character; they can also move the plot along. **'Find some more then,' he bellowed, as he reversed erratically down the lane.**

17

Y3 Term 3 S5

OBJECTIVES

S5 how sentences can be joined in more complex ways through using a widening range of conjunctions in addition to *and* and *then*, eg *if, so, while, though, since, when*;

Principles and explanation

Conjunctions are words which can link two short sentences (clauses) to create a longer one. **And**, **but** and **or** join clauses to create 'compound' sentences. The conjunction **and** is very common in speech where gesture and intonation enhance communication. In writing, conjunctions such as **if**, **so that**, **while**, **since**, **though** and **when** are necessary to make the link between clauses more precise; sentences containing clauses with these conjunctions are 'complex'.

Sentence level activities

Function (page 156)

Choose a page in a text which contains a number of conjunctions, eg *Ginger* by Charlotte Voake (Walker Books). The non-conjunction in this example is in *italics*.

Dear Mr Agard <u>and</u> Ms Nichols,
I like the book you wrote called Caribbean dozen. I say one of the poems <u>while</u> I am skipping. I've been saying that poem <u>since</u> I was four <u>but</u> now I say the version in your book. I look at the book everyday <u>so that</u> I can learn the last verse. Mrs Bradley reads us poems <u>when</u> we have finished our work. Martin likes the one about the chocolate bars <u>because</u> it is only five words long. I like writing poems <u>though</u> I'm not as good at it as Sheena. I am better <u>if</u> nobody bothers me. I *could* write you a poem about my friend's hamster <u>or</u> I could draw Mrs Bradley's cat for you. I like the picture of the rabbit <u>and</u> I like the poem too. I want a rabbit <u>but</u> I am not allowed one.
Love from
Gina

List

Start a list of conjunctions. Ask children to spot others during shared, guided and independent reading, and add to it. Keep it on display for reference during shared writing. Discuss purposes, eg **because** helps you to give a reason for something.

Rewrite

Rewrite a text for sharing so that it has no conjunctions at all. Set it out one clause per line, eg:

Once upon a time there were three bears.
There was a mummy bear, a daddy bear and a baby bear.
The mummy bear made some porridge.
The baby bear and the daddy bear came down to breakfast.
Mummy bear spooned some porridge into three bowls …, etc.

Reread and discuss the effect of writing in this way. Direct children to the list of conjunctions and ask them to choose conjunctions to join these short sentences into longer ones. Reread and compare, deciding which sentences need to stand alone and which benefit from combination. Discuss how some sentences need to be brief for dramatic impact, eg **The wolf howled**.

Ensure children apply this sentence level learning in their writing.

Shared writing

Related text level objectives: Y3 Term 3 T11–T14, T20, T22

- In shared writing, model how to choose suitable conjunctions. In writing from notes, show how you can join ideas, eg **Keep away – Bubonic plague v infectious. Cross on doors – plague in house**.

- Provide notes on a topic with which the children are familiar. Children expand them into a couple of sentences, using conjunctions.

- Write a paragraph in different coloured (rainbow) sentences to highlight the effect of long and short sentences. Consider the effects of variety in length. Sometimes it is more effective to use a short sentence, eg for emphasis or to create a dramatic effect. Compound and complex sentences may create more economical writing and can show relationships.

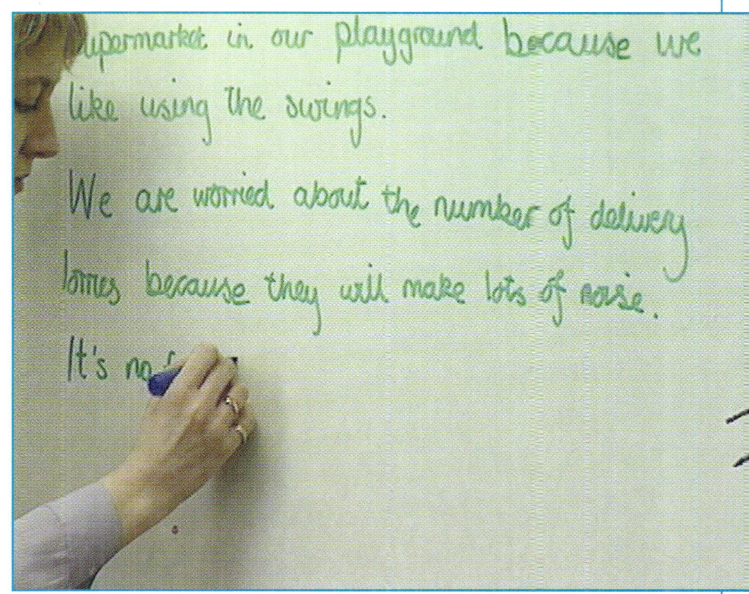

18

Y3 Term 3 S6

OBJECTIVES

S6 to investigate through reading and writing how words and phrases can signal time sequences, eg *first*, *then*, *after*, *meanwhile*, *from*, *where*;

Principles and explanation

- Some words and phrases at the start of sentences help to link or connect sentences together so that sentences follow on from each other in a time sequence, eg **suddenly**, **after that**, **finally**, **first**, **next**, **later**, **meanwhile**, **then**, **after a while**, **when I finished**.
- Children often use **and then** to link ideas, which can be dull. To avoid using **and then**, start a new sentence, join the sentences or start a new sentence with a connecting word or phrase,

  eg **They saw the dogs and then they looked at the cows** could become:

  They saw the dogs. Then they looked at the cows.

  After they saw the dogs, they looked at the cows.

  They saw the dogs. After that, they looked at the cows.
- In most stories the events happen in order. Certain words and phrases can help us tell the reader when things happen.

Sentence level activities

Cloze (page 157)

Choose a page of text with a number of connectives, eg **suddenly**, **after that**, **finally**, **first**, **next**, **later**, **meanwhile**, **then**, **after a while**, **when I finished**. Cover the connectives with Post-its®. Discuss suitable connectives to go in the spaces and then reveal the one in the text. The following example is an invented recount by the pilot who finds Brian in Gary Paulsen's book *Hatchet* (Macmillan Children's Books).

I was as amazed as anyone else when I found Brian. I was flying low over an area of forest, miles from anywhere, when I noticed smoke. **After that** I pulled round and flew in low for a better look. **First**, I noticed that someone had cleared an area of trees. **Then** I saw the camp. I had to circle round a couple of times. **After a while** I was ready to fly in low and put the plane down on the lake. **Next**, I paddled across to where Brian was standing, staring at me as if I was a ghost. **Suddenly**, he spoke and said his name. You could have knocked me flat when I realised that I had found the kid!

Sequence

Use a flow chart to identify the main sequence of events in a known story. Label each event with an appropriate temporal connective, eg **first**, **later on**, **after that**, **early**, **next morning**, etc.

And then

Play a game where children have to tell the story of a favourite book, film or TV programme without using the words **and then**. If they do so, someone else has to take over.

Collect and classify (page 156)

Analyse the use of connectives in books. Note the order in which connectives tend to be used in different text types: recounts, narrative, instructions.

Oral

Enlarge a page of a comic strip, eg *The Snowman*, *Father Christmas*. Describe the events as they occur in the pictures, using appropriate connectives to drive the narrative along.

Improve (page 161)

Create a page of text all strung together with **and then**.

I saw the plane and then it flew over and then it seemed to disappear and then just when I thought that it had gone it came back and I could hardly believe it and then just when I did not know if I was awake or dreaming it shot in over the trees and then it landed on the lake and then out climbed a man and then he was rowing across to me and then he spoke to me and then I found myself talking to the first human being that I had seen in months and then I knew that it was over.

Ensure children apply this sentence level learning in their writing.

Shared writing

Related text level objectives: Y3 Term 3 T12, T16, T22

- Write a letter to a friend recounting a recent school or local event.
  - Write the setting in advance and briefly show where it answers the questions: Who? Where? When? What? Why?
  - Run through the sequence of events together – four or five events. Make brief notes on sugar paper for display.
  - Compose the first two sentences, explaining your choice of connective. Ask the children what the next connective might be.
  - Compose the sentence. Let the children have a go at the final sentences and the close of the letter and take examples.

- Ask the children to work in pairs to recount the same event but as a story in the first person, using their dry-wipe boards or independently.
  When marking, isolate passages joined by **and then** and use these for whole class demonstration, showing how to improve the writing.

- Bring planning diagrams from other curricular areas for writing up into a report.

19

Y3 Term 3 S7

OBJECTIVES

S7 to become aware of the use of commas in marking grammatical boundaries within sentences.

Principles and explanation

- Commas help the reader make sense of a text, by showing where there is a break in the sense within a sentence. They help the reader 'chunk' up the sentence into meaningful units, mirroring the function of intonation in spoken language. Commas are used in lists (nouns, verbs, adjectives), to mark off extra information, eg **Jill, my boss, is 28 years old**; after a subordinate clause, eg ***Although it was cold*, we didn't wear coats**; with many connecting adverbs, eg **Anyway, in the end I decided not to go.**

- While commas are sometimes essential (and sometimes not necessary) there is often a degree of personal choice involved. Ensure pupils are aware that there is a difference between personal preference in aspects of punctuation and standard accepted conventions by which all writers are expected to abide.

Sentence level activities

Punctuate (page 159)

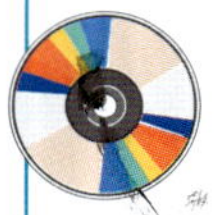

As revision, choose a page containing commas in lists, commas between adjectives, full stops, question and exclamation marks. Cover them up and ask the children to indicate what the covered punctuation should be using punctuation fans.

Function (page 156)

In a shared text, highlight all the commas. Consider where commas are used, and eliminate those used in lists. Ask the children to consider the function of the others.

Collect and classify (page 156)

Classify the use of commas in a text: lists – nouns, verbs or adjectives; demarcating extra information; demarcating meaningful units; demarcating adverbs.

Mr Crimp, a geologist, is able to read the history of rocks in a continent, rather like reading tree rings. Continents seem to have a core of very ancient rock, forming micro-continents, onto which younger rocks have been welded at various intervals ever since. Continents, though, are not fixed. They can move, merge or split. At times, molten rock from the earth's mantle bursts through the continental crust spilling the boiling, treacherous lava, rocks and gases into the air.

Mis-commas

In a shared text, put commas in the wrong places. Read the text aloud, pausing at the commas so the text is meaningless.

Find

Remove all the commas from a text. Try reading it aloud. Discuss where commas are needed, and ask pupils to add them. Each time, ask the children to note whether they think the comma is – very good; possible but not absolutely right; wrong. The children should look in their own writing for places where they could put commas or change/join/improve sentences, thus requiring the addition of commas.

Happy families

Give out cards from a pack of Happy Families. Show the children how to play the game. Read the card, eg **Mr Bun the baker**. Alter it to **Mr Bun, the baker, made us some excellent cakes**. Where each comma occurs raise a curled finger. Get into groups of about six. Continue round the group choosing some unlikely actions for the card characters.

Construct (page 158)

Give out the sentence (eg green), noun (eg red) and name (eg grey) cards. The children get into groups with one green, one red and two grey cards and see what sentences they make in the order grey, green, red, grey. Three of the children should have commas and hold them in the correct places, eg:

Peter, my sister, couldn't find his dog, Angel.

Mrs French, the plumber, went over to see her friend, the Prime Minister.

HEADLESS SENTENCES (EG GREEN)	NOUN PHRASES (EG RED)	NAMES (EG GREY)
went over to see her friend	my sister	Jan
was on his way to see his wife	the plumber	Fred
couldn't find his dog	my boss	Bozc
lost her cat	her aunt	Angel
bumped into the lamp post	your hairdresser	Mr Picnic
rang his father	our builder	Mrs French
walked towards her son	the queen	the Prime Minister
marched home to his mum	a little girl	the king
played at home with her rabbit	a small dog	Ellie
left home without his hat	the wise man	Flopsy
		Mary
		John
		Peter
		Jatinda
		Izzy
		Martin
		Craig
		Imran
		Sunny

Coloured information

Ask the children to write a sentence on dry-wipe boards, using a different colour pen for the extra information within the commas.

Ensure children apply this sentence level learning in their writing.

Shared writing

Related text level objectives: Y3 Term 3 T11, T12, T14, T20, T22

- Stress the importance of variety of sentence length in writing. Use longer sentences as an opportunity to focus on commas.

- Write the opening to a story. Use examples of the constructions practised to tell the reader more about a character, the place or time, eg **John, the dancer's father, was … They belonged to Mrs Jinks, his mothers' housekeeper. Meanwhile, the door opened …** Ensure correct punctuation for these constructions and wherever lists of nouns, verbs or adjectives occur.
- In independent time, children look in pieces of their own writing for places where they could put commas or change/join/improve sentences, thus requiring the addition of commas.

Year 4

Teaching units 20–32

Before working from these teaching units, please read the following sections:

- Introduction and rationale (page 7);
- How to use the teaching units (page 24).

A few reminders:

- Instructions for activities displaying page numbers are to be found in Section 3 of Part 3.
- For work on any grammatical feature in a previous or subsequent year or term, please refer to the grammatical subject index in Section 8 of Part 3.
- These units do **not** include the teaching for text level objectives.
- The activities in the units can be used, reused and elaborated.
- Sentence level learning should be applied in shared, guided and independent writing.

20

Y4 Term 1 S1

OBJECTIVES

S1 to reread own writing to check for grammatical sense (coherence) and accuracy (agreement); to identify errors and to suggest alternative constructions;

Principles and explanation

- Children have to consider so many different elements (eg spelling, handwriting, content) when they write, that they often 'lose track' in the course of writing. They should be encouraged to rehearse each sentence before committing it to paper, read it back after they have written it and read 'from the top' every so often to ensure there is cohesion in the writing.
- Writing for a genuine audience and/or 'publishing' work in scrap-books, anthologies, etc., helps children see the need to 'get it right'.
- The form of a verb changes according to its subject, eg **I want, he wants**. This is more obvious in the verb **to be** – **I am**, **he is**, **they are**, **I was**, **you were**. There are variations between many spoken dialects and written standard English.
- The most common construction of the simple sentence is subject/verb/object (SVO), eg **the dog** (subject) **digs** (verb) **a hole** (object) or subject/verb/complement (SVC), **the dog** (subject) **is** (verb) **tired** (complement).

Sentence level activities

Construct (page 158)

The children should first pair up red and green cards and then go off to find a child with a blue card which makes a sentence when placed between them in the order: green – blue – red, eg **He is happy.** (not **He are happy.**).

SUBJECT CARDS (EG GREEN)	VERB CARDS (EG BLUE)	COMPLEMENT CARDS(EG RED)
You	were	happy
She	were	sad
He	was	little
We	was	friendly
They	was	jolly
Her friend	is	busy
The teacher	is	tidy
The doctor	is	helpful
Mrs Bloggs	are	tired
We	are	bossy

Missing verbs

Give children fans (one between two) on which are written verbs. Say the subject and object of a sentence, eg **They bread**, and ask the children to find a suitable verb on the fan to fill the space, eg **sell**.

VERBS FOR FANS	SUBJECT – OBJECT		SUBJECT – OBJECT	
digs	They	the baby	I	dishes.
wash	I	houses.	They	football.
makes	He	a noise.	It	holes.
sell	She	curry.	He	the windows.
plays	We	cars.	They	bread.
build	She	the violin.	We	the bath.
	He	the garden.	She	potatoes.
	It	the dinner.	It	pies.
	I	clothes.	We	sandcastles.

Ensure children apply this sentence level learning in their writing.

Shared writing

Related text level objectives: Y4 Term 1 T11, T12, T24–T27

- Remind the children:
    - *Before they write*, to think through (rehearse) sentences to check that they make sense
    - *As they write*, to keep rereading to make sure that their sentences flow.
    - *After they have written*, to reread their work to check that it makes sense, that it cannot be improved and that it is accurate.

- At points during shared writing ask the children to decide what to write next and to write it down on dry-wipe boards. Check the dry-wipe boards for accurate sentences, with agreement correct. Alternatively, write down the next sentence on the white board with incorrect agreement. Ask the children to rewrite the sentence on their dry-wipe boards accurately.

Y4 Term 1 S2

OBJECTIVES

S2 to revise work on verbs from Y1 Term 3 and to investigate verb tenses: (past, present and future): compare sentences from narrative and information texts, eg narrative in past tense, explanations in present tense (eg *when the circuit is …*); forecasts/directions, etc. in future. Develop awareness of how tense relates to purpose and structure of text; to understand the term 'tense' (ie that it refers to time) in relation to verbs and use it appropriately; understand that one test of whether a word is a verb is whether or not its tense can be changed;

Principles and explanation

- See Teaching Units 2 and 37.
- The simple present is usually the base form of the verb, but with an **-s** added when it takes a singular noun or **he**, **she** or **it** as the subject, eg **I live**, **Jamila lives**.
- The simple past is usually the base form of the verb plus **-ed**, eg **He lived**, but irregular verbs form the past tense in a number of different ways, eg **I find – I found**; **I have – I had**; **I bring – I brought**; **I blow – I blew**; **I wake – I woke**.
- The most common way of referring to the future is to add **will** or **shall** to the base form, eg **I will live. I shall live**.

Sentence level activities

Tenses

Make cards which say **Today**/**Tomorrow**/**Yesterday**/**Last week**/**Next year**/**Last century**/**In the distant future**, etc. Make up a simple sentence in the present tense. (Or ask one or more of the pupils to mime a simple action, and then describe it.) Show the cards one at a time and ask the pupils to rewrite the sentence starting with that word (and consequently changing the tense). Award the card to the pupil who offers the first/best correct sentence. First work orally, then in writing on dry-wipe boards.

Today, **the man feeds (is feeding) the cat.** *Yesterday*, **the man fed the cat.** *Tomorrow*, **the man will feed the cat.** *In ten years time*, **he will not need to feed the cat because it will be dead.** *In the distant future*, **the man will be dead, let alone the cat!**

Improve (page 161)

1 "I expect it hurt when you cut your finger," said Mrs White to her three-year-old grandson. "I didn't cutted it, I shutted it in the door. It hurted a lot because I bursted the skin and splitted the nail as well. My Mum putted a big plaster on, but it still hurted. It upsetted me. So I went to the hospital and they setted it in plaster. Then they letted me come home."

2 He bringed a piece of metal which he finded at the tip. He bended it and builded a wonderful buggy. It was much better than the one you buyed from the shops.

3 He burned something on the fire which smelled really strange. It sended him to sleep and he dreamed that he had learned to do magic. In fact he had spilled the wizard's potion when he leaned on the tree and that had spoiled everything.

4 As soon as he awaked he arised from his bed and beginned to feel hungry. He bited a magic tomato and blowed the seeds out of his mouth. The seeds flyed through the air. They roded on the wind until they reached an enchanted tree. The tree shaked its branches and the magic bells ringed.

Ask the children to examine the corrected past tense verbs in each of the four boxes above to see whether they can see some similarities between them. In box 1, the past tense verbs are the same as in the present tense. In boxes 2 and 4, most of the past tense verbs have radically different spellings from the present tense. In box 3, most of the verbs have could be spelled with **-ed** or **-t**.

Ensure children apply this sentence level learning in their writing.

Shared writing

Related text level objectives: Y4 Term 1 T9, T10, T11, T14, T15

- Write a YESTERDAY-TODAY-TOMORROW story in three paragraphs. Think of a simple everyday situation which falls neatly into these three stages (eg **Yesterday you had a big falling out with your friend. Today you are feeling really lonely and have nothing to do. Tomorrow you will swallow your pride and make up with your friend.**)

    Plan it out in three boxes, corresponding to three paragraphs. See Teaching Unit 8. Paragraph 1 will start 'Yesterday …' and explain what happened previously (in the past tense). Paragraph 2 will start 'Today …' and explain how you are feeling now (in the present tense). Paragraph 3 will start 'Tomorrow …' and in it you will imagine what you are going to do to put matters right (in the future).

- Think of a story which you (and your readers) know very well. Pick a starting point somewhere in the middle of the original story.

    Write a non-rhyming poem, with three verses, on a TODAY-YESTERDAY-TOMORROW pattern (using appropriate tenses), where you share some of the thoughts and feelings of one of the main characters from that story.

    Give clues to the original story, but never actually say what it is. Get others to guess the story, eg:

Today, I have this island, my island;
Not for ever, perhaps, but for today.
Today I have the ring too, beautiful golden;
Not yet fully mine, but certainly not hers now;
(And us only twelve pence the poorer!)
How much better it suits my finger, than her nose.

And yesterday? Yesterday I had the sea,
The green sea and the green boat.
Yesterday I had the starlight,
The plucked strings, his crooning voice.
How smooth he was; all honey and flattery!
But I'd not have had him different. No.

And tomorrow? Tomorrow will be the day,
Better than Christmas. "I will. I will."
And afterwards? That night will be all feast and dancing;
Hand in hand, dancing by the sea's edge, dancing in the moonlight.
I will gaze for ever into his enormous eyes.
Tomorrow? Tomorrow will be quite … runcible!

Y4 Term 1 S3

OBJECTIVES

S3 identify the use of powerful verbs, eg *hobbled* instead of *went*, eg through cloze procedure;

Principles and explanation

A 'powerful' verb is one which conveys not just the bald or basic action but elements of character, atmosphere and mood. We tend to think of adjectives and adverbs as the 'describing words' in texts, but verbs are often vividly descriptive words. When trying to improve a dull text, substituting powerful verbs for weak ones can be more effective than lacing it with adjectives and adverbs.

Sentence level activities

Cloze (page 157)

Choose a shared text with many powerful verbs, eg *The Village of Round and Square Houses* by Ann Gripalconi (Macmillan), *The Sand Horse* by Ann Turnbull and Michael Foreman (Red Fox), and cover them with Post-its® or masking tape on which you substitute dull verbs. Discuss what the powerful verbs add in terms of character, atmosphere, mood.

Improve (page 161)

Gravella looked out of the window. She had never heard such a racket. From the parson's meadow the bull made a sound, while the piglet made a sound as if a thousand hot skewers had been put into her side. Without stopping to see any more, Gravella put on her clothes and went downstairs.

By the back door she went by Arthy doing his knives, sparks going as the grinding wheel spun. Jem's duster went as she did the pans till they looked good. But Gravella went past. She could get the high pitched shriek of an over excited pig.

"Just fancy," muttered Jem. "That was our Gravella, and not a good morning went on her lips."

Arthy did his head. And the two of them went on, grim-faced, while the pots and pans looked good in the sunlight and the sound of squealing piglet was in the morning's peace.

Changing verbs

Provide a series of sentences with weak verbs, eg **The king *went* across the room.** Discuss what the verb can tell you about the king's character and mood. Decide on a character/mood and ask one pupil to role-play *how* the king 'went'. Ask for suitable powerful verbs to convey his going, eg **stormed**, **clattered**. Suggested sentences: **She *got* into the car. Billy *ran* down the road. He *looked* out of the window.**

Collect

- Collect powerful alternatives for common verbs, eg **eat**, **look**, **say**, and discuss when and why you might use the alternatives.
- Spot powerful verbs in stories and poems and discuss why the author chose them. **Can you think of any alternatives?**

Ensure children apply this sentence level learning in their writing.

Shared writing

Related text level objectives: Y4 Term 1 T1, T11, T12, T14

Choose a character, give her or him a name and decide what sort of person she or he is. Decide with the class how the character is feeling and what has just happened that led to this. Decide a brief scenario involving the character, and ask pupils to act it out, given that the character is feeling angry, sad, happy, etc. Write an account, using verbs to show the reader how the character feels. For instance, if she is angry she might 'storm' through a room, whereas if she is miserable she might 'slouch'.

Marcie charged into the room … That's exactly how she came in, isn't it? 'Charged' is the right word to use because we want to show the reader that she is feeling angry. Now, how did she look at Mr Patel? **and she glowered at Mr Patel.** I don't need that **she**, do I? It'd sound better without it. **Marcie charged into the room and glowered …** Yes. Right, what was Mr Patel doing? I've said his name so I can just say 'He': **He was staring out of the window, but he heard her and turned round**. Turned is a bit dull. Show us how you did it again, Bruce. **Spun round** – good!

23

Y4 Term 1 S4

OBJECTIVES

S4 to identify adverbs and understand their functions in sentences through: identifying common adverbs with -ly suffix and discussing their impact on the meaning of sentences; noticing where they occur in sentences and how they are used to qualify the meanings of verbs; collecting and classifying examples of adverbs, eg for speed: *swiftly, rapidly, sluggishly*; light: *brilliantly, dimly*; investigating the effects of substituting adverbs in clauses or sentences, eg *They left the house … ly*; using adverbs with greater discrimination in own writing;

Principles and explanation

- Many adverbs answer the question 'How?' about what is happening in a sentence. These adverbs are usually formed by adding **-ly** to an adjective (though not necessarily, eg **fast**, **well**). Some words ending in **-ly** are adjectives, not adverbs, eg **woolly**, **lovely**.
- Some dialects use adjectives in place of adverbs, eg **He done it beautiful**.
- Adverbs can be placed in different positions in a sentence, and are thus useful for varying sentence structure.

Sentence level activities

Function (page 156)

The non-adverb in this example is in *italics*.

Bridie called <u>softly</u>. <u>Carefully</u> she picked up the candle and peered into the darkness. Shadows flickered. She stood <u>still</u> and listened. <u>Cautiously</u> she moved down the corridor. Her dress rustled, and she paused. A gust of wind blew <u>gently</u> and the candle flickered. <u>Fortunately</u>, it did not blow out. Her mind raced <u>madly</u>. I *will* arrive <u>soon</u>, she muttered <u>anxiously</u>.

Follow up by finding adverbs in texts and the verb or other adverb they are modifying, and discuss the effect on meaning of where the adverb is placed in relation to the verb.

Collect and classify (page 156)

Ask the children to find the adverbs in a text and try to find the verbs to which the adverbs relate. In *Suddenly* by Colin McNaughton the same adverb, **suddenly**, is used throughout.

Hetty came **quietly** from where she had been hiding. She crossed the lawn, not **slowly**, not **quickly**.

"Hetty," shouted her aunt, so **loudly** and **coarsely** that Hetty imagined a crow.

Hetty shook the dew out of her woolly hat. She gave a friendly smile at her aunt. But this only served to make her more angry.

"Stop it," she shouted **harshly**.

Hetty did not speak. She stared **calmly** at her shoes. Her mind drifted **easily** back into her own dream world. Looking up, she tossed her head **defiantly**.

Re-order (page 160)

Make a sentence on a washing line, sentence maker or on the computer (large screen). Move the adverb around in the sentence to see where it:

- could go without changing the meaning of the sentence;
- could go and change the meaning;
- couldn't go because the result would not be a sentence, eg **Quietly, he tiptoed out of the room. He quietly tiptoed out of the room. He tiptoed quietly out of the room. He tiptoed out quietly of the room**, etc. Look at possible implications for punctuation.

He tiptoed out of the room quietly.
Softly, she opened the door.
Sally walked slowly home.
You should think seriously about this problem.
She tripped accidentally over the cables.
Gravella complained loudly to the piglet but not a word passed its lips.
Jo scribbled rapidly on the wall and turned to run.
The policeman smiled calmly.
Bilbo slept fitfully with dreams of the dragon racing madly through his mind.

Construct (page 158)

NOUNS (BLUE)	VERBS (RED)	ADVERBS (YELLOW)
Birds	behave	badly
Men	sing	well
Dogs	walk	beautifully
Girls	swim	slowly
Boys	play	fast
Women	dance	softly
Footballers	shout	rudely
Teachers	eat	lazily
Giants	fly	smartly
Policemen	talk	sweetly
Doctors	cry	loudly
Babies	think	messily

Ensure children apply this sentence level learning in their writing.

Shared writing

Related text level objectives: Y4 Term 1 T1, T11, T12, T13, T14

In narrative use adverbs when writing dialogue, to show how characters speak. As you compose, ask the children to role-play your speakers, conveying *how* they spoke each line. Use this to devise suitable adverbs. In rereading your writing demonstrate that you can have too much of a good thing!

The children continue to write the dialogue, using adverbs and powerful verbs to convey how the speakers spoke. Some of the children could write on overhead transparencies so that their work can be discussed by the class. Consider the effectiveness of the verbs and adverbs, including whether they are under- or overused.

Y4 Term 1 S5

OBJECTIVES

S5 to practise using commas to mark grammatical boundaries within sentences; link to work on editing and revising own writing.

Principles and explanation

Commas help the reader make sense of a text, by showing where there is a break in the sense within a sentence. They help the reader 'chunk' up the sentence into meaningful units, mirroring the function of intonation in spoken language.

Sentence level activities

Construct (page 158)

GREEN	PINK	BLUE
Miss Jones,	our teacher,	is getting married on Saturday.
Seelawn,	the nanny,	was flying home today.
Mr Bloggs,	the plumber,	might run in the marathon.
Spud,	my hairdresser,	won't be able to go to the party.
ET,	your typist,	has too many teeth.

In this version, ask three children to come to the front of the class and hand them a card each. Ask them to form a sentence. Hand out the remaining cards to twelve other children. Ask three of these children to exchange with a child with the same coloured card who is standing at the front. The rest of the children read out the resulting sentence with suitable intonation to take account of the extra information inserted at the comma boundaries.

Ask three children to remain standing, eg to make the sentence **Miss Jones, my hairdresser, might run in the marathon.**

Ask the middle child to step forward and ask the children to expand the information about her being my hairdresser starting with the word **who …**, eg **who used to be my hairdresser**, **who wants to be my hairdresser**, **who hates being my hairdresser**. Discuss the need for commas to separate out this additional information about the subject of the sentence.

Substitute 1

Find a sentence from a text in which additional information is demarcated by commas, eg **'I am Roland, alone now with my mother, the lady of the castle.'** – from page 42 of *King of the Dark Tower*, by Alan Brown (Hodder & Stoughton). Think of some famous characters from novels or history and make up sentences with a similar construction, eg:

I am Harry Potter, flying around with my friends, the Weasleys.
I am Bananaman, amazingly transformed from the body of Eric, my everyday personality.

Substitute 2

Find a sentence from a text in which a list of actions is demarcated by a comma or commas, eg **'There was a ring at the back door. Uncle Albert stopped peeling potatoes, wiped his wet hands on the sides of his trousers and answered it.'** – from page 24 of *The Time and Space of Uncle Albert* by Russell Stannard (Faber). Suggest a replacement for the first sentence, eg:

There was a scratching on the window
There was a giggle from the back of the classroom
A hiss of steam emerged from the great engine
A light flashed in the darkness.

Ask the children to write a second sentence which copies as closely as possible the structure of the model, but also picks up clues from the first sentence and carries on in the same genre, eg:

A light flashed in the darkness. The sentry jerked out of his stupor, raised his head slowly above the barricade and scanned the night intently.

Substitute 3

Start from other sentences in texts and with the children create more sentences on the same pattern in order to build up children's repertoire and the attendant punctuation, eg 'The next morning when Ezzie looked under his pillow, there was no money.' – from page 54 of *The Eighteenth Emergency* by Betsy Byars (Puffin). Insert a different character and make up the remainder of the sentence, eg:

The next morning when Goldilocks woke up feeling so sick, she wished she hadn't eaten so much porridge.

or

The next morning when the Frog prince woke up and saw the face next to him on the pillow, he wished he was back in the pond.

Collect and classify (page 156)

Choose a page of text without dialogue, but with commas demarcating lists of actions and additional information. Ask the children to classify the uses of the commas.

Fix it

Remove all commas from a page of text and ask the children to insert them, discussing their usage.

Ensure children apply this sentence level learning in their writing.

Shared writing

Related text level objectives: Y4 Term 1 T11, T24, T25

Write a paragraph of a story or non-fiction text to demonstrate the use of commas and how to think in meaningful chunks, and insert commas as part of the first draft of writing. First, generate with the children on a large piece of paper the content for writing a paragraph. Construct sentences out of that information which require commas, preferably in lists of actions or extra information. You could write the sentences in two colours, with a different colour for the bit of the sentence between the commas. Talk aloud as you make your choices of words and phrases and talk about the need for commas as you are writing – not as an apparent afterthought. Invite the children to suggest the last two or three sentences.

Repeat this process with new information and ask the children to write sentences on their dry-wipe boards and share with the rest of the class, explaining their use of commas.

Y4 Term 1 T15

OBJECTIVES

T15 to use paragraphs in story writing to organise and sequence the narrative;

Related text level objectives:

Y4 Term 1 T4 to explore narrative order: identify and map out the main stages of the story: introductions → build ups → climaxes or conflicts → resolutions;

Y4 Term 1 T10 to plan a story identifying the stages of its telling;

Y4 Term 3 T3 to understand how paragraphs or chapters are used to collect, order and build up ideas;

Principles and explanation

- Refer to Teaching Unit 8.
- Year 4 pupils need to begin to understand how to organise more extended chronological narratives into several basic paragraph units which relate to story structure. They also need to be increasingly aware of, and be able to use, appropriate ways of introducing and/or connecting paragraphs in chronological narratives.

Shared writing

- **Collect and classify (page 156)**

  Using a variety of texts which provide chronological narratives written in paragraphs, identify the paragraph connectives which relate to time or narrative sequence. These may be words or phrases, and some may be more obvious than others, eg **The next day …**, **Later …**, **No sooner had he … than …**, **Meanwhile …**.

  Sort and classify them. Discuss their use. Ask why they are there, whether all paragraphs include them and whether they are always right at the beginning.

  Map some narratives against a time line, then 'box' them using these temporal connectives as labels for the boxes: **In the beginning**, **Many weeks later**, **Straight after that**, etc.

  Reconstruct the stories using the temporal connectives as 'paragraph prompts'.

- Select a text with a strong, interesting story structure. It can be advantageous to choose something in picture book format which isn't, as it stands, written out as a straight paragraphed narrative text. The example used here is *Where the Wild Things Are* by Maurice Sendak (Collins Picture Lions). Amongst many others, *Gorilla* by Anthony Browne (Walker) also works well at all the same levels.

  Through interactivity and discussion, 'box' the story in order to identify the main stages of the narrative, eg:

Max was naughty and was sent to his room.

A forest grew in his room.

An ocean appeared and he sailed across it.

He reached the island, tamed the wild things, and became king.

He got homesick and returned to his room.

Possibly, expand these boxes with notes about the principal 'events' within each.

Try mapping the boxes onto a timeline, exploring how long each took (or perhaps how long its seemed to Max that each took).

Discuss and add temporal connectives (or paragraph prompts) to each box, which can introduce each paragraph, eg:

One night …
(Max was naughty and was sent to his room.)

Later that night …
(a forest grew in his room.)

Quite suddenly …
(an ocean appeared and he sailed across it.)

After sailing for days, weeks, months and years …
(he reached an island, tamed the wild things, and became king.)

A lifetime later, or so it seemed to Max …
(he got homesick and returned to his room.)

- Using the **one box per paragraph** principle, base a piece of whole class composition on this. The outcome can be a 'straight' retelling of the narrative in different words, an elaboration, or one which provokes more originality by altering, say, the characters or setting. Whichever of these, it is however essential to retain the box/paragraph structure derived from the original.
- After appropriate interactive discussion and engagement with the original text, the level of such activity can be further significantly developed by using the 'boxes' to move from the superficial narrative to a more sub-textual level. You can then use this as a more generic frame for writing, facilitating movement into more original content, eg:

The protagonist is frustrated and angered by the restrictions of his home life.

He fantasises an 'escape' into another world.

He works through his anger and frustration in this fantasy world.

He is then ready to return to reality, and welcome its positive benefits.

Working in this way, the boxing of story segments provides the basis for a plan and the 'paragraph prompts', eg **Later that night …** can constitute a frame for subsequent individual writing or supported composition.

Y4 Term 2 S1

OBJECTIVES

S1 to revise and extend work on adjectives from Y3 Term 2 and link to work on expressive and figurative language in stories and poetry: constructing adjectival phrases; examining comparative and superlative adjectives; comparing adjectives on a scale of intensity (eg *hot, warm, tepid, lukewarm, chilly, cold*); relating them to the suffixes which indicate degrees of intensity (eg *-ish, -er, -est*); relating them to adverbs which indicate degrees of intensity (eg *very, quite; more, most*) and through investigating words which can be intensified in these ways and words which cannot;

Principles and explanation

- See the definition of adjective in the Glossary (Section 7 of Part 3).
- Adjectival phrases act as adjectives, eg **He's not** *as old as you*; **I'm** *really hungry*; **he's bigger than you**; **she's** *the tallest*.

Sentence level activities

Collect and classify 1: revision from Year 3 (page 156)

Find the adjectives in a page of text and discuss what they add to the narrative, eg:

They stopped and stared. The bridge hung across the **sluggish** river. It was made of **black metal** chains. **Dry** rushes had been woven between the **rusted** chains. On the **opposite** shore two **large**, **wooden** posts held the chains. The posts were decorated with **bright** feathers and **small** flags that shimmered in the breeze.

"Prayer flags," muttered Signi, "They are **afraid** of the river."

Dore looked down at the **dark** river. It was a **rich**, **brown** colour, swollen with the rain. A **white** mist hung across the **dull** skin of the river so that the **far** bank was barely **visible**. It would be like walking into a **white** cave of nothingness. Dore touched the **cold** hilt of his sword for comfort.

Note: **Prayer** is a noun, not an adjective although in this sentence it has an adjectival function.

Adjective plants

Draw a stem for a noun and write appropriate adjectives in each leaf.

Improve (page 161)

This text has a superfluity of adjectives in places or an overuse of the same adjective. There are also instances where a more precise noun would be better than some, or may be all, of the adjectives.

The tired, weary, sleepy rat ran down the steep, sloping bank, panting hard. It paused at the wet, damp ditch and waited. Not a sound came from the direction of the big road, so it began to make its way along the wet, damp ditch towards the nice, warm, snug, friendly burrow.

There was an uneasy, nasty, horrid silence from the burrow. It was dawn and the sun-light had already warmed the damp earth beneath the rat's damp paws. It stopped and sniffed. There was no trace of rabbit.

Degrees of intensity

Write a number of adjectives, eg **hot**, **warm**, **tepid**, **luke-warm**, **chilly**, **cold**, **frozen** on cards. Use a washing line or sentence maker to order these words by degrees of intensity. This activity could be carried out on the computer.

Ask the children to suggest words to describe something, eg light or speed, and place them on the scale as they are suggested, eg:

- light: **dazzling – dim**
- speed: **supersonic – snail's-pace.**

Collect and classify 2 (page 156)

Draw up a table with the headings: Adjective, Comparative, Superlative. Write the adjectives in Collect and classify 1 in the adjective column. With the help of the children, fill in the columns with the comparative and superlative forms. Notice the different ways this occurs, eg **difficulter** is not a word.

Ensure children apply this sentence level learning in their writing.

Shared writing

Related text level objectives: Y4 Term 2 T10, T11, T13

- Write brief openings to stories which introduce a character and describe a setting. The setting must include not only the place but also add in something about the weather, time of day or season to help create atmosphere. Emphasise the need to be precise with nouns (**robin** rather than **bird**) and to select adjectives with care, eg:

  Snow clouds hid the bright moon. Sandals Lane was quite dark. Snow whipped down from the North and ice frosted the window panes. It was so cold that locks froze and stones in the wall cracked. Latika poked her nose out of number thirty-two. She could see something glittering on the front path and it wasn't the snow.

  It is worth trying sentences out with and without adjectives to check whether embellishment does add to the force of the sentence. This can be done orally, before writing anything down. Avoid adjectives that are obvious and tell the reader what is already known.

- Compose a comparative poem where the purpose is to exaggerate, eg:

  He is funnier than Lenny Henry on a banana skin.
  He is slimmer than a stick insect on a diet.
  He is angrier than a bull who sees a red packet of beefburgers in a shopping bag ….

  Write down the initial comparison, eg **She is taller than a ladder.** Then add a further exaggeration, eg **She is taller than a ladder on stilts.**

- Invent a mythical creature and write a boastful poem, eg:

  The Zegreb is –
  Faster than a jet-powered cheetah,
  Cleverer than Einstein's father,
  Quieter than a needle dropped on velvet.

- It will be useful to some pupils to have thought out a list of adjectives to use. The skill is in thinking of an initial idea and then taking it one step further, eg **slower than a snail** might be an initial idea. This could be taken one step further, **slower than a snail with its brakes on, sitting on super glue!**

Y4 Term 2 S2 (Y5 Term 3 S5)

OBJECTIVES

S2 to use the apostrophe accurately to mark possession through: identifying possessive apostrophes in reading and to whom or what they refer; understanding basic rules for apostrophising singular nouns, eg *the man's hat*; for plural nouns ending in *-s*, eg *the doctors' surgery*; and for irregular plural nouns, eg *men's room* and *children's playground*; distinguishing between the uses of the apostrophe for contraction and possession; beginning to use the apostrophe in their own writing;

Principles and explanation

- Children need to be clear about the difference between the two functions of the apostrophe – possession and omission. See the Glossary entry for apostrophe (Part 3, Section 7).
- The term 'contraction' to indicate the use of an apostrophe to replace omitted letters, eg **can't**, **won't**, has been superseded by the more accurate term 'omission'.
- On the whole, the apostrophe of omission is used in informal writing such as a letter to a friend, or in direct speech.
- Children should be secure in the use of the apostrophe for omission before tackling this objective which deals with possession. (See Y3 Term 2 W15 and Y3 Term 3 W11.)
- The possessive words **yours**, **his**, **hers**, **ours**, **theirs** and **its** are *not* written with an apostrophe.
- Confusion between **its**, as a possessive word, eg **Its wing was broken**, and **it's** meaning **it is**, is common, eg **It's hot**.
- In cases of possession, using an apostrophe makes writing more economical, **the gloves of the girl** becomes **the girl's gloves**.

Sentence level activities

Collect and classify 1 (page 156)

Choose a page of text containing a number of apostrophes of possession and omission. With the children, pick out the words containing apostrophes, one by one. Classify each word containing an apostrophe and the subsequent word in two columns, eg possession, **Dad's coat**; omission, **Dad's forgotten**. The children should indicate which column each word belongs in by writing P or O on their dry-wipe boards. (They could equally well raise a finger for Possession or make a circle with their thumb and forefinger for Omission.) Before accepting an answer, insist on an explanation from the child as to why he or she chose that answer.

Jamila's father was late for work. He was rushing round the house like a fire brand. He upset Grampa's tooth mug and stood on the dog's paw.

'Won't you calm down?' said Mother. 'It's not as late as all that.'

'It is,' he snarled. 'I'll lose my job.'

He grabbed his sandwich box and slammed the door.

Jamila knelt by the dog, and stroked its paw.

'Dad's forgotten his coat,' said Mum. 'Jamila, jump up and take your Dad's coat to him. He can't have got far.'

'Mum, Dad's an Olympic runner. He'll be at the station by now.'

'Try anyway, the forecast's bad for this evening. I'll take your Gran's breakfast up. Oh, and I've got to polish the boys' shoes before they go to school.'

If the children have difficulty in deciding whether an apostrophe is one of omission or possession, ask them whether the word after the apostrophe, eg **coat** or **forgotten**, *belongs* to Dad. Where the apostrophe is used as omission, it can be replaced by the full version, eg **Dad has forgotten**.

Collect and classify 2 (page 156)

Look through other texts for apostrophes of possession to add to the list. Make certain the list contains some regular plurals, eg **boys**' and some irregular plurals, eg **children's**. Classify the words in two columns: Singular and Plural.

To illustrate the plural apostrophe rule, ask two or three boys to stand together. Ask them to hold a card between them on which is written **The boys**. Now put a card by their feet on which is written **shoes**. On the board write **the shoes of the boys** and ask the children for a more economical way of saying this. When they say **the boys' shoes**, put an apostrophe on the card which says **The boys** and put it in front of the word **shoes** on the floor – **The boys' shoes**. Repeat the process with two or three girls and then finally with both the boys and the girls and a card on which is written **children**.

P and O

Give half the children cards on which P is written and the other half cards with O. Say part of a sentence containing a word with an apostrophe of omission or possession or a word ending in **-s** which should not contain an apostrophe, eg *John's* **gone to hospital;** *John's* **friend is ill. Look,** *it's* **a sparrow;** *its* **wing is broken. She put four** *apples* **in her** *friend's* **bag; they are hers** The children raise the appropriate card, or not. Ask for an explanation of their decision.

Improve (page 161)

Write a short text in which some of the apostrophes are missing or in the wrong place. Restrict the use of apostrophes to possession. On a future occasion include apostrophes of omission and incorporate both **it's** and **its**.

Apostrophe

Say a sentence including a word with an apostrophe and ask the children to write two of the words on their dry-wipe boards, eg **I have to wash the** *men's football* **kit.** Give practice in using the possessive apostrophe in regular and irregular plurals as well as singular words.

Ensure children apply this sentence level learning in their writing.

Shared writing

Related text level objectives: Y3 Term 2 T10, T11, T13

- Children could write pattern poems along the lines of:
  My mother's cat is …
  My cousin's cat has …
- Plan a story which will necessitate using both apostrophes of possession and omission (probably using direct speech). Decide the names of the characters and agree to write the story about some of their belongings such as their animals or their family. Demonstrate the first part of the story and then ask for the children's contributions, eg:
  The wind was whistling through the trees. Jan could hear his father's voice downstairs, and could imagine his mother's patient smile as she listened. 'I've just about had enough. I've decided to pack it all in. We'll be all right. I've checked up on that.'

Y4 Term 2 S3 and S4
(Y5 Term 1 S1 and Term 2 S1)

OBJECTIVES

S3 to understand the significance of word order, eg some re-orderings destroy meaning, some make sense but change meaning, sentences can be re-ordered to retain meaning (sometimes adding words); subsequent words are governed by preceding ones;

S4 to recognise how commas, connectives and full stops are used to join and separate clauses; to identify in their writing where each is most effective;

Principles and explanation

- A clause is a group of words that expresses an event, eg **She drank some water**, or a situation, eg **She was thirsty**/**She wanted a drink**. It usually contains a subject and a verb, eg **she drank**/**was**/**wanted**.
- A sentence can be simple, compound or complex.
- A simple sentence consists of one clause, eg **It was late.**
- A compound sentence has two or more clauses joined by **and**, **or**, **but**, **so**. The clauses are of equal weight (they are both main clauses), eg **It was late but I wasn't tired.**
- A complex sentence consists of a main clause and one or more subordinate clauses, eg **Although it was late, I wasn't tired.**
- Economy in writing is achieved by bringing ideas or events together into compound sentences. Explicitness is achieved by the use of subordinate clauses. Interest for the reader is achieved by varying the length, complexity and word order in sentences. The occasional short, simple sentence helps to hold the reader's attention.
- The order of words within noun phrases is not flexible, eg **That big, grey sausage dog on the sofa**; none of the words could be moved. Generally the subject of a sentence precedes the verb, eg **The dog bit the man** is totally different in meaning from **The man bit the dog**. Some prepositional phrases which modify verbs and some adverbials can be positioned in different places in relation to the verb and retain the meaning, eg:
He was awake *during the night*./ **During the night, he was awake.**
He was *frequently* seen./ **He was seen *frequently*.**

Sentence level activities
Re-order (page 160)
Ask six children to hold up cards containing words and punctuation marks, eg:

| the cat | the dog | the horse | the cow | and | and | chased | so | kicked | , | . | . |

Make a human sentence by children holding up the words or put a sentence onto a large computer screen, eg **That big, grey sausage dog on the sofa wanders around the village all night long**. Move the words around, first within the noun phrase, and then around the verb. Establish which can be moved whilst retaining the same meaning and which cannot. Repeat with other sentences in order to construct a general hypothesis.

Ensure children apply this sentence level learning in their writing.

Shared writing

- Provide or generate from the children the elements of a story or a procedure, eg:

Abdi leaves his friend's house. He takes the route home. He whistles softly. He scuffs his feet in the dry leaves. He pretends to dribble a football up the pitch. He passes a derelict church. He hears a sound. He stops. He listens. He hears someone crying. He pushes the gate open. It creaks. etc.

Use conjunctions and connectives, commas and full stops to demonstrate how to create an interesting narrative out of these bald facts, eg:

Abdi leaves his friend's house and takes the route home. He whistles softly as he scuffs his feet in the dry leaves and then pretends to dribble a football up the pitch.

Ask the children to suggest the next sentence and discuss their contributions before writing one on the board. Continue interactively and then ask the children to write the next two sentences on their own maintaining the style you have established in the rest of the story.

- Find or create and enlarge an explanatory text some of which is cumbersome in its construction, eg:

Whirlwinds are smaller than hurricanes and so are tornadoes. Whirlwinds and tornadoes are about a hundred feet across. They start deep inside large thunderclouds. These thunderclouds are called supercells and inside they have a column of warm air which rises and high winds roar through the top of the cloud making the warm air in the cloud spin which becomes a spinning vortex which sucks up everything in its path.

Model for the children how to sort out the main statements and write them clearly. Let the children have a go by discussing it in pairs and trying it out on their dry-wipe boards.

- Model how you can play with a sentence to give differing effects, eg **The sinister man crept furtively up the gravel path.** How would you write that as if you were making a hurried phone call to the police? **Man – creeping – path!** Make it into a compound sentence to add some more information **The sinister man crept furtively up the path but the boy heard him.** Change the sentence to emphasise the cleverness of the boy. You may need to change the word order and/or make it into a complex sentence, eg **Although the man crept furtively, the boy heard him.** Demonstrate editing work to check that word order makes sense, gives the required effect and is brief when brevity is needed.

Y4 Term 2 T19

OBJECTIVES

T19 to identify how and why paragraphs are used to organise and sequence information;

Related text level objectives: Y4 Term 2 T24; Y4 Term 3 T24

Principles and explanations

- See Teaching Unit 8.
- For connectives, refer to Teaching Unit 32.

Shared writing

- For a variety of suitable non-fiction texts (for this purpose select ones written in continuous paragraphed prose):
  - Interactively explore and discuss why the writer has used paragraphs in the way he or she has.
  - Ask the children what each paragraph is about. Can they give a summative 'title' to each paragraph? Could they sum up the content of the paragraph in a single word?
  - Map out the progression of paragraphs through a whole piece or article. Use boxes for this to reinforce the one paragraph per box principle.
  - Stick or copy a non-fiction text into the middle of a large piece of paper. Make marginal annotations which comment on the content and organisation of the paragraphs. (**New paragraph here because he is now talking about a different country./This paragraph is about different kinds of weather./Uses this paragraph to introduce the idea of magnetism./This paragraph explains why leaves are green./Conclusion: this paragraph sums up the information given earlier./*However* used as the link word.**)
  - Contrast and compare different examples.
  - Summarise a text by replacing each paragraph by a single sentence.
  - Clarify an existing text by providing each paragraph with a subheading.
- **Collect and classify (page 156)**
  Using a variety of text types, collect and classify the connectives (words and phrases) used to link paragraphs. Are certain connectives more frequent in certain text types?
- For an 'explanation' text:
  - Summarise each paragraph into a 'box'.
  - Locate (or invent) an appropriate connective to act as the 'paragraph prompt' for each box.
  - Use this to generate a generic frame into which to fit other explanation writing, eg:

The first thing that happens is …

This means that …

After that …

As a result …

Then …

The final result is that …

- Now work backwards to fill out this frame with a new context, but within the same text type. Keep to the one paragraph per box principle.
- Bring to the lesson diagrams of information obtained in another curricular area, eg:

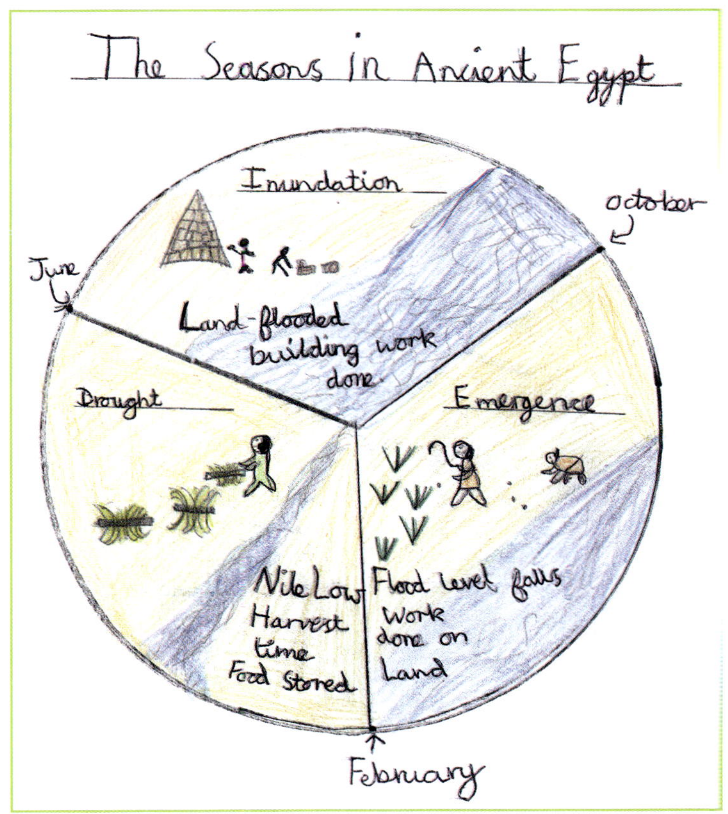

Y4 Term 3 S1
(Y5 Term 1 S1 and Term 2 S1)

OBJECTIVES

S1 to understand that some words can be changed in particular ways and others cannot, eg changing verb endings, adding comparative endings, pluralisation, and that these are important clues for identifying word classes;

Principles and explanation

- Certain endings are typical of certain word classes: **-ing** and **-ed** end many verbs, eg **wasting** and **wasted**; **-er** and **-est** make many adjectives into comparatives, eg **hotter** and **hottest**; **-s** is often added to plural nouns, eg **cakes** and is also used at the end of third person singular verbs, eg **takes**.
- However, there are exceptions in both directions, such as words ending in **-ing** which are not verbs, eg **He picked up the sizzling sausages**, and past tense verbs which do not end in **-ed**, eg **sunk**. There are words ending in **-er** which are not comparative, eg **runner**, and comparatives which do not end in **-er**, eg **more difficult**.

Sentence level activities

Endings

Make some large cards with various endings. Use **-ed**, **-ing**, **-er**, **-est**, **-s**, **-es**, **-ly**. Then, on a different colour of card, put a number of words. Create a grid like this:

NOUN	VERB	ADJECTIVE	ADVERB	NOT SURE	DOESN'T WORK

Emphasise that you can put words into more than one category, eg **farms**, but that generally some endings work with some words and not others. Which words fall into several different categories?

Give the children small versions of the above words, possibly one set between two. Ask them to make words which do work, and words which definitely do not work, eg **aftering**, **happied**.

Suggest sentences for the words which do work.

As a game, try to invent sentences using the words which do not work, eg **I am aftering this bus. Yesterday I happied my friend.** What kind of words have we created here? (verbs).

Same word sentences

Select some of the words from the activities above. Just for fun, try making sentences which contain as many different endings as possible for the same word. The sentences must make sense and be grammatically correct – although they will probably not be very 'elegant'.

Words that can act as both nouns and verbs are probably the easiest and most versatile for this, but try others as well, eg:

The farmer still farms the farm his family had farmed for generations and his daughter will soon be farming it too.
Remember, he remembers remembering what he never remembered before.

Improve (page 161)

Rachel has written a poem. She is having some difficulty with word endings. Ask pupils to act as 'editors' and help sort them out. (Remember there is not necessarily a single 'right' answer!) Which type of word is giving Rachel difficulty?

Trees

Trees Trees
Sways in the wind
Twists as bean round the net
Branch are tough and rough
Wraps around each other
Like a handly cuff
Rachel, Year 4

The children could be asked to take other texts, written by themselves or others, and create deliberate mistakes in word endings, for others to correct.

Ensure children apply this sentence level learning in their writing.

Shared writing

Related text level objective: Y4 Term 3 T15

Use some of the **same-word-different-ending** sentences generated above to create a word-play poem. Alliteration is necessarily built in to this activity, and some verses may even turn out as tongue-twisters!

The farmer, farming, farmed the farm.
The sailor, sailing, sailed the sea.
The workers worked through the working day.
But by just being did the bumble bee.

or

The playful player played the play.
The shoppers shopped for shopping in the shop.
The typist typed the typing in a type of daze
But just stopping up the bottle did the stopper stop.

Y4 Term 3 S3
(Y5 Term 1 S1 and Y5 Term 2 S1)

OBJECTIVES

S3 to understand how the grammar of a sentence alters when the sentence type is altered, eg when a statement is made into a question, a question becomes an order, a positive statement is made negative, noting, eg the order of words, verb tenses, additions and/or deletions of words, changes to punctuation;

Principles and explanation

- When a statement uses a verb string, it can be made into a question by re-ordering the words, eg **He has been making jam.** becomes **Has he been making jam?** In a verb string, all but the final verb are called auxiliary verbs, eg **has** and **been** are auxiliary and **making** is the main verb.
- When a statement uses just a main verb, auxiliary verbs are needed to make it into a question, eg **He made jam.** becomes **Did he make jam?** or **Has he made jam?** (**did** and **has** are auxiliary).

Sentence level activities

Re-order (page 160)

Hand five children the cards for the sentence:

| Mr Bloggs | is | going | to the library | . |

Hand a child a question mark and ask him or her to rearrange the children into a question and take up position. (Ask the child with the full stop to sit down.) Repeat with **Mr Bloggs has been to the library.** and then **Mr Bloggs went to the library.** Note that the last statement cannot be made into a question using the same words.

Compare (page 157)

First, with the children, compare the statements in the left column with the questions on the right and agree what makes it possible to make a statement into a question using the same words. Next, with the children, change the 'dog' statements into questions and see whether your theory holds out.

STATEMENTS	QUESTIONS
Mr Bloggs is going to the library.	Is Mr Bloggs going to the library?
Mr Bloggs was going to the library.	Was Mr Bloggs going to the library?
Mr Bloggs will be going to the library.	Will Mr Bloggs be going to the library?
Mr Bloggs might be going to the library.	Might Mr Bloggs be going to the library?
Mr Bloggs has been to the library.	Has Mr Bloggs been to the library?
Mr Bloggs had been to the library.	Had Mr Bloggs been to the library?
Mr Bloggs can go to the library.	Can Mr Bloggs go to the library?
Mr Bloggs goes to the library.	Does Mr Bloggs go to the library?
Mr Bloggs went to the library.	Did Mr Bloggs go to the library?

The dogs are digging a hole.
The dogs were digging a hole.
The dogs will be digging a hole.
The dogs might be digging a hole
The dogs could be digging a hole.
The dogs have been digging a hole.
The dogs had been digging a hole.
The dogs can dig a hole.
The dogs dig a hole.
The dogs dug a hole.

Change the statements

Repeat this activity but changing all the statements from positive to negative. Note that the same theory applies. **The dogs *are digging* a hole./The dogs *are not digging* a hole./ The dogs *dig* a hole./The dogs *do not dig* a hole.**

Convert

Convert any of these statements into an order and notice that the order is the same, regardless of whether the subject is singular or plural and regardless of tense because imperatives are always in the present tense: **Go to the library! Dig a hole!**

Asking questions

Take one of the questions, eg **Might the dogs be digging a hole?** Ask questions using the question hand (on each finger there is a different 'wh' word – **who? where? when? what? why?**), eg **Where might the dogs be digging? When might the dogs be digging? Why might the dogs be digging? Who might be digging? What might the dogs be digging?** Again, notice the construction of the question.

Quickmake (page 158)

Starting question: **Will Sam be going out to play?**
Starting order: **Cut carefully round the edge.**

Ensure children apply this sentence level learning in their writing.

Shared writing

Related text level objective: Y4 Term 3 T25

Examine and discuss the language of some simple advertising jingles. Write your own advertisement or radio jingle. Using the linguistic features explored above, try to include at least one **question**, one **positive** and/or **negative statement**, and one **imperative** (order).

Do your dogs have trouble digging? Blunter claws mean fewer holes. Buy our "DOGGY CLAW SHARP" nail file. DOGS DIG BETTER WITH "CLAW SHARP" CLAWS!

Alternatively:

Is your garden full of holes? Is doggy digging getting you down? Buy our "DOGGY CLAW CLIP" clippers. "CLAW CLIP" CLAWS DIG FEWER HOLES!

Y4 Term 3 S4

OBJECTIVES

S4   the use of connectives, eg adverbs, adverbial phrases, conjunctions, to structure an argument, eg *if … then*, *on the other hand …*, *finally*, *so*.

Principles and explanation

- Connecting adverbs (and adverbial phrases and clauses) maintain the cohesion of a text, eg to present an argument, to indicate a sequence of time, to show contrast.
- Connecting adverbs and conjunctions function differently. Conjunctions, eg **but** and **although**, join clauses within a sentence. Connecting adverbs, eg **however**, connect ideas, but the clauses remain separate sentences. The same meaning can be achieved in one sentence or by using two sentences, eg:

  I was angry *but* I didn't say anything. (**but** is a conjunction – one sentence)
  ***Although* I was angry, I didn't say anything.** (**Although** is a conjunction – one sentence)
  I was angry. *However*, I didn't say anything. (**However** is an adverb – two sentences).

- Commas are often used to mark off adverbial phrases or clauses, eg **First of all, I want to say … I didn't think much of the film. Helen, on the other hand, enjoyed it.**

Sentence level activities

Function (page 156)

Choose a discussion text and underline all the connectives and conjunctions and one near the end which isn't. The non-connective in this example is in *italics*.

One hot day my uncle, Professor Stanley Russell, came out of a shop carrying a delicious ice-lolly. He held it out.

"<u>Now</u>, I have something for you to think about, Ben," said Uncle Stan. "Is this ice-lolly really here? <u>Clearly</u>, your eyes are popping, <u>and</u> your mouth is watering, <u>so</u> we know that you can see it. <u>Therefore</u> you think that the lolly is real. <u>After all</u>, most people believe what they see. <u>On the other hand</u>, take its colour. <u>Almost certainly</u> you think it is orange, <u>but</u> you can see other colours. <u>For example</u>, where the sun is glinting, the lolly looks white. <u>Thinking about it</u>, why should orange be its colour and not white? <u>Moreover</u>, you call its shape a cylinder. <u>Yet</u> from different angles you see completely different shapes, such as a circle or a rectangle. <u>Consequently</u>, what you see keeps changing. <u>In the end</u>, can you be certain of anything? <u>In other words</u>, is the lolly really here at all?"

"Not any more," I said, *looking* sadly at the sticky pool at my Uncle's feet.

"No, Ben," continued Uncle Stan, "<u>but</u> is this stick really here?"

Replace (page 160)

- Write two sentences showing the reason for a school rule, eg lining up.

If children run all at once to the door, there will be a crush and someone might get hurt. On the other hand, if children line up in partners and walk in through the door, they will get to their classrooms quickly and in safety.

- Choose another rule and explain using the same two-sentence construction – **If, On the other hand.**
- Do the same with other constructions, eg **Children should wear plimsoles instead of shoes for PE because they are better for running. Besides, plimsoles are light and won't hurt other children.**

Ensure children apply this sentence level learning in their writing.

Shared writing

Related text level objectives: Y4 Term 3 T21–T23

List arguments, with contributions from the children, for and against, eg selling fruit or sweets in school to raise money for a new computer. **Sweets are bad for teeth. Fruit is not harmful to teeth.** etc.

Draw three boxes: one for arguments against sweets and in favour of fruit; the next for counter arguments against fruit and in favour of sweets; the third for a decision. Put the statements in the boxes, eg:

Sweets are bad for teeth. Fruit is not harmful to teeth. Sweets are fattening. Fruit is less fattening. Sweet papers would cause litter. Fruit cores and pips can be recycled for compost.

Fruit is messy to peel. Children won't put the peel in the compost bin. Children would buy more sweets than fruit because they like sweets better.

Sweets are so bad for children that the arguments against selling them are stronger than the arguments against selling fruit. Action should be taken to make the fruit attractive so children will want to buy it. Very messy fruits shouldn't be sold. There should be plenty of bins available.

Have an introduction, already written, explaining the need for a new computer and the proposal to raise money by selling snacks to the children.

Talk through the next paragraph, asking for and discussing suggestions. Write on the board.

Hand over to the children discussing possible openings for each sentence and taking feedback. Insist that they reread each sentence before composing the next.

Year 5

Teaching units 33–43

Before working from these teaching units, please read the following sections:

- Introduction and rationale (page 7);
- How to use the teaching units (page 24).

A few reminders:

- Instructions for activities displaying page numbers are to be found in Section 3 of Part 3.
- For work on any grammatical feature in a previous or subsequent year or term, please refer to the grammatical subject index in Section 8 of Part 3.
- These units do **not** include the teaching for text level objectives.
- The activities in the units can be used, reused and elaborated.
- Sentence level learning should be applied in shared, guided and independent writing.

Y5 Term 1 S2
(Y5 Term 2 S2 and Y5 Term 3 S1)

OBJECTIVES

S2 to understand the basic conventions of standard English and to consider when and why standard English is used: agreement between nouns and verbs; consistency of tense and subject; avoidance of double negatives; avoidance of non-standard dialect words;

Principles and explanation

- In most areas of grammar, standard and non-standard English are the same and often children whose spoken language includes some non-standard forms do not use them in writing. The few areas of difference should be discussed in class so that children are aware of the standard forms which should be used in writing.
- In discussing these differences, the words 'standard' and 'non-standard' should be used, rather than 'correct/incorrect' or 'right/wrong', as the non-standard forms are 'correct' in casual speech.
- Non-standard forms include different past tense and past participle formation for some irregular verbs which were discussed in earlier years (see Teaching Unit 2).
- Other frequently occurring standard/non-standard features of which children should be aware include the following:
  - adjectives as adverbs (Teaching Unit 23), eg **He ran real quick.**
  - subject–verb agreement with **was**/**were**, eg **He were. They was.**
  - **them** as determiner, eg **them books**
  - 'double' negatives (more accurately, multiply-marked negatives), eg **I didn't say nothing to no-one.**
  - **what** or **as** as relative pronoun, eg **the book what/as I bought**.

Sentence level activities

Verbs

Revise the list of verbs which have different past tenses or past participles in standard and the local dialects (the list will vary from place to place), and discuss the different situations in which the alternatives are used. This discussion should be handled sensitively, as children in the class may differ according to which forms they use in casual speech. Establish the names 'standard' and 'non-standard' for these forms.

Adverbs and adjectives

Discuss the use of adjectives or adverbs to show that the non-standard goes beyond verb forms. Make sure the children all understand the standard rule (adjectives can only modify a noun).

Subject–verb agreement

Do the same for subject–verb agreement with **was**/**were**, contrasting the use in the local non-standard with that in standard English; point out that **was**/**were** is the only past-tense verb that agrees with its subject in standard English and discuss the pros and cons of the two grammars.

Ensure children apply this sentence level learning in their writing.

Shared writing

- Select a passage of standard written English and invite the children to convert it into 'correct' local non-standard.

- Collect other examples of differences between the local non-standard and standard English as a class project and record them in a book. (The collection could be built cumulatively by successive Year 5 classes as a school project.)

- As a drama activity let two children simulate a conversation between two local people and tape the result; alternatively the teacher could tape a short conversation in non-standard speech between two local people and play it to the children (without revealing identities). The tape could then be transcribed accurately by the class and discussed in terms of its grammatical features.

- Use this transcription as material for two further exercises:
  - a playscript which replaces the non-standard features, for discussion of the effects of this change;
  - a prose narrative in which the non-standard features are preserved within direct speech.

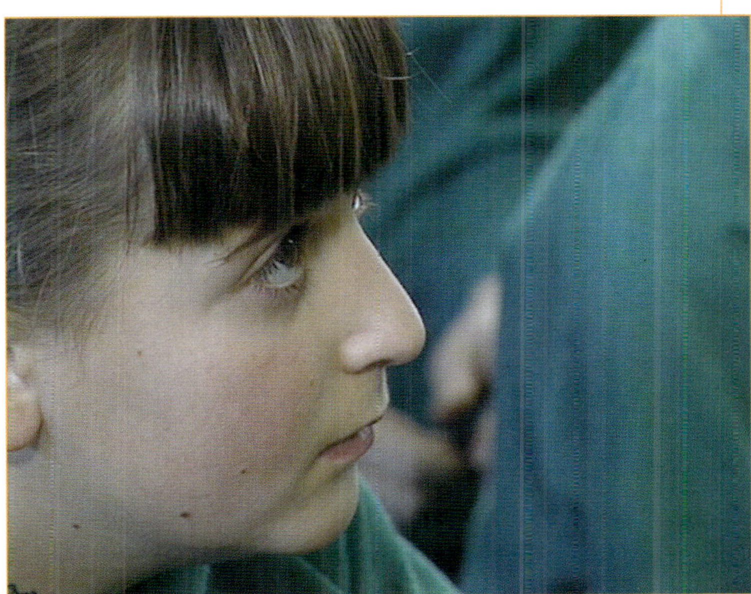

34

Y5 Term 1 S3 and S6

OBJECTIVES

S3 to discuss, proof-read and edit their own writing for clarity and correctness, eg by creating more complex sentences, using a range of connectives, simplifying clumsy constructions;

S6 to understand the need for punctuation as an aid to the reader, eg commas to mark grammatical boundaries; a colon to signal, eg a list;

Principles and explanation

- See the Glossary (Section 7 of Part 3) for an explanation of complex sentences and subordinate clauses.
- There is a tendency for weaker writers to write in simple and some compound sentences with a limited range of conjunctions within, and connectives between, sentences. Varied sentences occur when a conjunction is introduced, so it is helpful to draw the children's attention to the range of conjunctions available, eg **after, although, as, as if, as long as, as though, because, before, if, in case, once, since, than, that, though, till, until, unless, when(ever), where(ever), whereas, while**, and pronouns, eg **who, which, what, whose, where, when, why, how**.
- Commas are used after a subordinate clause which begins a sentence, eg **Although it was cold, we didn't wear our coats.** See the Glossary for other uses for the comma.
- Sometimes other punctuation can be used in much the same way as commas. Both dashes and brackets tend to indicate more of a break between subordinate and main clauses, and dashes are used in more informal writing.
- Note that simple sentences should not be linked by a comma. This is called the 'comma splice'; it has the effect of weakening both sentences and is a very common mistake in children's writing. Simple sentences may be joined by a semi-colon or a conjunction, or separated by a full stop.

Sentence level activities

Adding conjunctions

Put a list of subordinating conjunctions on display, eg **after, although, as, as if, as long as, before, if, in case, since, unless, when(ever), where(ever), whereas**. Start with a main clause, eg **we didn't wear our coats** and ask the children in turn to make up subordinate clauses to precede the main clause, eg **Before it was cold, we didn't …, Unless it was cold, we didn't …, Wherever we went we didn't …, In case it got hot, we didn't …** When they say the sentence, they should insert the comma with a curled finger and the rest of the children spot the verb in the subordinate clause.

Construct (page 158)

Give out clauses, conjunctions and commas. Children should make sentences starting with a subordinate clause so they need to get into groups of four in the order: red (conjunction) – green (clause) – blue (comma) – green (clause). The resulting sentence should make sense even though it may be unlikely, eg **In case there were rabbits everywhere, I went to the park. When I wanted to be alone, I escaped to my bedroom.** With the addition of the conjunction, the first clause in the sentence becomes the subordinate clause and the second is the main clause.

CLAUSE (EG GREEN)	CLAUSE (EG GREEN)	CONJUNCTION (EG RED)	COMMAS (EG BLUE)
I went to the park	there wasn't anyone around	Although	,
I wanted to be alone	there was a lot to be done	In case	,
I was feeling miserable	there was a strange sound	When	,
I could not eat my breakfast	there were rabbits everywhere	As	,
I climbed the staircase	it was deserted	Since	,
I wanted to finish reading my book	it was sunny	After	,
I escaped to my bedroom	it was going to be hot	Before	,
I managed to get out	it was a tight squeeze	Whenever	,

Complex sentence game (page 159)

Starter sentence: **As I leaned against the railing, it collapsed.**

Collect and classify (page 156)

Investigate other punctuation in sentences, such as dashes and brackets.

Punctuate (page 159)

Cover all the punctuation in a text. Use both punctuation fans, one for each child in the pair. Children confer to decide who has the appropriate punctuation mark on their fans.

Ensure children apply this sentence level learning in their writing.

Shared writing

Related text level objectives: Y5 Term 1 T15, T17, T24, T25

- **Writing for effect**

  Provide a structure for a short piece of writing using a strip cartoon, strip action stories, eg *Feelings* by Aliki, detailed action pictures, eg *Out and About Through the Year* by Shirley Hughes (Walker) and *Where's Wally* by Martin Handford (Walker).

  Ask children to write a story deliberately using different sentence structures, eg short, simple sentences, maximum six words; compound sentences, 10–20 words; complex sentences, minimum 25 words; a mixture of lengths of sentences; a particular, defined pattern of sentences such as short-medium-long-short-medium-long, etc.

  Discuss the effect of writing in these different ways, eg short sentences speed up the action or echo the heartbeat of a scared character.

- Ask children to write the first part of, eg a description, starting with a simple sentence such as **The girl had red hair** and adding a subordinate clause to give more information about the subject, demarcating it with commas, eg **The girl, who was standing by the door, had red hair.** Extend the description by adding another sentence with the subordinate clause in a different position, eg **Looking rather lost, she pulled a letter from her bag.** Finish the paragraph by adding some further information in the form of a list or simple sentences linked by semi-colons, eg **She read it twice; it seemed to cheer her up.**

Y5 Term 1 S4
(Y5 Term 2 S3 and Y5 Term 3 S2)

OBJECTIVES

S4 to adapt writing for different readers and purposes by changing vocabulary, tone and sentence structures to suit, eg simplifying for younger readers;

Principles and explanation

Writing can be adapted for different readers and purposes by varying:

- sentence length (including variations);
- sentence complexity;
- use of subordinate clauses and conjunctions;
- use of reported speech;
- use of first and second person pronouns;
- use of tenses;
- use of questions and other alternatives to ordinary statements (eg **suffice it to say …; …, don't you? …thought Wolfie …**);
- use of names (eg **Mr Wolf, The Big Bad Wolf, Wolfie**);
- use of vocabulary (eg **childish – scampered, prettiest**; **racey – chill out**; etc.).

Sentence level activities

Collect and classify (page 156)

Select three or four texts, each of which has clearly been written for a very different audience, eg a picture book written for very young children, a 'bedtime story'-type text written for 6–7-year-olds, a 'Horrible Histories'-type text written for 10–11-year-olds, a 'Point Horror'-type text written for teenagers. Identify and classify the main language features of each. (Perhaps this could be done as a group activity, with different groups looking at different texts and then reporting back to the whole class.)

Advice

Ask the children to write advice for someone writing for this particular age group (eg **Keep the sentences fairly short. Keep the tone informal and 'chatty'**.). Ask them to think of two or three 'Golden Rules'.

Ensure children apply this sentence level learning in their writing.

Shared writing

Related text level objective: Y5 Term 1 T15

- Take a scene from a well known story (perhaps one that is not usually elaborated in most versions) and on different occasions write up the same basic story line for each of the specific audiences studied earlier.

- Make a point of employing the language features identified and following the 'Golden Rules', eg for the scene from 'Little Red Riding Hood' where the wolf arrives at Grandma's cottage, eg:

Text for a picture book

Mr Wolf soon found Grandma's cottage. He opened the wooden door and peeked inside. There was Grandma in her cosy bed. She was wearing her best nightcap. She was wearing her new spectacles too. Poor Grandma was terrified. "Help!" she cried, but no one heard her. The wolf grinned his most wicked grin. Then he pounced into the cottage and ate poor Grandma all up. He was so greedy that he swallowed her whole. Nasty Mr Wolf licked his lips. Then he put on Grandma's best nightcap and her new spectacles. He hadn't eaten those. He slipped into Grandma's bed. It was still warm. He pulled up Grandma's covers, right up to his wicked chin. Then he waited. He just waited, grinning his wicked grin.

Bedtime story

Grandma's cottage was the cosiest you have ever seen. It had a roof of thatch, and the prettiest garden with yellow roses all around the door. The Big Bad Wolf didn't lose any time at all in getting there. He wanted to be sure that he was well ahead of Red Riding Hood. So he scampered through the forest and reached the cottage before you could say "Jack Robinson". Once there, he quietly turned the polished, brass handle and pushed open the wooden door. He peered around it sneakily. There she was, fast asleep and looking as warm as toast in her enormous four-poster bed. All that showed of Grandma above the covers was her wonderful lacey nightcap. Well, you know what happened next, don't you? We won't go into the nasty details. Suffice it to say that very soon it was the wolf, and not poor Grandma, who was lying in the cosy bed with a flowery nightcap pulled between his pointed ears.

As for Red Riding Hood, she was skipping through the forest without a care in the world. She hummed softly to herself as she went. Little did she know what awaited her at Grandma's house. But you know, don't you?

For 'streetwise kids'

It was all going to plan. Wolfie wrapped himself in an old red blanket, put on a squeaky, girlie voice and pretended to be that goody-goody, butter-wouldn't-melt-in-her-mouth granddaughter. His performance deserved on Oscar, I can tell you. As it turned out, she swallowed the whole performance whole, as you might say. (This was before **he** swallowed **her** whole, of course, we haven't got to that bit yet.)

"Like taking candy off a baby," thought Wolfie. "In fact that's a good idea. I was wondering what to do tomorrow."

The Granny's cottage bit did turn out to have its down side though. Parents, grandparents, teachers, other old fogeys … they all do it. As soon as they think they've got you cornered they go on and on at you. They say things like … when I was a young lad/lass/herring, just knee high to a grasshopper/space hopper/gobstopper … Well, Granny was no exception. Wolfie thought she would never shut up. Then, suddenly he remembered that he had a way of making her. Scrunch! Goodbye Granny!

"That'll teach you to go on at me," he mumbled with his mouth full.

Y5 Term 1 S5 and S7

OBJECTIVES

S5   to understand the difference between direct and reported speech (eg *she said, 'I am going',* *she said she was going*), eg through: finding and comparing examples from reading; discussing contexts and reasons for using particular forms and their effects; transforming direct into reported speech and vice versa, noting changes in punctuation and words that have to be changed or added;

S7   from reading, to understand how dialogue is set out, eg on separate lines for alternate speakers, and the positioning of commas before speech marks;

Principles and explanation

- See the Glossary (Part 3) for the definition of direct and reported or indirect speech.

- Reported speech is used in fiction and in non-fiction to create variety, so that the writer does not include long stretches of direct speech. If direct speech is used sparingly, it can have greater impact: writers tend to put their most forceful points in direct speech.

- Sentences in which there is reported speech are among the most common forms of complex sentence. **He said that he would come** has a main and a subordinate clause. Quite commonly, in speech and in writing, the connective **that** is omitted. **He said he would come** is a complex sentence which has no connective and no comma.

- Speech can imply character but can also slow down the pace of a narrative. Therefore, use of direct speech should be considered carefully.

- Reported speech is useful when the writer wants to contrast between what a writer says and what she or he is thinking.

- Reported speech is useful for summarising what the speaker says and therefore moves the action along more quickly.

- When direct speech is converted to reported speech, a number of changes are made, eg **'Are you ready?'** might be reported as **He asked if I was ready**. This requires removing the speech marks and making the following changes:

  - tense: **are** to **was**
  - person: **you** to **I**
  - subordinating words: **if** added
  - word order: **Are you** changes to **I was**
  - punctuation: **?** to **.**

Sentence level activities

Compare (page 157)

Ask the children to look at the sentences below, and describe what is happening when direct speech is transformed into reported speech.

DIRECT SPEECH	REPORTED SPEECH
'I hate you,' she whispered.	She whispered that she hated him.
The man shouted at the dog. 'Go home!'	The man shouted at the dog to go home.
'Did you find it in the tunnel?' she asked.	She asked whether he had found it in the tunnel.
'Let's find the others,' he suggested.	He suggested (that) they find the others.
'That's not fair,' he exclaimed.	He exclaimed (that) it was not fair.
He asked, 'How did you know?'	He asked her how she knew.
'Mending walls,' he said, 'is a specialist occupation.'	He said that mending walls was a specialist occupatio

The children should suggest similar features to those in the Principles and explanation section.

Ensure children apply this sentence level learning in their writing.

Shared writing

Related text level objectives: Y5 Term 1 T15, T18, T21, T24

- Explain that if there is a section of a story in which the characters talk a lot, it may be a good idea to use both direct and reported speech, eg:

  'I shouldn't have done it,' she sobbed. She said she was the one who had broken the window. 'It's all my fault, and no-one else's,' she said, looking the policeman straight in the eye.

  The effect here is to emphasise the direct speech, and so to emphasise the fact that the girl is taking all the blame. Perhaps it leads the intelligent reader to suspect that it's not entirely true that she was the only one to blame.

- Plan a story together as a class. Choose a moment in the story where there might be a large amount of dialogue. Ask the children to write this part of the story, but include only three sentences of direct speech. The rest of the information will have to be conveyed by other means, including reported speech.

- Try transforming a small part of a playscript into a story, and see what changes are required.

- Use dialogue to build character. See Teaching Unit 22. Allow the reader to infer a person's appearance and character from the verbs, particularly speech verbs, eg **muttered**, **gloated**, **spat**, **exhorted**, etc.

Y5 Term 1 S8 and S9

OBJECTIVES

S8 to revise and extend work on verbs (see Y4 objectives), focusing on: tenses: past, present, future; investigating how different tenses are formed by using auxiliary verbs, eg *have*, *was*, *shall*, *will*; forms: active, interrogative, imperative; person: 1st, 2nd, 3rd. Identify and classify examples from reading; experiment with transforming tense/form/person in these examples – discuss changes that need to be made and effects on meaning;

S9 to identify the imperative form in instructional writing and the past tense in recounts and use this awareness when writing for these purposes;

Principles and explanations

- See Teaching Units 2 and 21.
- English has only two inflected tenses: past and present. In other words, in English only the past and present can be made by changing the form of the verb itself. The present can also be used for future events, eg **The train *leaves* in five minutes.**
- In English, all other examples of tenses are created by using **auxiliary** verbs like **be** and **have** (see the Glossary).
- The future is formed with modal verbs (see the Glossary) like **will**/**would**, **shall**/**should**. Modal verbs are a special kind of auxiliary verb used to express shades of meaning and are very important in a wide range of genres, particularly argument and persuasion, since they allow the writer to qualify and refine thoughts and ideas.

Sentence level activities

Read

Read the poem 'The Commentator' supplied on the disk. (Ensure that you create the tone and rhythm of a real commentary.) This poem is by a pupil and is based on 'The Commentator' by Gareth Owen, which can be found in *Song of the City* (Collins). Ask the children to identify the tense of the poem. (Mostly the present, although there are some examples of the past, eg **'he said'** and **'He stopped stone dead …'**, etc. and some interesting uses of modal verbs for the future, eg **'Can he? Will he?'**) Why do commentators use the present tense? (Because the action is happening at the same time and the tense makes it sound exciting.) Take a short extract from the poem and ask children to cast it into the past tense. What effect does this have in describing the action? Make the point that in writing stories we tend to stick to the past tense and should try to be consistent.

Discuss

You could also discuss 'The Commentator' as an oral text, which creates the effect of speech (eg repeated use of **and**, with some short statements, eg **'Incredible! 0.62 seconds inside the world record.'**). One effect of putting the poem into the past tense might be to make it sound more like writing. Another might be the need for a wider range of adverbs of time to make it work as writing (instead of simply **and**), eg **then**, **next**, **later**, **meanwhile**, **suddenly**, **afterwards**. (You could make the point that it is important to be able to choose from a range of such words to make a narrative hang together in interesting ways.)

Mime

Get one or more children to mime a simple scene. One other can play the part of Commentator (always using the present tense). As the scene takes place, the Commentator provides the commentary, with support from other children/the teacher as appropriate. Now ask another pupil to be a journalist and retell what has taken place as a news report using the past tense. Another possibility is to choose a pupil, or group of children to adopt the role of interviewer and ask those who are about to mime the scene, what they will be doing (using the future). Draw out the contrasts in tense and the different functions from these three role-play activities.

Rewrite playscript

In discussing a playscript or narrative, identify the direct speech. Taking some examples of the dialogue, rewrite it as reported speech. Explain the shift from the present to the past tense. Ask children to identify which word in the verb chain changes to make this shift (the first one). Does this rule always work? Look at some further examples and test them out. (The answer is Yes.)

Ensure children apply this sentence level learning in their writing.

Shared writing

Related text level objectives: Y5 Term 1 T13, T15, T16, T18, T19, T20, T24, T25

- Use 'The Commentator' poem for shared reading, discussing the tense and how the writer contrasts simple actions with an exciting commentary. (Also discuss the repeated use of **And** and **But**, emphasising that normally they would not begin a sentence and so would not have a capital letter. Why has the writer deliberately broken this rule? (Main answer: To make the text more like speech.)

- Take a simple event, action or job and model producing the beginning of a commentary poem through shared writing. (An example, 'Tense Moments', based on the act of writing is provided on the disk for illustration, but this does not have to be used.) Ask children to choose their own action or event, the simpler the better being the guideline. Ask them to provide a sports commentary that makes it sound as if it is the most exciting event in the world, remembering to use mainly the present tense. The written task could be built up from oral work, eg in pairs or small groups children could improvise commentaries in independent time before producing written versions. Now cast a short part of the event as a narrative in the past tense. What are the differences in effect? Ensure that the past tense is used consistently. In the plenary read aloud some of the commentator poems. Do they work? Do they sound exciting? How well is tense used to create the desired impact?

- Having analysed a playscript with stage directions in shared reading (T5), ask the children to work in groups to produce a short playscript or scene with detailed stage directions in the present tense (T18). In groups, discuss how the scene might be turned into a story. Where would the changes in tense need to happen? What are the differences in effect in plot and character?

- Pursue the shared writing objectives indicated in other writing tasks, including non-fiction, drawing on and utilising the awareness of appropriate verb tenses derived from the sentence level activities; for example: Use the past tense for recounts (T13); or a range of modal verbs in the evaluation of scripts and performance (T20) or the present tense in annotations of scripts (T19).

UNIT **38**

Y5 Term 1 T14

OBJECTIVES

T14 to map out texts showing development and structure, eg its high and low points, the links between sections, paragraphs, chapters;

Related text level objective: Y5 Term 2 T22

Principles and explanation

- See Teaching Unit 8.
- Year 5 children need to begin to understand how to organise more complex chronological narratives into several basic paragraph units which relate to story structure. This should be further developed in respect of narratives which do not have a simple linear chronology. They also need to be increasingly aware of, and be able to use, appropriate ways of introducing and/or connecting paragraphs in these narratives.
- Year 5 children need to extend and develop the use of paragraph structures and connectives in a range of non-fiction text types, including recounts, procedures, reports and explanations and arguments.

Shared writing (narrative)

More complex chronological narrative

Select a text with a strong, interesting story structure, but preferably one which isn't too long to provide a realistic writing model for children. The example used here is a well known ghost story, retold as 'Room for one more' in *Short* by Kevin Crossley-Holland (Oxford).

Through interactivity and discussion, 'box' the story in order to identify the main stages of the narrative. Concentrate on the story structure, not necessarily on the paragraph pattern of the original eg:

The "hero" has difficulty sleeping in a strange bed.

He has a nightmare. He sees a hearse full of people. The driver says "Room for one more!". He is terrified.

He wakes next morning. The dream seems unimportant. He goes shopping. He tries to get on a lift. It is full.

The attendant says "Room for one more!" He is reminded of the dream and will not enter.

The lift plummets. The people are killed. The dream was a premonition.

Discuss and add temporal connectives (or 'paragraph prompts') to each box, which can introduce each paragraph, eg **During the night …**, **When he woke the next morning …**.

Using the one box per paragraph principle, base a piece of whole class composition on this. The outcome can be a 'straight' retelling of the narrative in different words, an elaboration, or one which provokes more originality by altering, say, the characters or setting. Whichever it might be, it is essential to retain the box/paragraph structure derived from the original.

Working in this way, the boxing of story segments provides the basis for a plan and the 'paragraph prompts' (**Later that night …**, etc.) can constitute a frame for subsequent individual writing or supported composition.

'Parallel' narrative structure

Proceed through all the stages above but with a model text which combines two parallel narrative threads, eg *The Meteorite Spoon* by Philip Ridley (Puffin).

An excellent introduction to this is *Dear Daddy* by Philippe Dupasquier (Puffin; available as big book) – having looked at the whole, use part, not all, of this narrative for writing.

Plan a box (paragraph) structure which runs the two narratives (alternately, at home, on the ship), combining them at the end when 'Daddy' returns.

Explore and consider very carefully the connections between the paragraphs. Find as many ways as possible of 'flagging' the narrative change, without using the same ones repetitively (*ie* **What else could we say instead of *Meanwhile, back on the boat?***).

Alternative story structures could be derived from traditional stories, eg telling 'Snow White' by narrating Snow White's actions, and the Wicked Queen's alternately. Is there an even more interesting structure than turn-and-turn-about?

Story within a story

Work as above but using a story-within-a-story model, eg the first half of *Knots on a Counting Rope* by Bill Martin Jr and John Archambault (Henry Holt Big Books). Boy and Grandfather talk./Grandfather narrates story of boy's birth./Grandfather discusses significance of story with boy.

How will the paragraph organisation, and the connective words and phrases used help clarify this structure for the reader?

'Time slip' narrative

Work as above but using a time slip story model, eg *Where the Forest Meets the Sea* by Jeannie Baker (Walker Big Books). Boy and father visit the forest in 'real time'./Boy imagines himself back in the 'stone age' forest and plays with Native Australian boy./Boy returns to real time./Boy pictures the forest projected into the future.

Again, how will the paragraph organisation, and the connective words and phrases used help clarify this structure for the reader?

Complex narrative with non-linear chronology

Look, for example, at the first chapter of *The Daydreamer* by Ian McEwan (Red Fox). 'Box' up the story structure trying to understand and clarify its shifts in time and place, and from reality into daydreaming. What devices (paragraphs, connectives, etc.) does the writer use to help the reader understand what is happening?

Can any of these ideas be used in children's writing?

In all the above contexts, continue to collect, classify and explore ways of linking paragraphs into a cohesive narrative (see Teaching Unit 25).

Shared writing (non-fiction)

Continue the approach to paragraph organisation and paragraph connectives outlined in Year 4 (Teaching Unit 29) extending this into more complex models from a range of text types.

Y5 Term 2 S4 and S10

OBJECTIVES

S4 to revise from Y4: the different kinds of noun; the function of pronouns; agreement between nouns, pronouns and verbs;

S10 to ensure that, in using pronouns, it is clear to what or to whom they refer.

Principles and explanation

- Nouns can be singular or plural. Collective nouns refer to a group, eg **crowd**, **team**, **flock**. Proper nouns, eg names of people, places towns begin with a capital letter.
- The term 'noun phrase' can refer to just one word, eg **Tom**, **she**, or a group of words, eg **a lot of money**, **the best team in the world**, that functions in the same way as a noun in a sentence.
- A noun phrase can include a determiner, eg *these* **hats**, *a* **baby**, as an adjective, eg *sad* **face**, *watery* **grave**, as an additional noun which acts like an adjective, eg *library* **book**, as a prepositional phrase, eg **man** *in* **the moon**.
- Pronouns are words which stand in place of noun phrases. The most obvious ones are the personal pronouns, eg **I**, **she**, **they**, **me**, **it**, but other words also fall into this class, eg **this**, **those**, **one**, **someone**.
- Children sometimes overuse pronouns so that it is not clear to the reader who is being referred to, and sometimes fail to use pronouns when they would have been appropriate. Changing person mid text, eg from third person to first person, is also a common feature in immature narrative and recount writing. Encouraging children to reread each sentence as they write and to reread the previous group of sentences or paragraph will reduce the incidence of these problems.
- Many adverbs are formed by adding **-ly** to an adjective (though not necessarily, eg **fast**, **well**). Some words ending in **-ly** are adjectives, not adverbs, eg **woolly**, **lovely**, **friendly**.
- In many cases, adverbs tell us: *how* (manner), eg **slowly**, **happily**; *where* (place), eg **there**, **away**, **outside**; *when* (time), eg **now**, **soon**, **later**; *how often* (frequency), eg **ever**, **regularly**.
- Adverbs can be placed in different positions in a sentence, and are thus useful for varying sentence structure.

Sentence level activities

Determiners

Find a singular noun phrase in a text, eg **the long, hot summer**. Change the determiner to **a**, **this**, **my**, **that**, **each** and consider the differences in meaning; notice that specificity varies according to determiner.

Collect and classify (page 156)

Choose a text containing varied types of noun phrases including some phrases containing adjectives or nouns behaving like adjectives, some phrases in which the noun is modified by a preposition, eg **the girl in the pink hat**. Underline the noun phrases.

Ask the children to find the main noun in each phrase and then to see how this noun has been modified. Classify according to whether the noun has been modified in front, eg **the red** *hat*, afterwards, eg **the** *girl* **with the dog**, or both, eg **the strange** *plant* **in my garden**, eg:

As Snow White entered the dwarves' cottage one night, she heard snoring from the adjacent woodshed. Upstairs, she found six exhausted dwarves fast asleep in the attic bedroom, but one of the miniature wooden beds was empty. She looked and thought carefully. The two dwarves with the yellow socks were both sleeping next to older brothers. The happy dwarf with the white beard was nearest the door. The chief miner dwarf would never sleep next to any of his younger brothers. The grumpy dwarf with the red beard was not wearing yellow socks. The youngest dwarf had not had a good wash for weeks. The dwarf in the end bed, who was the oldest, was not the chief miner. The dwarf with the red beard was sleeping next to the youngest dwarf's bed. Snow White used simple logic to identify the dwarf in the woodshed and to work out why he was there. Can you?

Cloze 1 (page 157)

Choose a page midway through a narrative text with which the children are familiar. Cover the noun phrases and replace by a single common noun. Discuss the alternative uses of strong descriptive nouns, determiners, adjectives, additional nouns or prepositions to use in place of the common noun.

Pronouns

Use a narrative or recount text written by a child in which the use of pronouns is ambiguous. Enlarge it and ask the children to read it and work out why it is difficult to understand what is happening in the story.

Function (page 156)

Choose a text containing adverbs of manner, eg **largely**, **merrily**, **well**, place, eg **here**, **there**, **home**, **outside**, time, eg **now**, **yesterday**, **later**, **soon**, and frequency, eg **often**, **never**, **usually**, **regularly**. Underline the adverbs and include one near the end which is not an adverb. Children should find the verb that each adverb relates to. As adverbs can occur at different points in a sentence, often away from the verb, this will engender a certain amount of discussion. The non-adverb in this example is in *italics*.

Later, Douglas went outside. He was standing nonchalantly beside the Magic Swingboat, as he often did, when Brendan the slug slid morosely up to him.

"Salutations, old pal," said Brendan gloomily. "Do you know I was viciously assaulted here recently? A hippy rabbit hit me repeatedly with his guitar."

"Assaulted, little gastropod?" said Douglas disinterestedly. "It happens regularly does it? Well, now you know how a peanut must feel."

"Peanut?" mused the *puzzled* slug. "Life is often rotten."

"Oh. I don't know. It's usually swings and roundabouts," said Douglas philosophically.

Cloze 2 (page 157)

Using the same text, discuss the necessity of using adverbs. Which ones are indispensable to maintain the sense? Which, if any, could be replaced by a more powerful verb?

Ensure children apply this sentence level learning in their writing.

Shared writing

Related text level objectives: Y5 Term 2 T11, T12, T13

Write a **'Somewhere today …'** poem. Concentrate on finding strong verbs and nouns, and perhaps one apposite adverb or adjective for each.

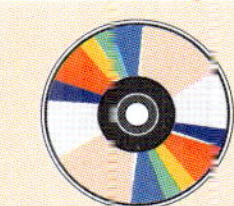

Somewhere in our school **today** …
A class of paint-splattered artists is excitedly exploring the work of Jackson Pollock.
Twenty-four happy infants are floating precariously, pretending to be bubbles.
A vital game of football is being cut short frustratingly by the playtime bell.
Two intense authors are skilfully building suspense into their mystery story.
A cluster of children is avidly engrossed with the creation of a web page.
A blushing poet is glowing proudly because his writing is being read aloud.
etc.

Amongst many other possibilities are 'Somewhere on my dad's farm today …', 'Somewhere in the world today …', 'Somewhere in our town, today …'. However, make sure that children write about things they really **know** and understand, or the result will just be a string of clichés.

Y5 Term 2 S5, S7, S8 and S9

OBJECTIVES

S5 to use punctuation effectively to signpost meaning in longer and more complex sentences;

S7 to explore ambiguities that arise from sentence contractions, eg through signs and headlines: *police shot man with knife, Nothing acts faster than Anadin, Baby Changing Room*;

S8 to construct sentences in different ways while retaining meaning, through: combining two or more sentences; re-ordering them; deleting or substituting words; writing them in more telegraphic ways;

S9 to secure the use of the comma in embedding clauses within sentences;

Principles and explanation

- A complex sentence contains a main clause and one (or more) clauses whose meaning is dependent on or subordinate to the first, eg **I asked if he could tie up my shoe laces. I asked** is the main clause. The main clause could stand alone as a simple sentence. Subordinate clauses cannot.

- Links between the main clause and the subordinate clause will clarify which is the subordinate clause. Words such as **although**, **if** and **unless** clearly place the words that follow in a subordinate position.

- The main clause makes independent meaning. The subordinate clause tends to qualify it by saying, for example, when, where, or why it is true.

- Subordinate clauses may have a whole verb chain, eg *As he <u>was tired</u> of waiting on his own*, **he followed the queue into the theatre** or just part of the verb chain, eg *<u>Tired</u> of waiting on his own*, **he followed …** The subordinate clauses are in *italics* and the verbs are <u>underlined</u>.

- When sentences start with a subordinate clause, the clauses are separated by commas.

- A subordinate clause can stand in place of a noun phrase, in which case it is called a noun clause, eg **He wondered *whether they would be getting any tea***. Children rarely use a noun clause to open a sentence, but it can be an effective way to vary the beginnings of sentences, if used sparingly, eg ***Climbing up lamp posts* was not in his repertoire of pranks.**

Sentence level activities

Making complex sentences

Write four or five sentences, eg **The man was waiting in the queue. He was a sailor. He wanted to buy some stamps. He needed stamps to send his parcel. He hadn't any money.** Discuss the best way to combine these sentences into one to retain the same meaning. Repeat with other groups of sentences.

Collect and classify 1 (page 156)

Make a collection of ambiguous statements from newspaper cuttings and joke books. Consider what creates the ambiguity by filling in the missing words to ensure the intended meaning, eg **Police shot man with knife = Police shot a man who was carrying a knife** (pronoun needed to link the knife with the man). **Baby changing room = Room for changing babies' nappies** (preposition provides clarity).

Collect and classify 2 (page 156)

Find complex sentences in texts, write on long strips of paper (old wallpaper is excellent), cut into clauses. Move the clauses about. Where can a main clause break to let in a subordinate clause? Write up sentences created and discuss punctuation.

Complex sentence game (page 159)

Starting sentences:

- **She promised** *that we could go to the theme park*.
- *To drive on the wrong side of the road* **is not a good idea**.

The subordinate (noun) clauses are in *italics*.

Ensure children apply this sentence level learning in their writing.

Shared writing

Related text level objectives: Y5 Term 2 T21, T22

Gather the information to write a short report on a subject in another curriculum area. Write on the board in short, concise sentences, eg:

The moon spins on its axis like the earth. The earth takes a day to spin on its axis. The moon takes over 27 days to spin on its axis. It takes the same amount of time to circle the earth once. This is why we always see the moon from the same side. People say the craters look like a face. They call it 'the man in the moon'. The moon has no light of its own. It reflects the light of the sun. The moon has a day and night side. We see the moon from different angles. We see the full day side of the moon for only part of each month. The rest of the time, we see part of the moon. We can only see the moon when the sky is reasonably clear of cloud.

Demonstrate how to show the relationship between some of these pieces of information by joining them in sentences using conjunctions, eg **As it circles the earth, we see the moon from different angles so we see the full day side of the moon for only a part of each month.**

Y5 Term 2 S6

OBJECTIVES

S6 to be aware of the differences between spoken and written language, including: conventions to guide reader; the need for writing to make sense away from immediate context; the use of punctuation to replace intonation, pauses, gestures; the use of complete sentences;

Principles and explanation

- Written language is different in many ways from ordinary unscripted speech, so writing is not simply a change of medium.
- There is no immediate context which defines 'here', 'now', 'you' and 'I'; the writer must define an 'internal' context and maintain it consistently.
- The production process is much slower and more conscious, so it is difficult to maintain the internal context and writers often have difficulty in using pronouns (Teaching Unit 39) and tense (Teaching Units 36 and 37) consistently.
- Writing can be revised and subjected to conscious scrutiny.
- Writing is structured in terms of larger units which have no equivalent in speech, eg paragraphs, bullet points, headings and punctuation; speech is interactive and is organised primarily in terms of 'turns', where pauses, body language and eye movements are important signals.
- Intonation can be expressed by punctuation, but the two systems do not correspond precisely.
- Writing, like speech, may vary in style from casual to formal, eg from notes and family letters to essays, published texts and official letters. Formal writing is governed by relatively strict conventions including the following:
  - It must be in standard English (Teaching Unit 33).
  - Sentences as shown by punctuation must normally be complete, ie they must contain a main clause (Teaching Unit 34).

Sentence level activities

Transcription

Find a tape-recording (or even better, a video) of a commentary on a football match, and transcribe it faithfully, without punctuation but with some convention to indicate pauses. In the following example (D. Freeborn *et al.*, *Varieties of English: An Introduction to the Study of Language*, Macmillan Education, 1986) pauses are signalled by ( ): (.) for a short pause; (1.0) for one that lasts a second.

and again it's Wilkins high across the area looking for Keegan Keegan gets the header in (.) not enough power (.) Ceulemans fortunately for Belgium is there to clear (.) not very far though (.) Sansom comes forward a yard in from the touchline the England left (.) long ball from Sansom high across the area Pfaff is there (.) punches the ball away (.) not very far but effectively (1.0) and Cools the (.) Belgian captain picks it up in space (.) far side from us the Belgian left (.) he's tackled fiercely though (.) and he loses the ball to Copple (.) to Brooking (.) tall Brooking (.) of West Ham (.) touches the ball on (.) Wilkins (.) good ball too to Brooking …

Find a volunteer in the class to read the transcription in the style of the original, and discuss any problems that arise, eg from the lack of indication of intonation. Ask how accurate a picture of the game the commentary gives.

Collect and classify (page 156)

Prepare collectively for a translation into a written account to be included in a newspaper article.

- Collect the verbs and classify them for tense. Discuss the reasons for the choice of tense and how the tenses would be different in writing?
- Collect the references to players and classify them as proper nouns, common nouns or pronouns. Discuss the reasons for the choices and how the written account will differ.
- Collect examples of patterns that are specific to football commentaries (eg **It's ... to ...**). What would happen to these in writing?
- Collect 'incomplete sentences', discuss how effective they are and ask how they should be treated in writing.

Ensure children apply this sentence level learning in their writing.

Shared writing

Related text level objectives: Y5 Term 2 T11, T22

- Write a coherent written report of the section of the match reported in the commentary, and compare the two line by line.

- Build a collection of differences which follow automatically from the difference between speech and writing.

- To encourage the children to reflect on the writing process, discuss what these differences show about the **processes** of speaking and writing.

- Do the same for the processes of listening and reading.

- Discuss the ways in which the writer can help the reader as reader, and how.

42

Y5 Term 3 S3

OBJECTIVES

S3 to search for, identify and classify a range of prepositions: *back*, *up*, *down*, *across*, *through*, *on*, etc.; experiment with substituting different prepositions and their effect on meaning. Understand and use the term 'preposition';

Principles and explanation

- A preposition is a word like **at**, **over**, **by** and **with** which is usually followed by a noun phrase, eg **We got home at midnight.**
- Prepositions often indicate time (*at midnight*, *during the film*, *on Friday*), position (*at the station*, *in a field*) or direction (*to the station*, *over the fence*). There are other meanings, eg possession (*of this street*), means (*by car*) and accompaniment (*with me*).

Sentence level activities

Function (page 156)

Choose a text containing a range of prepositions. Underline them and underline one other word near the end which is not a preposition. The non-preposition in this example is in *italics*.

"Now this is what you do <u>in</u> the obstacle race, children. Are you listening carefully? First you run <u>towards</u> the bath <u>of</u> jelly, then you jump <u>into</u> it, wade <u>across</u> it and climb <u>out of</u> the bath <u>at</u> the other side. Then you run <u>to</u> the string of sausages, and skip <u>over</u> them twenty seven times. Next you climb <u>up</u> the twenty foot pole, ride carefully <u>along</u> the tightrope <u>on</u> a unicycle, and abseil <u>down</u> the rope <u>at</u> the other end. <u>After</u> that you balance the bowl <u>of</u> tomato soup <u>on</u> top <u>of</u> your head, climb <u>over</u> the live alligator, and creep <u>under</u> the baby elephant, <u>between</u> its back legs. Then all you have to do is *run* backwards <u>to</u> the finishing line, carrying me. If anyone gets there, they win."

"No chance, Miss! You're much too heavy."

Cloze (page 157)

Cover all the prepositions. List all the words possible to replace them. Classify them according to whether they indicate time, position, direction, possession, instrument, purpose or accompaniment and present on a chart for the children to refer to when writing.

"I think Rev. Rhinoceros went **to** the aquarium **after** breakfast and murdered Mr Panther **behind** the shark tank **with** a fish hook."

"No. I think Miss Anaconda, working together **with** Miss Python, killed him **inside** the terrace café just **before** lunch. They strangled him **with** a feather boa."

"Never. It was Professor Panda. He was walking **towards** the chimpanzee house **in** time **for** tea when he shot Mr Panther **between** the ears **with** his revolver."

"You're all wrong. I think it was Colonel Camel, **behind** the picnic area **near** the car park. He hit Mr Panther **over** the head **with** an enormous fish belonging **to** the sea lion."

"What are you playing?"

"Zoodo."

Construct (page 158)

When the children have made their sentences, ask them to re-order them to see whether they are still acceptable sentences, eg **Mrs Bloggs was standing in the mud. In the mud, Mrs Bloggs was standing** (No). **My dog couldn't sing at midnight. At midnight, my dog couldn't sing** (Yes).

SUBJECT (BLUE)	VERB (RED)	PREPOSITIONAL PHRASE (GREEN)
Mrs Bloggs	was standing	in the mud
Mr Cheese	shopped	during the night
the lion	couldn't sing	behind the school
the frog	was hopping	by the table
his friend	ate	over the wall
Cinderella	didn't swim	with a gorilla
the old lady	fished	at midnight
the dinosaur	could play	on 11 May
my dog	wanted to fly	at the fire station
the trumpet	may depart	before Friday
this small child	is working	since the weekend
the footballer	laughs	throughout the day

Ensure children apply this sentence level learning in their writing.

Shared writing

UNIT **43**

Y5 Term 3 S4, S6 and S7

OBJECTIVES

S4 to use punctuation marks accurately in complex sentences;

S6 to investigate clauses through: identifying the main clause in a long sentence; investigating sentences which contain more than one clause; understanding how clauses are connected (eg by combining three short sentences into one);

S7 to use connectives to link clauses within sentences and to link sentences in longer texts.

Principles and explanation

- Complex sentences link ideas together. They contain main and subordinate clauses. A main clause is one that is self-contained, that can act as a free standing sentence. Subordinate clauses start with either a subordinating conjunction or relative pronoun (or they suggest one) and they cannot act as free standing sentences, eg **They played happily *until it started to rain*. Nathan, *filled with despair*, left the pitch.** In this sentence, the subordinating words **who** and **was** are suggested. (The subordinate clauses are in *italics*.)

- Many subordinate clauses begin with a conjunction (eg **while**), which suggests the relationship between the ideas (**while** indicates a time relationship). Each clause is a 'chunk of meaning', and punctuation is sometimes needed to show the boundaries between them. This is particularly the case when the subordinate clause comes at the beginning of the sentence, eg **While he was paying for his petrol, his car was stolen.**, or when the subordinate clause splits the main clause, eg *Nathan, filled with despair, left the pitch*.

- Connectives are words and phrases which help bind a text together, eg **however**, **finally**, **on the other hand**. The use of connectives is a distinctive feature of effective writing.

Sentence level activities

Making complex sentences

Write on the board two simple sentences, eg **The bully was on the phone to her gang. The victim was crying on her bed.** Discuss how to join these two elements into one sentence and show how the subordinate clause can go at the beginning or the end, eg:

The bully was on the phone to her gang, while the victim was crying on her bed.
While the victim was crying on her bed, the bully was on the phone to her gang.

Discuss whether the comma is as necessary when the subordinate clause follows the main clause.

Collect and classify 1 (page 156)

Find complex sentences in texts and underline the main clauses. Find the subordinating conjunction or pronoun, if there is one, and list for future reference on a poster. Look at the remaining clauses when the subordinating word has been removed, eg **As it was raining, I stayed in.** becomes **It was raining. I stayed in.** Consider the effect of the two versions, and in what circumstances one might be preferred over the other. Try changing the conjunction or reversing the clauses. Consider the effect.

Conjunctions

Provide three sentences on strips of card and a selection of conjunctions, and see how many different ways you can link the sentences, eg:

It was raining.   Fred went for a walk.   He was eaten by a monster.

It was raining and Fred went for a walk and was eaten by a monster.
Although it was raining, Fred went for a walk and was eaten by a monster.
Fred went for a walk in the rain and was eaten by a monster.
Whilst walking in the rain, Fred was eaten by a monster.
Walking in the rain, Fred was eaten by a monster.
Despite the fact that it was raining, Fred, who went for a walk, was eaten by a monster.
A monster ate Fred when he was walking in the rain.
It was raining when Fred went for a walk and was eaten by a monster.

Commas

Write a complex sentence on the board without punctuation. Ask the children to read it indicating with their curled fingers where the commas should be.

Collect and classify 2 (page 156)

Collect adverbial phrases creating links between sentences, eg However …, Therefore …, Consequently …, Meanwhile …, In consequence …, On the other hand …, Later that afternoon …. Classify adverbial phrases according to whether they indicate links of: time, sequence, cause and effect, condition, counter-argument.

Connectives

Between sentences, identify adverbial connectives. Consider their purpose and effect. Take them out/change them. Consider the effect.

Ensure children apply this sentence level learning in their writing.

Shared writing

Related text level objectives: Y5 Term 3 T9, T10, T15, T19

- Demonstrate using complex sentences in writing and then ask the children to include complex sentences in their own writing, making their own choice of conjunctions. They must check that they have at least two clauses and decide whether they need a comma. They should indicate where they have used complex sentences, then pass their work over to a response partner, who checks that the punctuation makes the meaning clear.
- Plan a discussion text. Discuss the sorts of links you need to make between ideas, eg On the other hand, conversely, however, therefore.

Create writing frames for text types, based on your analysis of connectives in texts you have read. There are three stages in the use of writing frames:
- Children use a writing frame worked out in a group.
- They create their own writing frame, to meet their own particular needs.
- They are sure enough of how they want to write that they do not need a writing frame at all

Year 6

Teaching units 44–54

Before working from these teaching units, please read the following sections:
- Introduction and rationale (page 7);
- How to use the teaching units (page 24).

A few reminders:
- Instructions for activities displaying page numbers are to be found in Section 3 of Part 3.
- For work on any grammatical feature in a previous or subsequent year or term, please refer to the grammatical subject index in Section 8 of Part 3.
- These units do **not** include the teaching for text level objectives.
- The activities in the units can be used, reused and elaborated.
- Sentence level learning should be applied in shared, guided and independent writing.

Y6 Term 1 S1

OBJECTIVES

S1   to revise from Y5: the different word classes, eg prepositions; re-expressing sentences in a different order; the construction of complex sentences; the conventions of standard English; adapting texts for particular readers and purposes;

Note: For complex sentences, see Y6 Term 1 S5; for conventions of standard English, see Y5 Term 2 S2; for adapting texts for particular readers and purposes, see Y5 Term 3 S2.

Principles and explanation

- We tend to take the term 'adverb' (see Teaching Unit 39) literally to mean 'adding meaning to or modifying the verb', but adverbs can also add meaning to other adverbs, adjectives and whole sentences as the adverb **really** illustrates below:

  I *really enjoyed* the party.   adverb + verb;
  She's *really nice.*   adverb + adjective;
  He works *really slowly*.   adverb + adverb;
  Really, he should do better. adverb + sentence.

- In many cases, adverbs and adverbial phrases tell us: *how* (manner), eg **slowly**, **happily**, **in a strange way**; *where* (place), eg **there**, **away**, **outside**; *when* (time), eg **now**, **soon**, **later**, **a few days ago**; *how often* (frequency), eg **ever**, **regularly**. Other adverbs show degrees of intensity, eg **very slowly**, **fairly well**; the attitude of the speaker to what she or he is saying, eg **perhaps**, **obviously**; connections in meaning between sentences, eg **however**, **furthermore** (see Teaching Unit 32).

- Nouns are modified by adjectives (see Teaching Unit 39), eg **the *big* hat**, and other nouns which behave like adjectives, eg **a *library* book**. Some adjectives are derived from nouns, eg **a *watery* grave**.

- Prepositional phrases and adverbials can occur at various points in sentences so allowing for emphasis and stylistic effect.

Sentence level activities

Adverb generation

Take a simple sentence, eg **He walked slowly**. Generate adverbs by replacing the given adverb with others which would make sense, eg **He walked quickly**, **hastily**, **swiftly**, **purposefully**, **crossly**, **awkwardly**, **grudgingly**, **merrily**, **sulkily**. Now ask the question *where?* – **away**, **nowhere**, **off**, **there**, **everywhere**, **outside**, **inside**, **upstairs**; or the question *how often?* – **very often**, **frequently**, **regularly**, **hardly ever**, **never**.

In shared reading, look for powerful verbs, eg *Sea Tongue* by Kevin Crossley-Holland (Longman).

Descriptive writing

Choose a narrative text or poem. Ask the children to underline the phrase which describes the subject of the sentence.

Nine off-white sheep with handlebar horns stood plaintively with their backs to the driving rain. **Tom** pulled his cape more tightly round him as he struggled past. Up ahead, **thunderous clouds** churned over and round. Suddenly **a bright streak** tore across the sky. **Flames** rose from a tree to Tom's left as **thunder** crashed and boomed, throwing him to the ground.

Discuss the distribution in the text of unmodified nouns (eg **Flames**) and the different ways of modifying them (eg ***a bright* streak**). Take suggestions as to why the author chose to modify or not in each instance.

Collect and classify (page 156)

Examine some instructional, persuasive and explanatory texts for the use of noun modifiers. Underline the subject of the sentence. First classify the noun as modified or not. Then classify the modified nouns by the method of modification, ie adjective, determiner, noun, preposition.

Construct (page 158)

Write a series of sentences using a prepositional phrase, eg:

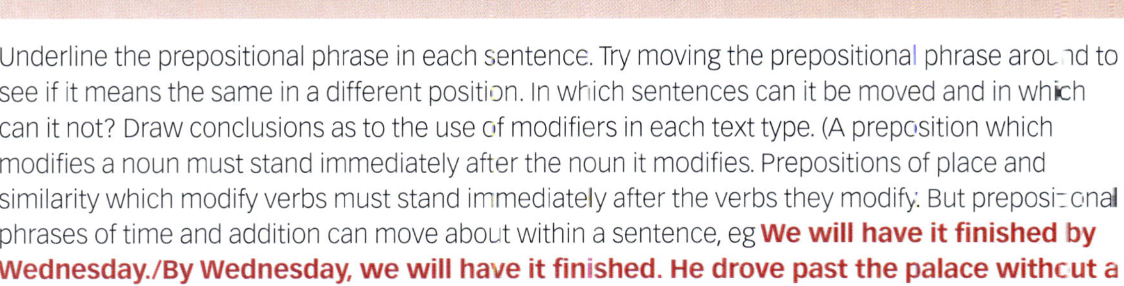

The man *in the red* suit ran away.
The girl was living *in France*.
They returned *at midnight*.
We will have it finished *by Wednesday*.
The boy *from space* cried all night.
He gave her some perfume *from France*.
The cat *with no whiskers* meowed all the time.
They were burgled *during the night*.
She walked *across the grass*.
They went *inside the tower*.
He went away *with his friends*.
She drove *past the palace without a second thought*.

Underline the prepositional phrase in each sentence. Try moving the prepositional phrase around to see if it means the same in a different position. In which sentences can it be moved and in which can it not? Draw conclusions as to the use of modifiers in each text type. (A preposition which modifies a noun must stand immediately after the noun it modifies. Prepositions of place and similarity which modify verbs must stand immediately after the verbs they modify. But prepositional phrases of time and addition can move about within a sentence, eg **We will have it finished by Wednesday./By Wednesday, we will have it finished. He drove past the palace without a second thought./Without a second thought, he drove past the palace.** Note the use of the comma when the prepositional phrase starts the sentence.)

Ensure children apply this sentence level learning in their writing.

Shared writing

Related text level objectives: Y6 Term 1 T10, T17

After planning a short non-chronological report, consider the effective use of nouns and their modifiers (determiners, adjectives, nouns and prepositional phrases). Choose the most precise and economical method of expressing the facts. For example, in a short report on frogs, the first paragraph may describe the particular frog being studied in the classroom. Description of the frog will be restricted to what is immediately observable, not conjecturing on how the frog may be feeling. It will include adjectives of colour and size and possibly some comparatives. The determiners may be **the** or **this**.

The next few paragraphs will lose any determiner and refer to **frogs** in general – their habitat, what they eat, reproductive cycle, etc.

This type of writing is in sharp contrast to a poem. Ask the children to describe the frog again, but in a poem. Discuss the freer use of language in this medium, the opportunity to consider the attitude of the frog being scrutinised by a sea of 11-year-old faces, the use of noun phrases to capture the essence of the colour and action of the frog swimming, which was denied in the report format.

Y6 Term 1 S2 and S3

OBJECTIVES

S2 to revise earlier work on verbs and to understand the terms 'active' and 'passive'; being able to transform a sentence from active to passive, and vice versa;

S3 to note and discuss how changes from active to passive affect the word order and sense of a sentence;

Principles and explanations

- A sentence using the active voice is one where the subject of the sentence is the 'agent' of the action expressed in the verb, and the object of the sentence is the 'recipient' of that action, eg **The mouse frightened the elephant.** (agent – verb – recipient).
- In using the passive voice, the sentence is turned around so that the normal object becomes the subject, ie the subject is now the 'recipient' of the action instead of the 'agent'. If the agent (the former subject of sentence) is retained, it is usually added after the verb and introduced with **by**, eg **The elephant was frightened by the mouse.** (recipient – verb – *by* agent). However the agent can sometimes be omitted completely, eg **The elephant was frightened.**
- The active voice is far more common than the passive, in both speech and writing.
- Passive sentences including the agent can sound clumsy and unnatural. They are often best avoided. Passive sentences which withhold or conceal the agent, eg **This window has been broken**, are much more useful. See also Teaching Unit 48.

Sentence level activities

'Who-did-what-and-to-whom?' game

Get two pupils very quickly to mime a simple action (No physical contact!). A must be doing something to B.

Create a sentence to describe the action from A's point of view (active). Then swap it around to B's point of view (passive). Work orally first and then in writing (dry-wipe boards). Keep it lively, active and fun.

> Shazia is painting a dog.
> No! A dog is being painted by Shazia.
> A monster is eating Cynthia.
> No! Cynthia is being eaten by a monster.

Extend this (literally, as well as educationally) by getting a number of pupils to form a row (or even a circle). Each person can be doing something to the one on their right. 'Read' the row or circle in one direction (the active one). 'Read' it again in the opposite direction (the passive one).

> Kate is speaking to Ahir. Ahir is helping Emma. Emma is shouting at Matthew. Matthew is eating Kate's apple.
>
> Ahir is being spoken to by Kate. Emma is being helped by Ahir. Matthew is being shouted at by Emma. Kate's apple is being eaten by Matthew.

Write out some of the sentences (on cards) to use later.

Investigate and hypothesise

- Ask pupils to collect examples of active and passive sentences, and write them on cards (possibly some from the previous game).
- Distribute the cards. Ask pupils to cut up the sentences and attempt to rearrange them to change active into passive, and vice versa.

- Hypothesise 'rules' for what happens when you change from one to the other. What happens to the order of the words? What word or words do you have to add or take away?
- See if pupils can explain for themselves what the difference between active and passive is, and how the sentences change.
- Practise changing sentences both ways to test the pupils' rules. Do they work or do they need to be revised in the light of further experience?

Sort and classify

Sort and classify these **passive voice** sentences according to the ending of each.

The window was broken **by a group of girls playing football**.
The window was broken **by a stone which had been carried from the beach.**
The window was broken **by giving it a sharp tap near the top right corner**.
The cup final was won **by the best team in the country.**
The cup final was won **by sheer grit and determination.**
The cup final was won **by dominating the opposition in mid field.**
The little monster was tripped up **by the big hairy monster.**
The little monster was tripped up **by his own big feet.**
The little monster was tripped up **by tying a string of sausages across his doorway.** .

In these sentences the passive voice is quite **useful**. Why? What different things do the different endings tell us? (Who did it?/What was used to do it?/What method was used to do it?) Could the word **by** be replaced by any other word in any of the sentences? Can you write some more examples for each category?

Ensure children apply this sentence level learning in their writing.

Shared writing

Related text level objective: Y6 Term 1 T6

Write a brief episode from the life of Mr Hasbean (a relation of Mr Bean, now deceased). Mr Hasbean is seriously accident-prone. Write in the voice and style of the example text, using the passive to show how Mr Hasbean is constantly the 'victim' of things **which happen to him**. Hint: Don't overdo it!

Mr Hasbean at the Seaside

No sooner had Mr Hasbean stepped off the coach than he fell foul of all the hazards of the seaside. First his best hat was blown away by gale-force sea breeze. Then, within seconds of reaching the promenade, his bald pate was splattered by a low-flying seagull. "Oh no, a souvenir from Scarborough already," he sighed. When he tried to walk along the beach his shoes were soaked through by the sneakiest of waves. When he tried to eat candyfloss his face became coated with sticky pink goo. Even worse, when he tried to buy himself a sixpenny donkey ride he was berated by the donkey man, and laughed at most cruelly by most of the people on the beach. Some nasty children even kicked sand at him. As he turned away in shame, he was hit sharply on the back of the head by a flying hat. "I wouldn't care," he grumbled, "but that was my hat."

If you have no better ideas, you could try 'Mr Hasbean on the farm' or 'Mr Hasbean goes back to school'.

Now what things could happen **to** Mr Hasbean in this situation? Let's make a list. Remember if we are using the passive voice, Mr Hasbean, or something belonging to him, has to be the subject of the sentence. **Yes, Mr Hasbean was bitten by…** that's the idea. Now we have to make these into a well balanced paragraph. We need to vary the sentence length, and we will mix some active voice sentences in as well, so that the pattern doesn't get too monotonous.

Y6 Term 1 S4

OBJECTIVES

S4   to investigate connecting words and phrases: collect examples from reading and thesauruses; study how points are typically connected in different types of text; classify useful examples of different kinds of text – for example by position (*besides*, *nearby*, *by*); sequence (*firstly*, *secondly…*); logic (*therefore*, *so*, *consequently*); identify connectives which have multiple purposes (eg *on*, *under*, *besides*);

Principles and explanation

- Connectives are used to help 'stick texts together' by referring and making links to what has gone before, to create links between sentences, eg **He went over the wall and lay still. *Later*, when he was sure no-one was around, he slithered forward**. **Later** is the connective.
- Connectives can be words or phrases, eg **Later**, **In spite of**.
- Different types of text may use particular types of connective, but some connectives can be used in more than one type of text. The kind of connective used is often a key identifying feature of a particular kind of text and used for a particular purpose:
  - addition (**also**, **furthermore**, **moreover**);
  - opposition (**however**, **nevertheless**, **on the other hand**, **but**, **instead**, **in contrast**, **looking at it another way**);
  - reinforcing (**besides**, **anyway**, **after all**);
  - explaining (**for example**, **in other words**);
  - listing (**first of all**, **finally**);
  - indicating result (**therefore**, **consequently**, **as a result**, **thanks to this**, **because of this**);
  - indicating time:
    subsequent (**just then**, **next**, **in due course**, **in the end**, **after that**, **later**, **finally**, **eventually**);
    prior (**at first**, **before**, **in the beginning**, **until then**, **up to that time**);
    concurrent (**in the mean time**, **simultaneously**, **concurrently**, **meanwhile**).
- Connectives do not necessarily open a sentence, eg **However, he was not satisfied.** ; **He was, however, not satisfied.**

Sentence level objectives

Collect and classify (page 156)

Distribute different kinds of non-fiction text to pairs or small groups of children and ask them to highlight connecting words and phrases. Collect these under different headings (eg 'connectives from instructions') on whiteboard or easel. Classify useful examples for different kinds of text, eg by position (**beside**, **nearby**, **by**); sequence (**firstly**, **secondly**); logic (**therefore**, **so**, **consequently**); identify connectives which have multiple purposes, eg **on**, **under**, **besides**. Try substituting one set of connectives for another. Which ones can you swap and still make sense? Which are not inter-changeable? Why? Collect examples from reading and thesauruses; study how points are typically connected in different kinds of texts.

Cloze (page 157)

Cover connectives with Post-its® in a fiction or non-fiction text. Read through the sentences before the first connective and, before reading the next sentence, discuss what connective would be appropriate to open it and why. Then read the sentence and consider whether the original suggestion is still appropriate. Finally reveal the connective. Repeat with subsequent sentences.

Replace (page 160)

Turn a set of numbered instructions for a recipe into a recount, changing the tense and substituting appropriate connectives for the numbers.

Ensure children apply this sentence level learning in their writing.

Shared writing

Related text level objectives: Y6 Term 1 T17

- Look at a number of reporting styles. Notice that in reports which describe a process there will be temporal connectives, eg the life-cycle of a butterfly or a football match, eg **First, three weeks later**. The connectives may well open paragraphs rather than connect sentences within paragraphs. On the other hand, reports which describe different facets of a subject might use subheadings or bullets to organise the text and very few verbal connectives between paragraphs, but they are more likely to use connectives to link or contrast ideas within paragraphs, eg **On Saturdays there are street markets where you can buy all sorts of goods. However, some children do not have places where they can play.**

- Link report writing to the content of another curriculum area, eg History. Gather the facts together, eg life in rural Britain in the 1930s. Decide the specific subjects for each paragraph and then work on each paragraph in turn. Use shared writing to work up one paragraph

47

Y6 Term 1 S5 and S6
(Y6 Term 2 S3 and Y6 Term 3 S4)

OBJECTIVES

S5 to form complex sentences through, eg using different connecting devices; reading back complex sentences for clarity of meaning, and adjusting as necessary; evaluating which links work best; exploring how meaning is affected by the sequence and structure of clauses;

S6 to secure knowledge and understanding of more sophisticated punctuation marks: colon, semi-colon, parenthetic commas, dashes, brackets;

Principles and explanation

- See Teaching Unit 43 for principles governing complex sentences.
- Subordinate clauses may have a whole verb chain, eg **The girl, who *was smiling* through the window, was enjoying one of the happiest days of her life**, or only part of the verb, eg ***Smiling* through the window, the girl was enjoying one of the happiest days of her life.** This last construction, in which a non-finite verb is used outside the verb chain is very useful for providing variety in writing, eg ***Loaded* to the full with contraband, the Skoda eased its way out of the warehouse.**
- Colons introduce lists, quotations or summarising statements. In parenthesis, commas create the least degree of separation; dashes are next, creating a jerky effect; brackets cut off part of a sentence very firmly.
- Semi-colons are used in place of connectives to separate two clauses. They tend to be used to join clauses which are semantically linked, eg **I liked the book; it was a pleasure to read.** They are also used to separate items in a list, where the items are phrases or clauses rather than single words, eg **Children should learn to form complex sentences through using different connecting devices; reading back complex sentences for clarity of meaning, and adjusting as necessary; evaluating….**

Sentence level activities

Crazy clauses

Use a complex sentence as a model, eg **Although Harry knew the way to Hogwarts, it would still be difficult.** Ask the children to write sentences starting with **although, because of, despite, after**, using the key words **humbug** and **zebra**, eg:

Although the *zebra* was on a strict diet, she still couldn't resist the *humbug*.
Because of the *humbug*'s relatively small size, it was only rarely mistaken for a *zebra*.
Despite the fact that the *zebra* hadn't eaten for days, it just couldn't bring itself to consume the stripey *humbug*.
After sucking a *humbug*, the *zebra*'s stripes became more prominent.

Construct (page 158)

On three pieces of card write:

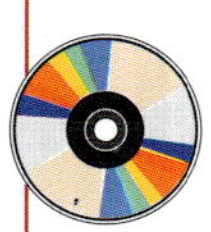

Ask pupils to hold up the cards to make **Although he was scared, he walked on.** Then ask them to re-arrange themselves into: **He walked on, although he was scared.** Discuss the effect of the order of the clauses: the first version emphasises the fear; the second the walking.

Discuss situations in which writers might want to use the first version, and situations in which they might prefer the second. For example, the first version might lead on to another sentence about fear, whereas the second might lead to a description of where he was going.

Ask pupils to invent similar complex sentences which can be manipulated for different effects, write them on strips of wallpaper and cut them into two clauses, which can be re-arranged. Then ask pupils to write down both versions and follow each with another suitable sentence, depending on the effect of the clause order.

Collect and classify 1 (page 156)

Find complex sentences in texts and underline the main clause in each one and look for the word which begins the subordinate clause. Classify these words according to whether they are verbs or subordinating words, eg *Shovelling* (verb) **snow as fast as possible, the rescue team managed to reach him. The rescue team managed to reach him** *because* (subordinator) **they shovelled snow very fast.** Collect the subordinating words into a list for future reference. Collect the examples of subordinate clauses which start with non-finite verbs (eg **Shovelling**) and display them.

Construct (page 158)

SUBORDINATE CLAUSE (GREEN)	MAIN CLAUSE (RED)
Linking arms,	the thief managed to escape
Shovelling snow as fast as possible,	the rescue team managed to reach him.
Growling in disgust,	he slunk along the corridor
Shrouded in a thin white veil,	the girls danced down the street.
Moulded onto the edge of the window,	the Prime minister called an election.
Encouraged by this response,	the boy's life appeared before him.
Falling through the air,	they could identify nothing.
Tortured by recollections of last night,	our dogs raced around the field.
Peering into the darkness,	her eyes appeared even bigger.
Fighting a way through the crowd,	the carvings were exquisite.

Complex sentence game (page 159)

Opening sentence: **Grinning from ear to ear, Paolo leaped off the balcony.**

The object of this activity is to give the children oral practice in constructing subordinate clauses beginning with a non-finite verb (see Principles and explanation above). In this activity the *subordinate clause* should always start with a *non-finite verb*, eg **Failing to notice the junction**; **Encouraged by this response.**

Examples

Encourage the children to look for examples of good use of complex sentences in each other's writing and to suggest occasions where linking simple sentences to form complex sentences might improve composition.

Collect and classify 2 (page 156)

Collect and classify semi-colons as 'unspoken' connectives, eg **It was a very cold day; she had to wrap up warmly**, or to demarcate phrases in lists, eg **On our picnic, we took fresh, green celery, cool and crisp; onion bhajis, large, round and spicey; orange and lemon slices floating in sparkling punch.**

Collect and classify 3 (page 156)

Collect and classify the use of colons, brackets and dashes.

Collect and classify 4 (page 156)

Collect and classify the use of commas: lists (verbs, adjectives, nouns); demarcating additional information, demarcating subordinate clauses, demarcating adverbials.

Punctuate (page 159)

Choose a text with a range of punctuation such as full stops, capital letters, commas, speech marks, question and exclamation marks, colons, brackets, dashes, semi-colons.

Ensure children apply this sentence level learning in their writing.

Shared writing

Related text level objectives: Y6 Term 1 T6, T14, T17

- **Teacher demonstration**

  Explain that we need to know how to write complex sentences so that we can write sentences which hold more than one piece of information. For instance, contrasting two characters in a story can be done very effectively and quickly in one sentence, eg **While Jenny was laughing with her friends, Sonia was crying alone on her bed.** Or balancing two opposing thoughts in a discussion piece, eg **Although foxhunting is cruel, the alternatives may be worse.**

  Explain that most effective writing is a mixture of simple anc complex sentences. Simple sentences are direct. Complex sentences, allowing the interweaving of ideas, express clearly the relationship between ideas, eg:

  I walked down the street. Lights came on in several windows. A dog howled. I shivered with fear. I walked on.

Enlist the aid of the children in the next sentence; tussle with the advantages and disadvantages of the form of sentence: complex versus simple and the different structures of complex sentences including non-finite verbs.

- Practise the use of semi-colons in a piece of biographical writing, eg:

Charles Dickens was born in 1812; when he died in 1870, he was the most popular writer in the country.

Consider all the other ways in which this sentence could be written, without a semi-colon, eg:

Charles Dickens was born in 1812 and died in 1870. By that time, he was the most popular writer in the country.

Consider the effect of the semi-colon: its formality and that it creates a balance within one sentence by inviting the reader to consider Dickens' birth and death as one, to think about how much he had achieved by the end of his life.

- Ask pupils to consider what effects these punctuation marks could achieve in their next piece of writing. Afterwards, they should judge whether the desired effects have been achieved. They could involve other pupils in making these judgements, by asking others what the effect of a particular use of punctuation is, before revealing their intentions.

Y6 Term 2 S1 (Y6 Term 3 S3)

OBJECTIVES

S1 to investigate further the use of active and passive verbs: secure the use of the terms 'active' and 'passive'; know how sentences can be re-ordered by changing from one to the other; identify examples of active and passive verbs in texts; experiment in transformation from active to passive and vice-versa and study the impact of this on meaning; consider how the passive voice can conceal the agent of a sentence, eg *the chicks were kept in an incubator*;

Principles and explanations

See Teaching unit 45.

Sentence level activities

Collect and classify (page 156)

Collect examples of the passive voice where the agent has been hidden or withheld. What different reasons might the writer have for doing this? (The agent is unknown. The writer does not want the reader to know who the agent is. The agent is unimportant or irrelevant in the context. The writer wants the reader to focus on the person [thing] who is acted upon, rather than on the agent.) eg:

The glass had been shattered. (We don't know how, why or who did it.)
The butler was murdered. (By whom?)
The parcel was delivered. (It doesn't matter who delivered it.)
The king was flattered. (It is the king who is important here, not the person doing the flattering.)

Play 'Who done it?'

Drawing on well-known stories, write single-sentence 'Who done it?' scenarios. Use the passive voice to conceal the perpetrator, eg:

Who done it?
1   A young bear's breakfast has just been eaten up, and his bed slept in.
2   An apple is being shot off the head of a very frightened looking young boy.
3   A rich man has been robbed, and a poor one rewarded with the loot.
4   A frilly nightcap and a pair of spectacles, no longer needed by their owner, are being worn by someone else.
5   A tiny, golden ball has been caught, and a sticky, aerial game won.

Model and discuss the writing first. If pupils still have difficulty, provide a potential list of perpetrators, or generate one as a class activity. Write each sentence in the active voice first, eg **Dr Who navigated an old police telephone box through time and space.** Then turn these around into passive voice sentences, including the 'by (who-ever-it-is)'. Form the final puzzle by crossing out the 'by…', eg **An old police telephone box was navigated through time and space (by Dr Who).**

Play games where other pupils have to guess 'who done it'.

Identify and change

- How is the passage altered by the changes from passive to active? Which is the more effective? Why?
- Identify and mark all the passive verbs in the following passage.

- Try to change the relevant sentences into the active voice. How easy is this? Is it easier for some sentences than for others? Which ones? Why? What word or words do you need to keep adding? Why?

Chapter Three: "Boom! Boom!"

This message **is being written** by me, the author. I know that we are only up to Chapter Three, but this story **will have to be cancelled**. You see it **was being written** as a detective story, a "Who done it?". Unfortunately, however, my detective **has** just **been killed**. You will remember that Chapter Two **was rounded off** when our hero went to bed in a guest room in the isolated mansion. Well, it turns out that he **was murdered** in the middle of the night. I **was surprised** myself, I can tell you. His bedroom door **was forced** and his room **was entered** at about three in the morning. The poor chap **was hit** over the head. He **was killed** with one almighty blow. It **has been discovered** that the deadly deed **was done** with an enormous drumstick. The weapon **had been stolen** from an eminent doctor whose bedroom was just along the corridor. I **have been informed** that she played the kettledrums in her spare time.

So now my story **has been ruined**. How can a detective story **be continued** without its detective? My creativity **has been murdered**. My great novel **can** never **be finished**. I **have been devastated** by the events of the last few hours. It has come as a resounding blow for me – as well as for the detective. My story **would have been enjoyed** by so many people! THE END.

Ensure children apply this sentence level learning in their writing.

Shared writing

Related text level objective: Y6 Term 2 T10

In a selected genre, and drawing on models previously examined, write a short passage where the protagonist is acted upon by outside circumstances. Make use of the passive voice to convey the feeling of the protagonist responding rather than acting, eg:

In the middle of the night Sebastian was woken by the most hideous scream. He jerked upright and his eyes sprang open. He was even more terrified by what he saw then. His flesh turned to goose bumps and his very blood curdled. His body was gripped by a paroxysm of horror.

The Oscars! Gemma could hardly believe it. She was overwhelmed by the glamour of the occasion. Her eyes were dazzled by the sequins, the lights, the glitter. More than that, her mind was dazzled by the sheer wonder of being part of it all. She had never before been made to feel so special, never in all her short life.

Simon was soothed by the tranquillity of the landscape. His busy mind was calmed by the scudding clouds. His temper was cooled by the quiet running of the stream. He began to feel human again, and his faith in life was restored by the naturalness, the tangible reality of everything around him.

Think where he (or she) is and what he is feeling. How do you want him to be affected by what he sees around him or what is happening around him? Now make him the subject of a passive verb, to show the way he is being affected. Don't overdo it. You will need to mix in some active verbs as well, or it will start to sound very contrived. Is it working? Are we getting that feeling of him being controlled or changed or in some way affected by things outside?

Y6 Term 2 S2 (Y6 Term 3 S3)

OBJECTIVES

S2 to understand features of formal official language through, eg collecting and analysing examples, discussing when and why they are used; noting the conventions of the language, eg use of the impersonal voice, imperative verbs, formal vocabulary; collecting typical words and expressions, eg *those wishing to…, hereby…, forms may be obtained…;*

Principles and explanation

- Some of the principal features of formal language are impersonality and 'distance' in approach (objectivity, avoidance of personal involvement), use of the passive voice, studied politeness, and the employment of formal vocabulary, including 'technical' words, and 'stock', conventional phrases.
- Whilst a degree of formality is sometimes called for in the context of a particular audience and purpose, this can easily be overdone. Too much formal language becomes gobbledegook and needs to be avoided. When unduly exaggerated, formal language can produce a comic effect – intended or otherwise!

Sentence level activities

Collect and classify (page 156)

Use a formally written text (eg a solicitor's letter) in shared reading. Highlight and discuss the formal features of the language and how they are used.

Over a period of time collect examples of formal texts. Get pupils to extract and classify examples of formal language.

Draw up a class glossary of formal language, explaining what is meant by each word or phrase and providing quotations to exemplify use (much as the original *Oxford English Dictionary* was compiled – but don't take forty years!).

Identify and change

COLE, MUFFAT, WINKIE & CO.
SOLICITORS
347A SHORT STREET, WETWANG
EAST RIDING OF YORKSHIRE WET1 4ME

Ms Keziah White,
Exterior Annexe,
17, Providence Street (Rear),   1st April 2000
Wetwang WET1 SHD

Dear Ms White,
    We write to you on behalf of our clients, Mr and Mrs S. White of 17, Providence Street, Wetwang.
    It has been brought to our attention that you have, in the very recent past, ceased to reside with our clients at the above address. Our information is that, subsequent to a domestic dispute with your sibling Nathan White, the youngest son of our aforementioned clients, you have taken up residence in an outbuilding of the said premises, a detached edifice formerly utilized for the storage of fossil fuel, now disused, and hereinafter referred to as The Coal Shed.
    We are therefore charged to enquire from you whether this domestic arrangement is to be regarded as permanent or temporary. Bearing in mind the fact that my clients are, jointly, the legal owners of the said occupied premises, namely The Coal Shed, you are asked to bear carefully in mind the circumstance that, if the former arrangement is to apply, a formal leasing agreement will need to be drawn up, subject of course to yourself, as tenant, making the necessary provision for regular payments of the required rental and service charge.
    We would be grateful for your speedy response to the above address.
            Yours sincerely,
            L.M. Muffat

    L.M. Muffat,
    for Cole, Muffat, Winkie & Co.

- Identify the formal language and discuss its use.
- 'Translate' Ms Muffat's letter into 'ordinary' language.

Ensure children apply this sentence level learning in their writing.

Shared writing

Related text level objective: Y6 Term 2 T20

The Coal Shed
Home

Dear Mum and Dad,

I hate you, and I really, really hate Nat. You set your solicitors on me! Well, I'm not coming home. Never. I'm never coming back until you make Nat give me my turn on the computer. I'm never coming back whatever the solicitors say. And I'm not paying any rent either. That's a joke. It's filthy in here. A bag lady wouldn't live here. Anyway, I haven't any money. I'm only six and a half, or have you forgotten. I'm hungry. Please leave a peanut butter sandwich and a Mars bar outside the back door. If you don't I'll report you to the social services for neglect. Can I have a torch, too. It's dark in here. And a blanket. I'm cold.

Your still very, very, very cross daughter,

Kezie. xxx

P.S. No kiss for Nat, definitely not.

Imagine Kezie had employed her own solicitor instead of writing back herself. Write the solicitor's letter responding on her behalf (perhaps as a teacher demonstration, or a whole class composition). Plan ideas in straightforward language first and then 'translate'.

Continue the correspondence by writing Cole, Muffat, Winkie & Co.'s reply to the above (perhaps as supported composition). Perhaps set some pupils the challenge of incorporating specific words or phrases drawn from the class collection.

50

Y6 Term 2 S4

OBJECTIVES

S4   to revise work on contracting sentences: summary; note making; editing;

Principles and explanation

- There are three main reasons why you might want to make a sentence shorter:
    - to summarise it, ie reduce a text to its most important points, without going into details;
    - to make notes about it, ie taking the important information from it and recording it in shorter form;
    - to edit it, so that it is more effective.
- **Summarising** involves writing a complete sentence, but getting down to the essence of a longer sentence, eg:

  Anybody wanting to conquer part of the country would have to capture the castles in it before they could move on to other areas, because the soldiers who lived in the castle controlled the surrounding countryside by riding out to frighten anyone who complained about the local baron.

  Summary:

  Whoever controlled the castle controlled the surrounding countryside.
- **Note making** does not require the writing of full sentences, eg **soldiers use castle as base to frighten complaining neighbours so, control the castle = control the countryside**.
- **Editing** means making judgements about the effectiveness of the original writing, and deciding that you can improve on it, eg **If a baron wanted to take over part of the country, he first had to take control of the castle, so that he could use it as a base to intimidate local inhabitants**.

Sentence level activities

- Look at old newspaper headlines of stories that the children know about from the previous week. Analyse how the writer has reduced the information into so few words.
- Consider a current news topic of the day. Write a headline which captures the essence of the subject on the basis of the above analysis.
- Find headlines on the same subject from different newspapers which shed different perspectives on the story. Compare them. Discuss how the authors have achieved differences in so few words.

Ensure children apply this sentence level learning in their writing.

Shared writing

Related text level objectives: Y6 Term 2 T14, T19

- Display a page of non-fiction text and ask the children to skim read it. Summarise the first part of the text and ask the children if they agree with your version. Ask them to contribute the rest.

- Explain that summarising a piece of fiction is possibly more difficult than most non-fiction, because there are different aspects to consider, eg plot, setting, characterisation, author's intention, theme, implicit meanings, issues. Discuss how to go about summarising a fiction paragraph, eg the first paragraph of *The Secret Garden* in five sentences. Decide how much space to give to the facts and how much to Mary's character; how to link the two together, through cause and effect; whether to write about why the author wants a main character like this; why she has chosen to start the book with this long attack on Mary.

- Encourage pupils to summarise by starting with note making. The notes are for personal use, while the summary is for an audience.

- Use the idea of editing in shared and guided writing, drawing most of your examples from pupils' work. Ask pupils to speak and sometimes to write commentaries on the editing process, explaining why they made the changes they did and how they feel the changes have led to an improved end product.

Y6 Term 2 S5

OBJECTIVES

S5 to use reading to: investigate conditionals, eg using *if…then*, *might*, *could*, *would* and their uses, eg in deduction, speculation, supposition;

- use these forms to construct sentences which express, eg possibilities, hypotheses;
- explore use of conditionals in past and future, experimenting with transformations, discussing effects, eg speculating about possible causes (past) reviewing a range of options and their outcomes (future);

Principles and explanation

- A conditional sentence is one in which one thing depends upon another.
- Conditional sentences often contain the conjunction **if**, eg **I'll help you if I can. If the weather's bad, we might not go out**. Other conjunctions are **unless**, **providing**, **provided** and **so long as**.
- A conditional sentence can refer to an imaginary situation, eg **I would help you if I could.** (but in fact I can't) **What would you do if you were in my position?**
- The term 'conditional' is sometimes used to refer to the form **would** + verb, eg **would go**, **would help**.

Sentence level activities

The 'If' game (modelling conditional sentences)
Model: If I do this, I will (may, might, can) (be able to) do this.
Or: Unless I do this, I will not (may not, might not, cannot) (be able to) do this.
Following the pattern of the model, ask the children to create sentences explaining what they will do if they win the lottery. (Or what they will not be able to do if they do not win it.) Who can create the most tear-jerking sentence? Who can create the silliest one? Remember, they must follow the pattern of the model. Give the children 5 minutes to do this.

If I win the jackpot on the lottery, I will buy a budgie for every lonely old person in the country.
If I win millions on the lottery, I will cut a Mars bar in half lengthways, suspend it in a glass tank, and exhibit it at the Tate.

Model: If this happened, then this would (could, might) happen.
Following the pattern of the model, the children should create a sentence speculating about what might happen (or not happen) if they were a particular famous person of their choice. Who can create the funniest sentence? Who can create the most topical one?

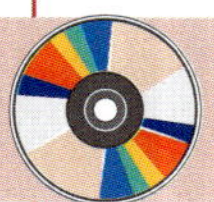

If I were David Beckham, I would always have spice in my life.
If I turned into the Iron Man, I think I could fall apart.

Model: If this had (or had not) happened, then this would (could, might) have (or have not) happened.
Following the pattern of the model, the children should create a sentence providing an excuse for not having done their homework (or something else some grown-up has been asking them to do). Who can come up with the best excuse? Who can think of the zaniest one?

If my Mum hadn't crashed the car on the way home and been so shaken up that she forgot to buy any dog food, then the dog probably wouldn't have eaten my pencil and I would have finished my homework.

If you'd bought me a goat when I wanted one, then you wouldn't have needed anyone to mow the lawn.

Model: If you do that, then this will (may, might, could) happen.
Following the pattern of the model, create a sentence which advises someone about what to do or how to do something. Alternatively, they could threaten someone as to what will happen if they do (or don't do) something. Who can come up with the most useless piece of advice in the world? Who can think of the most meaningless threat?

If you stay in that bath too long, you'll turn into a rubber duck.
If you make a face and the wind turns, it'll stay like that.

Ensure children apply this sentence level learning in their writing.

Shared writing

Related text level objectives: Y6 Term 2 T13, T14

- When reading a story, stop at a crucial point. Discuss what the characters could have done differently and the consequences, eg **If John had only…then….** Alternatively, speculate on the choices facing the characters and their consequences, eg **If Gill decides to …then….** Write up a short paragraph, using and discussing conditional sentences.
- Read and discuss Rudyard Kipling's poem 'If'. Write a parody of it, centred on notions of what you need to do to succeed/survive in your school, eg:

IF you can go into assembly and sit on a hard floor for hours with a ramrod straight back …
IF you can keep your hand in the air all day without even getting asked one question …
IF you can get all your own kit back into your PE bag and not end up with two left plimsoles,…
THEN…what?

52

Y6 Term 2 T2

OBJECTIVES

T2 to analyse how individual paragraphs are structured in writing, eg comments sequenced to follow the shifting thoughts of a character, examples listed to justify a point and reiterated to give it force;

Related text level objectives: Y6 Term 2 T1; Y6 Term 3 T21

Principles and explanation

- See Teaching Unit 8.
- Year 6 pupils need to understand how to organise more complex chronological narratives into several basic paragraph units which relate to story structure. This skill should extend to narratives which do not have a simple linear chronology. They also need to be aware of, and able to use, a range of appropriate ways of introducing and/or connecting paragraphs in these narratives.
- Year 6 pupils need to extend and develop the use of paragraph structures and connectives in a range of non-fiction text types, including recounts, procedures, reports and explanations, arguments and persuasive writing. They also need to understand how individual paragraphs can be structured, and begin to use this understanding in their own writing.

Shared writing (non-fiction)

Structuring of individual paragraphs within a text

Revisit the non-fiction paragraphing activity used for Year 3 (See Teaching Unit 9) where a list of information about Indian elephants has to be rendered into a cohesive non-chronological report. However, this time concentrate on the potential structuring of each individual paragraph within the report as a whole. For example, consider the three versions of a potential third and final paragraph.

An elephant can break branches with its trunk. It breathes through it. It also uses its trunk to drink. It sucks up water and squirts it into its mouth. Its trunk is really a nose with which it can pick up a single berry.

The elephant's trunk is really its nose. It breathes through it. It uses its trunk to drink, by sucking up water and then squirting it into its mouth. It can pick up a single berry with its trunk, and can also use it to break branches.

The elephant's trunk is a remarkable thing. Despite its great length, it is really a nose. The elephant breathes through it. It also uses its trunk to drink, sucking up water and squirting it into its mouth. Although its trunk is strong enough to break huge branches, it is also so sensitive that it can pick up a single berry. Can you do either of these things with your nose?

- With the children consider how these versions are different and how each of the three writers has gone about the task. Is what is communicated to the reader altered by the way it is written? Which is more effective and why? What lessons can be learned from this about how to put a paragraph together? Consider whether there are any more things to do to improve this paragraph.
- Try to apply the lessons learned to the task of writing the two preceding paragraphs about Indian elephants.

- Apply the same processes to other collections of related information, trying to meld them into a coherent 'rounded' paragraph.

Shared writing (narrative)

- Using a variety of suitable fiction texts (for this purpose select texts written in continuous, paragraphed prose rather than picture books):
  - Interactively explore and discuss why the writer has used paragraphs in the way he or she has.
  - What is each paragraph telling us about? Can you give a summative 'title' to each paragraph? Could you sum up the content of the paragraph in a single word?

- Map out the progression of paragraphs through a whole story. Use boxes for this to reinforce the one paragraph per box principle.

- Stick or copy part of a story text into the middle of a large piece of paper. Make marginal annotations which comment on the content and organisation of the paragraphs. (**New paragraph here because he is now talking about a different person.**/**This paragraph is describing the landscape.**/**Uses this paragraph to move to later in the morning.**/**This paragraph explains why she feels the way she does.**/**This paragraph surprises us by suddenly introducing a new situation.**/*Later that day* **used as the link phrase.**)

- Continue the approach to exploring paragraph organisation and paragraph connectives through writing, as outlined in Year 5 (see Teaching Unit 38). Extend this into more complex models from a range of genres, styles and periods.

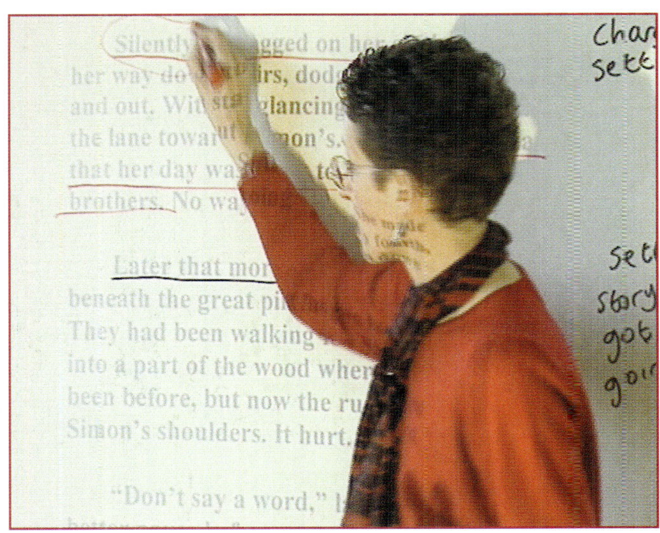

53

Y6 Term 3 S1

OBJECTIVES

S1 to revise the language conventions and grammatical features of the different types of text such as: narrative (eg stories and novels); recounts (eg anecdotes, accounts of observations, experiences); instructional texts (eg instructions and directions); reports (eg factual writing, description); explanatory texts (how and why); persuasive texts (eg opinions, promotional literature); discursive texts (eg balanced arguments);

Principles and explanation

- When we read, we should read as a writer. We should pick out the techniques which writers use and store them up, so that we can use them in our own writing.
- Being able to identify the techniques, however, is only half the battle. We have to be able to say what the effect of those techniques is, to say why the author used them. And we have to get beyond answers like: **He used it to make it more interesting** and **He used it to make us read on**. These answers are not good enough, not because they are not true, but because they could apply to every situation. We need to be more specific.
- The list of techniques which can be analysed is drawn from objectives throughout the NLS *Framework for teaching*, eg:
  - from word level: choice of vocabulary; use of obscure or unusual words; repetition; imagery; rhythm; alliteration; assonance;
  - from sentence level: simple/compound/complex sentences; writing inferentially; connectives; parts of speech; punctuation; tense; active/passive voice; person; paragraphing; linking devices;
  - from text level: audience; purpose; form; structure; author's intentions; theme; issues; design; layout; use of illustrations.
- Refer to Sections 1 and 2 in Part 3.

Sentence level activities

Analysis 1

Give pupils extracts from a selection of text types. Ask which text type each is, how they know, and what are the key features of each.

Non-fiction texts

Review with pupils the descriptions of the six non-fiction text types provided in Module 6 of the Distance Learning Materials and in Section 2 of Part 3 of this book. Look at examples of text which conform precisely to the types, and others which do not, eg explanations which do not contain causal connectives or which contain elements of instruction texts.

Narrative and poetry

Using the descriptions in Section 1 of Part 3 of this book, analyse narrative and poetry.

Analysis 2

Take a short text and do a detailed analysis. For example, use an advert as an exemplification of a persuasive text, eg **RODEO: RIDE THE RANGE** (magazine advert for new range of cars). Divide the analysis into word, sentence and text levels, ie:

	TECHNIQUE	EFFECT
Word level		
Vocabulary	Uses words which suggest cowboys	If you buy this car, you'll be a rugged man.
Alliteration	Repetition of 'R'	An attempt to make the phrase memorable?
Sentence level		
Verb	Uses imperative form	As if ordering you to buy
Colon	Used to separate name from imperative	Cuts out words like 'with this car you can…' but implies them
Text level		
Format	Block capital letters	Makes message seem important, almost vital
Layout	Most of page filled with photo of car	Picture has more impact than words

Ensure children apply this sentence level learning in their writing.

Shared writing

Related text level objectives: Y6 Term 3 T15, T19, T22

Now I'm going to decide which of the effects I want to achieve and therefore which of the techniques I want to use in my advert. I think my advert will be in a magazine too, and it will be trying to persuade teenagers to buy a particular kind of trainer.

First, at Word Level, I want to suggest that if you buy these trainers, you'll be really fashionable, just as, in the car advert, they were trying to suggest that, if you bought the car, you'd be a real man. What vocabulary could I use? **Cool** – that's a good idea, because it means fashionable, but it also suggests that the trainers are good for your feet. I'll use alliteration, too, to make the advert memorable.

Secondly, Sentence Level, I'll use an imperative verb, as if I'm ordering the readers to buy the trainers. Instead of a colon, perhaps I'll put a dash. I think it's more trendy.

At Text Level, typeface and layout will be very important.
Train hard – keep cool.

- Ask pupils to create their own advert, using the strategy outlined above.
- Ask pupils to analyse their advert in spoken and written form.
- Use the same strategies in reading and writing other text types.

54

Y6 Term 3 S2

OBJECTIVES

S2 to conduct detailed language investigations through interviews, research and reading, eg of proverbs, language change over time, dialect, study of headlines;

Principles and explanation

- Investigating the language is the best way to find out how it works, how it has changed and is changing.
- The English language is almost infinitely flexible.

Sentence level activities

Language spotter

Introduce pupils to a range of material which will draw their attention to language itself, eg some proverbs, a piece of Chaucer or 'Gawain and the Green Knight' in their original form, a recording of someone speaking in dialect, some examples of newspaper headlines where the meaning is telescoped or where there is a play on words.

Discussion

Discuss the different ways your pupils speak in different situations.

Collect and classify (page 156)

Collect some examples of young children speaking, either on tape or on video, and transcribe them. Enlarge some of the examples and discuss with the children. For example, John at 3½ said **I goed in the garden**. Discuss why John may have said **goed** instead of **went**. Explain that far from simply making a mistake, John was applying his knowledge of spoken language from words such as **played**, **waved**, etc. John has identified a verb (even though he didn't realise it) and added **-ed**. Other investigations could include:

- specific language associated with particular places or people, eg teachers, popstars;
- making a language map of the school, by walking round it and transcribing any talk which you hear;
- 50 different ways of saying the same thing, eg **yes**, **no**, **go away**;
- specific language features of soap operas, advertising, magazines, etc.;
- clichés:
  - the effects of ICT on language;
  - the puns in newspaper headlines and the names of companies, eg a hairdressing salon **'Hair Today; Gone Tomorrow'**;
  - examples of 'incorrect' English;
  - jokes and how they work, eg **'Doctor, Doctor, I think I'm a pair of curtains!' 'Pull yourself together, man!'**
  - a comedian's routine, including catchphrases, eg **'You couldn't let it lie…'**
  - rewrite a classic text in modern idiom or a rap poem in standard English;
  - write a story without using the letter 'e';
  - collect examples of dialect and look at a dialect map;
  - slang;
  - new words and new meanings, eg **naff, wannabe, awesome**;
  - compare the language of boys' and girls' magazines;
  - analyse the text of a pop song.

Insist that pupils describe, analyse and explain as well as collect.

Ensure children apply this sentence level learning in their writing.

Shared writing

- Children can use their discoveries from the sentence level investigations above as a model for a piece of writing of their own, eg to write their own pop song, newspaper headlines, jokes.

- Experiment with writing dialogue using dialect and possibly incorporating accent into the spelling. This may necessitate changes in the use of vowels. It will certainly require a creative use of the apostrophe to signify omission. The important thing to remember is consistency: **'You're not going out'** becomes **'Thaa's not gaan aat.'**.

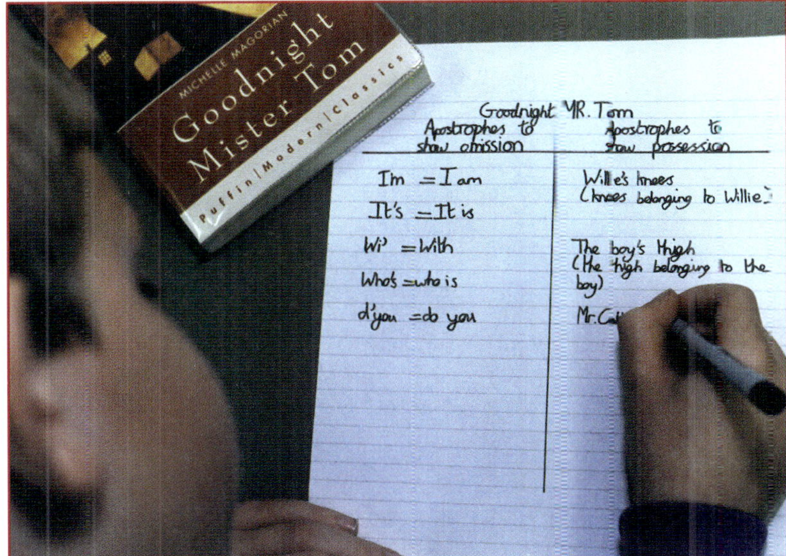

Part 3

Summary of organisation and language features: fiction and poetry

TEXT TYPE	PURPOSE	GENERIC TEXT STRUCTURE	SENTENCE/WORD LEVEL FEATURES
Retelling traditional tales	• To entertain and to pass on traditional culture	• Opening that includes a setting (of place and time) and introduces characters • A series of events that build up • Complication(s) • Resulting events • Resolution and ending	• Written in first or third person • Written in past tense • Chronological • Main participants are human or animal contrasting 'good' and 'bad' • Use of motifs, eg principle of three, younger son as hero • Connectives that signal time, eg *early that morning, later on, once* • Dialogue in differing tenses • Verbs used to describe actions, thoughts and feelings • Language effects used to create impact on reader, eg adverbs, adjectives, expressive verbs, similes, etc. • Some use of repetitive structures, eg *…but the first tasted too hot…but the second tasted too cold*
Adventure	• To entertain and enthral • To allow escape from reality – the humdrum	• Opening that includes a setting (of place and time) and introduces characters • A series of events that builds up • A complication and series of 'cliffhangers' • Resulting events • Resolution and ending	• Written in first or third person • Written in past tense (occasional use of present) • Chronological; possible use of time shifts • Main participants are human, or animal, contrasting 'good' and 'bad' • Use of stereotypical characters, settings and events, eg nightmares, nightime events, being lost or chased • Connectives that signal time, eg *First thing, later that day, early that morning* • Connectives used to shift attention, eg *meanwhile, at that very moment* • Connectives used to inject suspense, eg *suddenly, without warning* • Dialogue, in differing tenses • Verbs used to describe action, thoughts and feelings • Language effects used to create impact on reader, eg adverbs, adjectives, precise nouns, expressive verbs, metaphors, similes, etc.
Free verse	• To entertain • To recreate experience • To create an experience	• Opening and closure • Range of possible structures • Words used to create a varied pattern on the page	Possible use of: • internal rhyme and rhythm • half or near rhyme • alliteration and onomatopoeia • assonance and dissonance • metaphor and simile (personification) • expressive adjectives, adverbs and verbs • unusual word combinations • use of patterns, repetition
Haiku	• To entertain • To recreate the essence of natural experience • To capture a profound experience in a few words	• Opening and closure • Three lines	Possible use of: • alliteration, onomatopoeia • assonance/dissonance • metaphoric language • simile • expressive vocabulary • careful use of punctuation to add meaning • unusual word combinations

WRITER'S KNOWLEDGE

- Borrow words and phrases to link the tale together.
- Rehearse by constant retelling before writing.
- Be clear about the few key events.
- Add in detail to embellish – but do not add in too much or you may distract the reader from the main events.
- Try to see the story happening in your head as you retell events/write.
- Use some repetitive lines, eg so he huffed and he puffed…, especially if you wish the audience to join in.
- Keep the main characters distinctively good, bad, lazy, silly, etc.
- You can alter the setting and many details but the main events in the plot have to stay, eg Snow White in New York.
- Reread the tale aloud to see if it 'reads well'. Try it out on small groups.

- Avoid telling the reader what to feel, eg it was scary, but make the reader feel it through concrete description.
- Avoid telling the reader what a character feels, eg she was sad, but show how characters feel through what they say or do, eg her lip trembled.
- Know your ending so that events can be planned and written that converge at the end – otherwise some irrelevant details will creep in or the story may ramble.
- Do not plan too many characters or you may lose control of them.
- Give your main character some sort of flaw and make him or her interesting.
- Give your character a 'feeling' at the start of the story as this will influence events.
- Keep thinking as you write 'what would this person do/say?'.
- Plan just a few details about the character that tells the reader something about their personality.
- Include the weather, season and time of day as part of creating the setting.
- To create suspense, lull the reader into a false sense of security – get characters doing something pleasant and then introduce a dilemma.
- Use exclamations for impact, eg Help!
- Use questions to draw the reader into events, eg Where should they look now?
- At the end, show how the main character has changed as a result of the narrative.
- At the end, have the narrator or a character make comments on what has happened.

- Avoid abstract nouns, such as love, eternity, etc.
- Describe in a concrete way what you think you are writing about.
- Keep rereading to capture flow and rhythm.
- Only use simile if it comes swiftly, otherwise it sounds false.
- Metaphor is more powerful than simile.
- Use unusual but revealing word combinations to surprise the reader.
- Play with words and ideas.
- Hold the subject in your mind as you write.
- Observe very carefully the details of your subject.
- Use your senses.
- Select words which are linked to the senses, eg click, crack, greasy, jagged.
- Write very quickly in a totally focused way.
- Write about subjects that you know a lot about and that matter.
- Have the subject in front of you so you can observe it.
- Use the shape on the page to emphasise words and ideas.
- Avoid clichés.
- Read aloud to hear how it sounds.
- Be ruthless in revision so that each word is fresh and each word counts.

- Use careful observation of events and scenes.
- Create a verbal 'snapshot' to capture precisely the essence of a moment.
- Possible focus on a seemingly insignificant detail that suggests more than it states.
- Use a few words to evoke more than is described, eg suggesting the season.
- Use language to capture a sense of wonder or surprise about simple things.
- Select one or two details only.
- Use a 'sound effect' to emphasise loneliness or isolation.
- Begin by making notes outside of small details.
- Try to use words to help the reader see something familiar in a new light.

Summary of organisation and language features: non-fiction

TEXT TYPE	PURPOSE	GENERIC TEXT STRUCTURE	SENTENCE/WORD LEVEL FEATURES
Recount	• To retell events	• Orientation – scene setting opening, eg I went to the shop… • Events – recount of the events as they occurred, eg I saw a vase… • Reorientation – a closing statement, eg When I got back, I told my mum. (with elaboration in more sophisticated texts)	• Written in the past tense, eg I went • In chronological order, using connectives that signal time, then, next, after, meanwh… • Focus on individual or group participants, eg we, I

Non-chronological report	• To describe the way things are	• An opening, general classification, eg Sparrows are birds.
		 • More technical classification (optional), eg Their latin name is…
		 • A description of the phenomenon, including some or all of its:
		   – qualities, eg Birds have feathers.
		   – parts and their function, eg The beak is…
		   – habits/behaviour or uses, eg They nest in…
			• Written in the present tense, they nest
			 • Non-chronological
			 • Initial focus on generic participants, eg sparrows in general, not Sam the sparrow
			 • Moves from the general to the specific

Instructions and procedures	• To describe (or instruct) how something is done through a series of sequenced steps	• Goal – a statement of what is to be achieved, eg How to make a sponge cake • Materials/equipment needed, listed in order, eg 2 eggs, flour • Sequenced steps to achieve the goal, eg Cream the sugar and butter. • Often diagrams or illustrations	• Written in the imperative, eg Sift the flour • In chronological order, eg first, next • Use of numbers, alphabet or bullet points and colour to signal order • Focus on the generalised human agents rather than named individuals.
Explanation	• To explain the processes involved in natural and social phenomena, or to explain how something works	• General statement to introduce the topic, eg In the autumn some birds migrate. • A series of logical steps explaining how or why something occurs, eg Because hours of daylight shorten… • Steps continue until the final state is produced or the explanation is complete	• Written in simple present tense, eg Many birds fly south. • Uses connectives that signal time, eg then, next, several months later • Uses causal connectives, eg because, so, this causes
Persuasion	• To argue the case for a point of view • To attempt to convince the reader	• Thesis – an opening statement, eg Vegetables are good for you. • Arguments – often in the form of point plus elaboration, eg They contain vitamins. Vitamin C is vital for… • Reiteration – summary and restatement of the opening position, eg We have seen that…so…	• Simple present tense • Focus mainly on generic participants, eg vegetables, not a particular vegetable • Mainly logical, rather than connectives which signal time, eg this shows, however, because • Movement usually from the generic to the specific
Discussion	• To present arguments and information from differing viewpoints	• Statement of the issue plus a preview of the main arguments • Arguments for, plus supporting evidence • Arguments against, plus supporting evidence (alternatively, argument/counter argument, one point at a time) • Recommendation – summary and conclusion	• Simple present tense • Generic human (or non-human) participants • Logical connectives, eg therefore, however • Movement is from the generic to the specific, eg Hunters agree…, Mr Smith, who has hunted for many years,…

- Details are vital to bring incidents alive.
- Use specific names of people, places, objects, etc.
- Pick out incidents that will amuse, interest or that in some way are significant.
- You can write as if you were 'telling the story' of what happened.
- Plan by thinking, noting or drawing – when? who? where? what? and why? Use a flow chart to plan the sequence.
- End by commenting on events.

- Plan under paragraph headings in note form.
- Use a range of resources to gather information.
- Select facts from a range of sources to interest the reader, eg books CD-ROM, interviews.
- Possible use of a question in the title to intrigue the reader, eg Yetis – do they exist?
- Be clear, so that you do not muddle the reader.
- Open by explaining very clearly what you are writing about – take an angle to draw the reader in.
- Use tables, pictures, diagrams to add more information.
- Possibly end by relating the subject to the reader, eg Many people like whales…
- Reports are factual but you could add comments or use questions to draw in the reader.
- Reread as if you knew nothing about the subject to check that you have put the information across successfully.

- Before writing instructions be clear about what is needed and what has to be done, in what order.
- Think about your readers. You will need to be very clear about what to do or they will be muddled – if they are young, you may have to avoid technical language or use simple diagrams.
- The title should explain what the instructions are about – using how to… helps, eg How to play cricket.
- In your querying you may need to say when the instructions are needed, eg If your computer breaks down…, or for whom it is best suited, eg Young children may enjoy this game….
- Use bullet points, numbers or letters to help the reader.
- Use short clear sentences so the reader does not become muddled.
- Use the end statements to wrap up the writing – evaluate how useful or how much fun this will be.
- Make your writing more friendly by using you, or more formal by just giving orders.
- Use adjectives and adverbs only when needed.
- Tantalise the reader, eg Have you ever been bored – well this game will….
- Draw the reader in with some 'selling points', eg This is a game everyone loves….
- Make instructions sound easy, eg You are only four simple steps away….
- Finally, ask yourself whether someone who knows nothing about this could successfully use your instructions.

- Decide whether diagrams, charts, illustrations or a flow chart would help to explain.
- Use a title that indicates what you are writing about.
- Using how or why in the title helps. Try to make the title intrigue the reader, eg Why do sloths hang about?
- Use the first paragraph to introduce your subject to the reader.
- Organise the writing and illustrations to explain: what you need, how it works, why it works (cause and effect), when and where it works, and what it is used for.
- Add in extra, interesting information.
- Try to end by relating the subject to the reader.
- If you use specialised terminology, a glossary may be needed.
- Interest the reader with exclamation, eg Beware – whirlwinds can kill! Or use questions, eg Did you know that…?
- Draw the reader in, eg strange as it may seem…; not many people know that…,etc.
- Reread your explanation, pretending to know nothing about the subject – is it clear?

- Use good reasons and evidence to convince your readers.
- Use facts rather than just persuasive comments.
- You may wish to counter arguments.
- Try to get the reader interested and on your side – appear reasonable!
- Tantalise your readers so that they agree with you.
- Use strong, positive language.
- Short sentences can help to give emphasis.
- Make the reader think that everyone else does this, agrees or that it will make them a better, happier person, eg Everyone agrees that…, We all know that….
- Draw the reader in, eg At long last…the x you have been waiting for.
- Be informative, persuasive and sound friendly.
- Alliteration can help to make slogans memorable, eg Buy British Beef.
- Use humour as it can get people on your side.
- A picture that tugs at the heart-strings can be more effective than 1,000 words.
- Finally, reread and decide whether you would be persuaded.

- You can turn the title into a question, eg Should we hunt whales?
- Open by introducing the reader to the discussion – you may need to add why you are debating the issue.
- Try to see the argument from both sides.
- Support your views with reasons and evidence.
- In your conclusion you must give a reason for what you decide.
- If you are trying to present a balanced viewpoint, check you have been fair to both sides.

Instructions for the generic sentence level activities

Function

PURPOSE

To give children the opportunity to investigate the function of a word class, sentence structure or punctuation mark.

RESOURCES

Page of enlarged text with all the words (approximately 10) of the particular focus (eg adjectives), underlined and one word near the end which is underlined but not in the word class

INSTRUCTIONS

- Tell the children the objective of the lesson.
- Read through the text and then read again the first sentence which contains an underlined word.
- Discuss the function of the underlined word in the text, eg *the wise man – wise* is telling us more about the man.
- Ask the children to discuss in pairs the function of the next underlined word; take responses.
- Relate the function of this word to the function of the first word to see the commonality.
- Do the same with the next few words until you are sure that most children have understood.
- Tell them the name of the word class if no one has suggested it already.
- Ask the children to carry on to the end to find the underlined word which is not in the same class. This word is also in *italics* in the book, but not on the disk.

FOLLOW-UP

The children can look out for words in this category in their reading.

Collect and classify

PURPOSES

- To give children practice in identifying elements such as word class, sentence structure or punctuation marks.
- To give children the opportunity to investigate their subtypes or different functions of words.

RESOURCES

Depending on the objective, either a page of enlarged text containing a number of examples of the feature to be taught, or a collection of examples from a number of texts

INSTRUCTIONS

- Tell the children the objective of the lesson and highlight the first two examples of the focus for the activity.
- Ask the children to name the focus element (eg commas).
- Find all the examples of the focus element.
- Classify according to categories defined in the teaching unit.

Compare

PURPOSE

To give children the opportunity to deduce principles governing a grammatical feature by comparing two texts containing different facets of the same feature.

RESOURCES

Two versions of the same text illustrating the feature of the lesson, eg one in the present tense, the other in the past tense

INSTRUCTIONS

- Tell the children the objective of the lesson and underline/highlight the first example of the difference(s) between the two versions.
- Discuss the differences with the children.
- Highlight and discuss the next two or three examples.
- Where appropriate make a list to categorise the differences, eg past tense can be present tense with **-ed** added (**work/worked**) or it can be a different word entirely (**catch/caught**).
- Between you, highlight the remaining examples in the text.
- Discuss the merits of one form over another in terms of writing purpose.

Cloze

PURPOSE

To give children the opportunity to consider the effectiveness of a particular word within a sentence and to practise using effective language to suit the audience and purpose of the text.

RESOURCES

- Page of enlarged text with all the examples of a particular word class obscured with concealing tape
- Dry-wipe boards, one between two

INSTRUCTIONS

- Tell the children the objective of the lesson and point to the first concealed word.
- Ask the children, in pairs, to discuss what word the tape might be obscuring and to write down their suggestion on their dry-wipe boards.
- Discuss alternative suggestions.
- Compare with the original word, and discuss its effectiveness.
- Encourage divergence of response, eg for later work in poetry, rather than clichés.

VARIATION

Leave some of the words at the end uncovered so that children have an opportunity to identify examples of the word class.

Construct

PURPOSE

To allow children to experiment with sentence structure to reinforce knowledge of word classes and sentence construction.

RESOURCES

Coloured word/phrase cards to construct the focus sentence in the lesson, one word per child, eg noun-verb-adverb **dogs bark loudly**, or one phrase per child, eg subject-verb-object/complement **The friendly Alsatian is swimming in the lake.**

INSTRUCTIONS

- Give out cards to children. (Any extra children can be used to monitor the activity and could be given the task of being the scribe and writing down the sentences.)
- Put large pieces of paper and thick felt tip pens around the room.
- Ask the children to get together to make sentences according to the stipulated colour sequence of cards.
- When all are sitting down in their sentence groups, one child from the group (or a scribe) writes the sentence on a large sheet of paper.
- Ask the children to get up again and find different children to reform into new sentences and write them down.
- Repeat once more.
- Choose children to read out the three sentences on the sheets and all check that they are proper sentences and then vote for the most ludicrous sentence of the day. Write this up on a 'ludicrous sentence sheet'. (On the last day of term you can vote for the most ludicrous sentence of the term/year.)

VARIATION (TEACHER-DIRECTED WHOLE CLASS ACTIVITY)

- Place all the shuffled cards face down in piles, eg subject, verb and object/complement.
- Divide the class into three groups, eg subject, verb, object/complement.
- One child from the first (eg subject) group takes the top strip from their pile and stands and holds it.
- Next a child from the second (eg verb) group joins him or her and finally a child from the third (eg object) group.
- The children decide whether each sentence describes something which is possible. They then vote for the silliest sentence.

Quick make

PURPOSE

To give children oral practice in sentence construction.

RESOURCES
Washing line/sentence maker and coloured words

INSTRUCTIONS
- Make a sentence, eg *The shy child cries*.
- Ask a child to **say** a word to replace the first word (eg *A shy child cries*.)
- Ask the next child to replace the next word (eg *A cross child cries*.)
- Continue round the class replacing the words, keeping a brisk pace (eg *A cross baby cries, a cross baby bounces, that cross baby bounces, that beautiful baby bounces, that beautiful car bounces, that beautiful car crashes*, etc.).
- Continue until all the children have had a go. Write up the final sentence and compare it with the original.

Punctuate

PURPOSE
To give children practice in punctuation.

RESOURCES
- Page of text in which punctuation marks (as specified in the teaching unit) are concealed
- Punctuation fans

INSTRUCTIONS
- Display the text.
- Give out punctuation fans, one between two.
- Read the first half of the text together.
- Go back to the beginning and read just beyond the first concealed punctuation mark.
- Children discuss in their pairs which punctuation mark is appropriate and find it on their fans.
- Children hold up the fans and the teacher chooses a response either because it is correct or because she or he wishes to make a teaching point.
- The teacher exposes the punctuation mark and the activity continues.

VARIATION 1
In addition to concealing all the punctuation, put some concealing tape in places where there is no punctuation. The option for the children is increased to deciding whether there should be punctuation or not, as well as what punctuation it should be.

VARIATION 2
- Write out a text without punctuation.
- The children raise their hands to suggest between which two words the punctuation should occur.
- All the children then decide which punctuation mark it should be and raise their fans.

Complex sentence game

PURPOSE
To give children oral practice in constructing subordinate clauses. Decide on groups of preferably no more than five. Give the same set of instruction cards to each group, shuffled and placed face down.

RESOURCES
A set of instruction cards for each group of children (no more than five groups):

Change first word (or phrase) of subordinate clause 4 points	Create a completely new sentence 6 points
Change subordinate clause 4 points	Change subject in main clause 2 points
Change main clause 2 points	Move the subordinate clause 6 points
Change verb in main clause 2 points	Miss a turn 0 points

INSTRUCTIONS

- Write the complex sentence, given in the teaching unit, on the board.
- A child in the first group picks up a card and reads the instruction on it.
- He or she suggests an answer and checks with the group.
- Meanwhile, the other groups consider an answer in case the first group's answer is incorrect.
- The child offers an answer and the other groups and the teacher judge its suitability.
- The teacher keeps the score and can award full, half or no points for an answer.
- The teacher may need to record the sentence on the white board as it is modified.
- The first team to score 10 is the winner.

EXTENSION

When the group has agreed their answer, one child says it, another says 'comma' at the appropriate point(s) in the sentence.

Replace

PURPOSE
To give children the opportunity to see the connections between the same word in different forms and to realise the implications of changing the form of one word in a sentence on other words in the same sentence.

RESOURCES
A page of text as indicated in the teaching unit

INSTRUCTIONS
As required in the objective, replace specified words in a text with the same word in another form, eg change verb tenses, noun number.

Children can be actively involved in this by suggesting changed form of word on dry-wipe boards. Almost always, the replacement of one word in a sentence necessitates changing others. This activity encourages children to read and reread to check for agreement between words.

Re-order

PURPOSE
To help children understand that some words, phrases and clauses are fixed in relation to others in a sentence whereas certain classes or functions can be moved around to provide variety and emphasis.

RESOURCES

- Washing line, sentence maker or computer with large screen
- Coloured words, phrases or clauses, as specified in the objective

INSTRUCTIONS

This activity can take many forms. You could give the children words or phrases to hold and they could discuss the order they stand in. Alternatively, the children could stand and be directed by a 'circus master'. Children could be asked to hang the words on a washing line or put them onto a sentence maker. A child could operate the computer at the instructions of specified members of the class. Whatever device is available, the idea is to experiment to find out which words can be freely moved and which cannot.

Improve

PURPOSE

To give children practice in editing their writing by considering the choices open to them and discussing the merits of alternative words and structures.

RESOURCES

- A 'first draft' piece of text (possibly from previous year group) which is weak on the specific elements of the chosen teaching objective
- Dry-wipe boards between two; pens and erasers

INSTRUCTIONS

- Ask the children to read through the draft either in unison or silently.
- Explain what aspect(s) of the writing you want the children to focus on (eg weak verbs, monotonous sentence openings, longwinded constructions).
- Discuss the first instance of the focus element and change accordingly.
- Ask a child to find the next instance.
- Ask the children to suggest alternatives by writing them on their dry-wipe boards.
- Ask the children to hold up their dry-wipe boards, and choose a pair to read out their version.
- Ask the class to discuss the version given.
- Possibly choose another version.
- Decide which version to insert on the draft on the board, always discussing reasons for decisions or asking the children for reasons for their decisions.
- Continue through the draft.

Some grammatical terminology

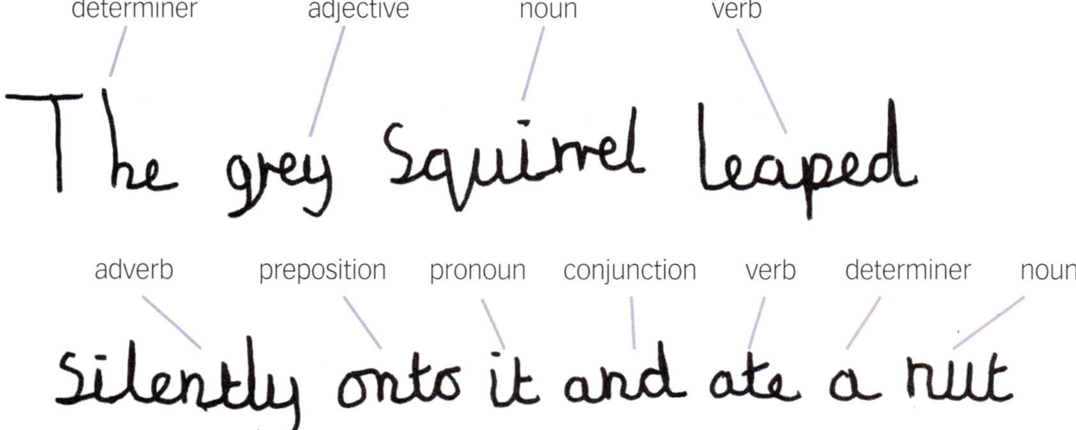

subject	verb	object
The boy	ate	his sandwich.

subject	verb	complement
The boy	was	in the garden

Simple sentence

It was a beautiful day

Compound sentence

main clause

Mrs. Eves was scrubbing her front

conjunction · main clause

step and Mrs. slater was polishing

main clause continued

her windows

Complex sentence

main clause · subordinate clause

Mary Davies, who had just got over

subordinate clause continued · main clause

the mumps, was playing hopscotch

main clause continued

on the pavement.

Complex sentence

main clause

Her mother was busy cooking

conjunction · subordinate clause

while the baby slept fitfully in the

subordinate clause continued

back room.

A teacher's description of a unit of work based on a cluster of text and sentence level objectives in Year 5 Term 3 using the novel *The Midnight Fox* by Betsy Byars

OBJECTIVES

Text level objectives: Y5 Term 3 T9

T9   to write in the style of the author, eg writing on to complete a section, resolve a conflict…;

Sentence level objectives: Y5 Term 3 S4, S6 and S7

S4   to use punctuation marks accurately in complex sentences;

S6   to investigate clauses through: identifying the main clause in a long sentence; investigating sentences which contain more than one clause; understanding how clauses are connected (eg by combining three short sentences into one);

S7   to use connectives to link clauses within sentences and to link sentences in longer texts.

I work in a large town school, with 32 Year 5 children. They are a pretty mixed bunch, and when they came to me in September their writing lagged behind their reading.

Year 5 has a lot of sentence level work in it. I find that it is important to group objectives where I can. In my planning I always like to plan sentence and text level objectives together so that the sentence level work is linked to text. I look for good quality texts that will interest the children, as I think that this motivates them as readers. I always have a class novel on the go, which I read outside the Literacy Hour. Every now and again, I 'raid' it to teach particular objectives during the Literacy Hour as well as using extracts from other books.

This unit of work focused on looking at clauses, writing (and punctuating) complex sentences. It involved using connectives to make links between sentences and using conjunctions within sentences. There was quite a lot to it but most of my class do use complex sentences so I wasn't starting from scratch.

THURSDAY

I began the block of work on a Thursday. We had previously done some work on writing and performing poems. This had culminated in an assembly when each group performed a poem that one group member had written. It had been great fun. I had planned to move on to this work on complex sentences as a bit of a contrast. We had been reading Betsy Byars novel, *The Midnight Fox* (a quality novel from another culture), so I used that as a basis for the work.

My main objective was to explore clauses within complex sentences and use this to write, in the style of the author, a further passage starting near the beginning of Chapter 17 with the words, 'I opened the window, pushed out the screen, reached out into the rain, and…' This is the episode when Tom takes his courage into his hands to free the baby fox. He goes out at night, into the storm, and defies his uncle's wishes. For me, it is a key incident because at the end of the chapter it reveals how Tom has misunderstood his uncle just as much as the uncle has misunderstood Tom.

So, we began the Literacy Hour with shared reading; that took us up to the end of Chapter 16. We discussed the reactions of the different characters and spent some time looking at how Betsy Byars had managed to make the chapter so tense – especially through the way that she handles sentences. This took about quarter of an hour.

To tune the children back into the notion of clauses and conjunctions we quickly had a go at sentence combination. I play this game quite a lot, as a rapid activity, to warm us up. In the game the children have to join together three simple sentences. On this occasion they had to select from a range of conjunctions. This was building on previous work so I kept it swift. We then looked at various sentences and underlined the clauses. I find that sometimes I can begin by looking at a paragraph from a text as a starting point, but there can also be great advantages with extracting sentences. It makes the grammatical point easier for some children if they can easily see a string of sentences that contain a certain feature. It makes it easier to extract the patterns.

We spent some time taking sentences with three clauses and seeing whether they could be written in a different order. I emphasised the need to think about using a comma to mark off a subordinate clause, when it comes at the start of the sentence. This sentence level work was pretty quick-fire and took about 15 minutes to get through. I try to keep it lively so that it is more like grammatical gymnastics! I followed this with an independent activity, basically reinforcing the combining of sentences, identifying clauses and re-ordering. At the end of the lesson we defined what we had learned.

FRIDAY

In Friday's Literacy Hour, I began by focusing upon the first three paragraphs of Chapter 17. We looked at the way in which Betsy Byars handles sentences. She varies considerably her use of simple, compound and complex sentences, sometimes including a number of clauses within a sentence. We looked at her use of punctuation, which is often used to give emphasis to certain clauses. We discussed the impact that all this has on the reader – especially the 'job' of the sentences – some for impact or to emphasise a point, some for flow, or to explain things, some to add tension, to create links or to help the reader imagine what is happening, and so on. This took up most of the first half hour of the lesson, combining the sentence level work within the shared reading discussion.

To consolidate, I asked the children to analyse several paragraphs, annotating the text and listing different uses of sentences and clauses. For instance, some of the shorter sentences added impact, while others contained a number of clauses, sometimes to explain, sometimes to present information economically. At the end of this session we added to our definition, making points about using sentences, clauses, commas and re-ordering sentences to gain different effects.

MONDAY

The third session was on Monday. We began rereading the end of Chapter 16, and into the first part of Chapter 17, to revisit the events that lead up to Tom climbing out of the window. We responded to this by thinking about what might happen next – most of the class was sure that Tom would rescue the baby fox. But would Uncle Fred hear him, come down and shoot the fox or would he get away with it? Suppose Tom was caught, what would his uncle's reaction be? This shared reading took up the first part of the whole class session.

I followed this by demonstrating how to write a short paragraph, using the same style as Betsy Byars – that meant varying the sentences, using 'I' a lot, fairly straightforward language, revealing what Tom was thinking. I used demonstration on this occasion as I wanted to emphasise points about Betsy Byars' style – I tend to use demonstration writing whenever I am introducing something new or difficult. (I use collaborative writing when we are handling a topic that most of the children are becoming familiar with.) I made sure that I focused my explanation on the way in which I was handling the clauses, shifting them round for different effects, linking them together or isolating them for effect.

As soon as I had demonstrated the paragraph, the children were bursting to continue with their own. They wrote silently and solidly for the rest of the session, which ended with a few examples being read aloud as the rest of the class listened and made notes to provide feedback.

TUESDAY

The fourth session was on the Tuesday. I began by looking at some examples of writing by different children. I like to enlarge some of their work onto an OHT so everyone can see the writing. We focused upon the ways in which successful paragraphs varied the sentences, using different connectives to link within and between sentences. We noticed sentences that really did sound like a 'Betsy Byars' sentence' and some places where clauses had been shifted around to give emphasis. This took about 15 minutes.

After this we read the rest of Chapter 17 and moved into exploring why the different characters react as they do to what Tom had done. The whole class discussion took up the rest of the shared time and then the children moved into an independent activity. I did this through the children working in pairs to take a character, identify clues from the text, and write a diary entry that shows how their character reacted, and their motives. We ended the session with children reading out their entries.

The sequence of children's sentence level work and writing

Reading and writing journal entries

Keeping a reading and writing journal is a useful strategy for making links between reading and writing. In such a journal children could:

- evaluate their own writing
- reflect on different processes needed for different types of writing
- make notes about the structures and features needed to write effectively for different audiences and purposes
- write 'hints' and 'tips', perhaps gained from an author's visit
- note different strategies for opening or closing texts
- note how to vary sentences
- make lists of effective vocabulary
- make lists of special effects that poets use
- note how to use language persuasively
- note key points to remember when writing
- evaluate their work and set themselves specific targets, etc.

After studying certain types of writing, charts can be made, listing all that has been learned that might inform the children's own writing (eg **To write a good discussion you must remember to…**). In this way, the children read both for the experience of reading, as well as with a 'writer's eye', identifying how to write effectively.

1 The Way I Write

a Three pupils reflect on the ways in which they like to write poetry (Year 6).

The Way I Write

> Sometimes if a poem is more complicated it helps me to have an example read out to me or if it is a more descriptive piece to have a picture in front of me that I could refer too. It also helps me to write pieces of writing out in rough because then I can get better ideas and I can add more feeling to it and change words that I don't need or that I don't want.
>
> Lynn Eldered
>
> Age 11 Years.

> Before I start a piece of writing I find it helps to talk about it first, because it sort of 'makes my mind clear of what I've got to do. Some of my best ideas come from my imagination. If an idea appears in my head I quickly jot it down in my rough book and when I have a series of fairly good ideas I begin to construct a piece of writing. I prefer to work in a noisy room because sometimes the words people use in their speech can help create a realistic atmosphere in my poetry. I usually write in rough first, because then I can change words that I think are boring or just don't make sense.
>
> by Allison Crook
>
> 11 years old

> I like doing a poem in a quiet place so that I can think of words to put in the poem. And I would do it in rough first so that I could change the words if it doesn't fit in with the rest of the poem. My best ideas come from the other poems I've done and from the mistakes I've made. I get my ideas sometimes from the scenery around me and sometimes from places I've been to. If I discuss how to do a poem it might help me sometimes when I haven't got an idea.
>
> Leyla Abdullah
>
> 11 years old

b Writing
A pupil advises others on how to write effectively (Year 6).

> Writing.
>
> When I start to write a piece of writing I always build on a central idea, I prefer to work in quietness. If the piece of writing has to be good then I'm always concentrating. First of all I jot down ideas then I arrange them into the piece of writing. I then start to change words, I change non-interesting words for interesting ones. Make your work eye - catching and set it out so it looks good. Check for spelling mistakes. Never waste a good word, always try and fit it in. I like to read others work and grasp ideas from it. Look at ideas from all sides and find their best meaning and use. Use words that fit well in the piece of writing. Never stop conantrating, sometimes it helps to discuss your ideas with a friend.
>
> John Manwaring.
> 11 years of age

c Adverts
Following a range of lessons in which adverts have been studied, the children have made a summary of points about what makes an effective advert – in order to inform their own writing (Year 5).

> <u>Adverts</u>
> <u>Wednesday 15th September</u>
> <u>1999</u>
>
> A good advert 1.) has a snappy title to grab, your attention. eg. 1.) 'The Best sucker in town.' 2.) 'Golden time!' 3.) Get a tick tock today.
>
> 2) gives you plenty of information about the product and what it can do.
>
> 3.) may offer you something. eg. a free gift or a guarantee.
>
> 4.) concludes with a memorable remark. eg. Hurry whils* while stocks last. Come to my offe-* shop and you'll be the coolest person ever. dont miss the bargain offer.
>
> 5.) A good advert may have alliteration. eg. Get a tick tock today.
>
> 6.) A good advert has short, sharp sentences to catch your attention.

d 'Ingredients' needed for biography writing

A quick summary of key points, made after a series of lessons studying different examples of biographical writing. This lesson was followed by children planning and drafting biographies of their friends, using the key features that had been learned from their study of a range of biographical writing (Year 6).

> Biography Planning
>
> Ingredients:-
>
> Dates
> Pronouns 3rd person
> Chronological - from beginning to end
> Non-fiction Factual
> Past tense / formal no slang
> E.g. / quote - back up
> Paragraphs

e Autobiography

A quick list of key points needed for autobiography, made after a series of lessons studying different autobiographical writings (eg *Boy* by Roald Dahl, *The Moon and Me* by Betsy Byars), plus an example of teacher marking, noting aspects that the pupil needs to focus upon. This lesson was followed by planning and writing their own autobiographical writing, using these features (Year 6).

> 1st December 1998
>
> Autobiography
>
> 1. Pronouns - personal I, my, we, me
> 2. ² can't I'd didn't Contractions / informal
> 3. Paragraphs
> 4. Past tense
> 5. Factual not much discription
> 6. Personal
> 7. " " for quotes
> 8 Chronological

2 Categorising, defining and practising

a Categorising story openings
Over time children build up an ever increasing repertoire of different strategies for aspects such as opening and closing writing.

<< Types of Story Opening >>

Scene Setting	Question	Speech	Introducing characters.
On a windy hill half hidden by trees and swirly mist, stood a stone cottage.	"Will my cousin Dicky be there?"	"Right, everyone", said Miss Monk.	Until the angel came there were three terribly unhappy children at Nitshill road school: Penny, Mark and Marigold.
At the far end of England, a land of rocks and moorland stretches itself out into a blue-green sea.	Remember?	"You keep away from the Birdman, Gracie; my father had warned me often enough.	Keith Chapman, a tall, fair boy in blue jeans and a tee-shirt, held his breath and hurried past number 51, the dirty house.
It was warm indoors. Mother had soup bubbling on the stove.			

b Making notes as a writer about what makes an effective opening. Listed as instructions, focused on how to write an effective opening, based on reading many examples (Year 6).

Tuesday 1st December '98

Story Openings

- Catch readers interest
- Make opening dramatic
- Make reader want to read on – Questions – Why did it happen to me?
- Take reader straight into the story
- Make it interesting and straight to the point
- Put some description in about characters.

c   Practising three types of opening
Practising writing three different ways to open a story – using a time opening
(**On Thursday…**), a name opening (**Jo stared…**) and a question opening
(**What are you doing?**) (Year 3).

Story openings

1. Days of the week.
On Tuesday morning Amys new dog arrived.
On Saturday afternoon Tom got punched   by
Bill the bully.

2. Name openings.

Dorothy said, "Goodbye everyone."
Annie went to Mr Warboxs house. but she left
behind her parents locked.
Kitty glaßed at a spaceship passing by,
. in horror her uncle was in it.

3. Questions

" Tidy your room now will you ? " Shouted
Mrs pew.

" Why do I smell wet dog? " growled Mr Warbox
staring angrily, at Annie.

3 From a focused activity into writing

a   Improving five sentences using powerful verbs
A swift activity to focus children on the impact of selecting different verbs and what this reveals about character (Year 4).

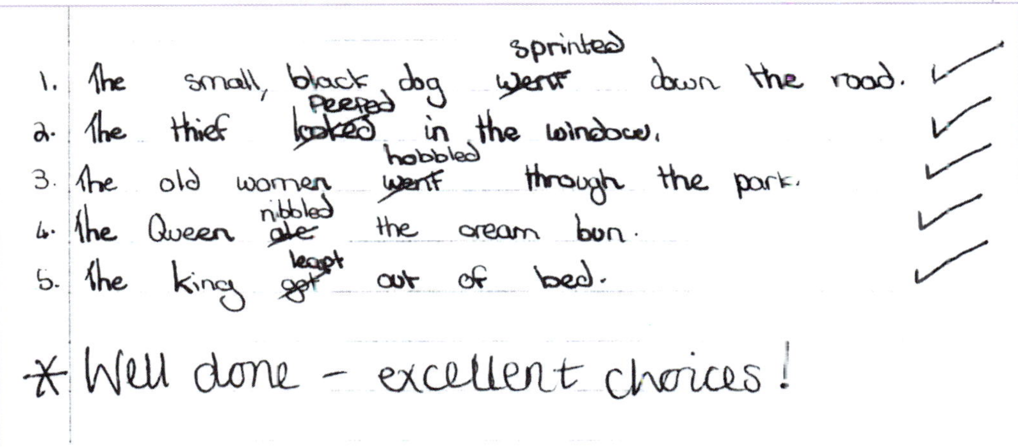

b   Drafting a first paragraph using powerful verbs
A follow-on in the same lesson as 3a (Year 4).

c Identifying features in a suspense paragraph
Analysing with a partner the different techniques that the writer has used to create suspense
(Year 6).

> *[Handwritten annotations surround the printed paragraph below]*
>
> Simple Sentence for impact
> what is it?
> one word
> Personification
> Phrase
> Simile
>
> Short sentence
> Question to draw reader in.
>
>   A door banged. Claire jumped. What was
> that? It wasn't Mr. Jakes because she could now
> hear him whistling at the other end of the
> playground. Out of the silence, she heard steps.
> Somebody was coming closer. Somebody, or
> something, was coming down the corridor. It
> Nearer. She stood still, so still that even the
> chairs and tables froze with her. Carefully, she
> peered round the edge of the door. A shadow
> slipped, quick as a knife, into the next
> classroom. Claire clenched her fist around the
> pen, her heart racing fast.
>
> who is it? hiding
> comma
> It / hiding
> adverb before the comma
> comma
>
> complex
> Sentence to tell reader
> how she is feeling.

d Drafting a suspense paragraph using identified features
A follow-on from 3c, using some of the features identified from reading, drafted onto a dry-wipe board (Year 6).

> *[Handwritten note on a Stabilo Plan Magic-Memo Board]*
>
> STABILO plan MAGIC-MEMO BOARD
>
> Daisy   16th February
>
> Simon dropped his lemonade.
> A twig snapped. Jo stood
> perplexed and still. What
> was it? Who was it? Simon's
> muscles tensed; he was
> petrified. A shadow slipped
> forward towards the
> children. Suddenly a hand
> grabbed Jo's shoulder In
> a flash a memory slipped back
> to Simon, was it the madman
> who killed his brother?
> as a wolf howled in the distance
>
> Schwan STABILO

4 Defining a feature, listing examples, into drafting

a Personification
Leading into a poem (Year 6).

6-3-00   <u>Personification.</u>

<u>Definition</u>: To make an object or thing seem more
real by giving it human feelings.

Eg. The sea <u>howled</u>.
The wind <u>whispered</u>.
The wind <u>whistled</u>
The wind <u>roared</u>.
The door <u>growled</u>.
The grass <u>blew</u>.
[shrieked] The door <u>shrieked</u>.
The flames ~~danced~~ hissed with anger
The flames ~~dodged in and out~~ shrieked with laughter.
The tree ~~waved~~ howled with old age.

<u>Autumn</u> 1st draft
                  [moaning]   [chattering]
The wind ripped through the trees, tearing the leaves
~~as it went.~~ as it went.
                    [fell]
The now-silent leaves ~~fall~~ to the ground which is
[growled] ~~growling~~ with side-splitting anger.

[Great so far.] The sun ~~smiles~~ [smiled] whilst shrivelling up the frightened
leaves, ~~making~~ [leaving] them delicate.
                                                  [squealing]
The raving rain hammered on the ~~squealing~~ guttering
                  [crafty]
The ~~roaring~~ fire whipped through the roaring wood,
gaining ~~to~~ power.

The hungry crops soaked up the running water left from
the ferocious flood.

The sly mist weaved in and out through the lively
houses, ~~kee~~ leaving them cold ~~and bo~~

The bitter frost freezed the ~~grumbling~~ ground, but
the savage sun freed the garden and field.

<u>Autumn.</u>
<u>Final draft.</u>

The wind ripped through the moaning trees,
tearing the chattering leaves as it went.

The now-silent leaves fell to the ground which
growled with side-splitting anger.

The sun smiled whilst shrivelling up the frightened
leaves, leaving them delicate.

The raving rain hammered on the squealing guttering

The crafty fire whipped through the roaring wood,
gaining power.

The hungry crops soaked up the running water left
from the ferocious flood.

The sly mist weaved in and out through the
lively houses, leaving them cold.

The bitter frost freezed the ground, but the
savage sun freed the garden and field.
<u>Very good personification. and quite a lot of effective alliteration</u>

b Onomatopoeia

Leading from lists of words, into sentences into two paragraphs (Year 6).

9-3-00

More imagery.

Splash, split, splodge, splat

Onomatopoeia

crash, crack, ~~crash~~ crank, croak, creak, crackle, crunch.
These 'cr' words are strong, powerful, sudden and jerky.

slither, slam, slop, slush, slosh, ~~slush~~, slap, slime, slip.
'SL' sounds words are usually softer, smoother, and said more slowly. ✓

clash, clap, clack, clatter, clop, click, clang, clink, clomp, clump, clip, clutch, cling, clamp.
'Cl' sound words are used to create a quick, sharp, loud and snappy sounds. ✓

Onomatop~~oric~~eia is used to show a word which sounds the same as its meaning. ✓

The man made a splash when he ~~jumped~~ splatted into the swimming pool, ~~then~~ split~~ting~~ his trousers.

The frog gave a loud croak when the creaking gate opened, before crashing into a crumbling gate wall

The snake slithered towards the vole, when he slapped him on the back, slipped ~~it~~ under ~~the~~ a rock and slamming it on the ground. ✓

The traffic warden clicked her fingers before clapping her hands, clamping a car and clipping a fining card onto the car window. ✓ ★

Very cleverly written

15-3-00   Onomatopoeiac paragraphs.

Mum
→ Marie clattered and clanged the saucepans, while her watch clinked against the metal. She clomped across the kitchen, before climbing up the stairs, and clapping her hands to wake up Jason.

I like the clink associated with metal.

?slumped → Lucy slammed the creaking door and slumped down in the chair. The fire crackled and spat. Her ginger cat creeped around the chair, slipped on the tiles and clutching the ~~too~~ ripped rug.

I like the alliteration

5 Revising

a Gather ideas for a first draft of an observation poem, focused on an autumn leaf (Year 4).

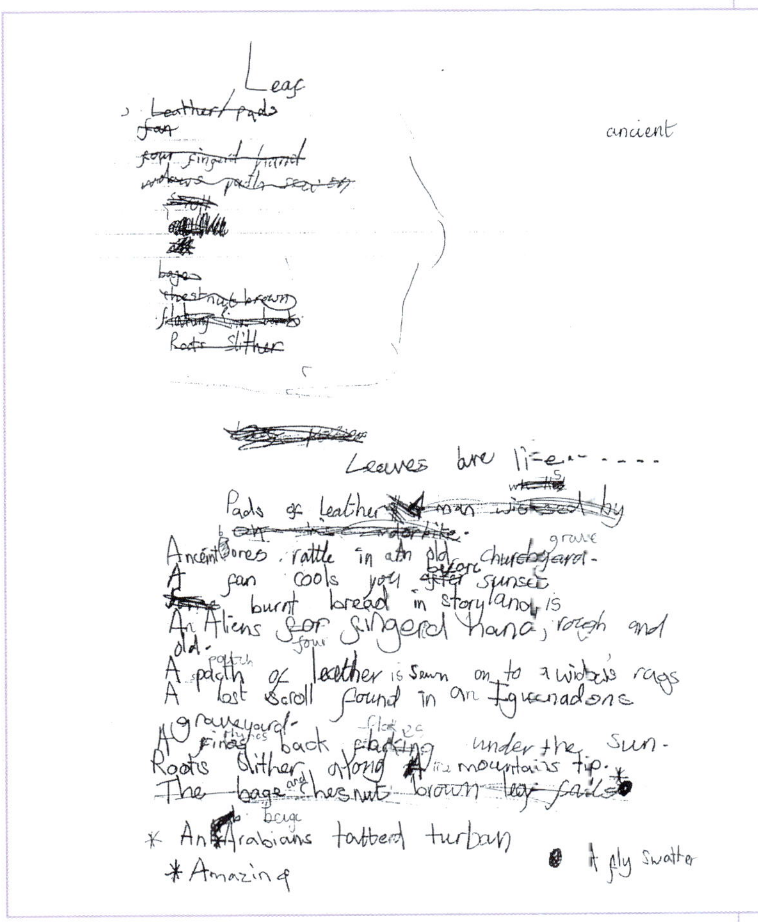

b First and final draft of a poem based on observing road repairs (Year 5).

Glossary

This glossary lists and explains terms used in the National Literacy Strategy *Framework for teaching* and associated training materials. It is intended for teachers. Examples have been given where possible. Historical or etymological information has been included where this may be useful.

This glossary is also located on The Standards Site: http://www.standards.dfee.gov.uk/literacy/glossary/

---

abbreviation

An abbreviation is a shortened version of a word or group of words. For example:

> *Co. (Company)*
> *approx. (approximately)*
> *PR (public relations)*
> *PTO (Please turn over)*

Some common abbreviations are of Latin terms:

> *etc (et cetera = and so on)*
> *eg (exempli gratia = for example)*
> *NB (nota bene = note especially)*
> *ie (id est = that is)*

Names of organisations are often abbreviated using the initial letters of each word. For example:

> *the EU (European Union)*
> *the NHS (National Health Service)*
> *IBM (International Business Machines)*

Some such abbreviations (for example, *NATO*, *FIFA* and *UNESCO*) are **acronyms**.

Some words are abbreviated so that only a part of the original word is used. Examples are:
> *phone (telephone)*
> *fridge (refrigerator)*
> *bus (omnibus)*
> *exam (examination).*

---

accent

features of pronunciation which vary according to the speaker's regional and social origin. All oral language, including standard English, is spoken with an accent. The term **accent** refers to pronunciation only.

see also **dialect**

---

acronym

An acronym is an **abbreviation** which is made up of the initial letters of a group of words, and is pronounced as a single word. For example:

laser (<u>l</u>ight <u>a</u>mplification by the <u>s</u>timulated <u>e</u>mission of <u>r</u>adiation)
Aids (<u>A</u>cquired <u>i</u>mmune <u>d</u>eficiency <u>s</u>yndrome
NATO (<u>N</u>orth <u>A</u>tlantic <u>T</u>reaty <u>O</u>rganization)
RAM (<u>R</u>andom <u>A</u>ccess <u>M</u>emory

Acronyms are to be contrasted with abbreviations in which the separate letters are pronounced:

USA (pronounced as U-S-A)
POW (P-O-W)
EMI (E-M-I)

acrostic

a poetic form which is organised by the initial letters of a key word, either at the beginning of lines, or with lines arranged around them:

Whistling wildly	Blo**w**ing
In a	ra**i**n
Northern	rou**n**d
Direction	an**d** round.

active and passive

Many verbs can be active or passive. For example, *bite*:

The dog bit Ben. (active)
Ben was bitten by the dog. (passive)

In the active sentence, the subject *(the dog)* performs the action. In the passive sentence, the subject *(Ben)* is on the receiving end of the action. The two sentences give similar information, but there is a difference in focus. The first is about what the dog did; the second is about what happened to Ben.

All passive forms are made up of the verb *be* + past **participle**:

active   *Somebody <u>saw</u> you.*
         We must <u>find</u> them.
         I <u>have repaired</u> it.
passive *You <u>were seen</u>.*
         They must <u>be found</u>.
         It <u>has been repaired</u>.

In a passive sentence, the 'doer' (or agent) may be identified using *by ...*:

Ben was bitten <u>by the dog</u>.

But very often, in passive sentences, the agent is unknown or insignificant, and therefore not identified:

The computer <u>has been repaired</u>.

Passive forms are common in impersonal, formal styles. For example:

It <u>was agreed</u> that ... (compare We agreed that ...).
Application forms <u>may be obtained</u> from the address below.

adjective

An adjective is a word that describes somebody or something. *Old*, *white*, *busy*, *careful* and *horrible* are all adjectives. Adjectives either come before a noun, or after verbs such as *be*, *get*, *seem*, *look* (linking verbs):

> a <u>busy</u> day   I'm <u>busy</u>
> <u>nice</u> shoes   those shoes look <u>nice</u>

Adjectives (and adverbs) can have comparative and superlative forms. The comparative form is adjective + *-er* (for one-syllable adjectives, and some two-syllable) or *more* + adjective (for adjectives of two or more syllables):

> old - old<u>er</u>
> hot - hot<u>ter</u>
> easy - easi<u>er</u>
> dangerous - *more* dangerous

The corresponding superlative forms are *-est* or *most* ...:

> small - small<u>est</u>
> big - big<u>gest</u>
> funny - funni<u>est</u>
> important - <u>most</u> important

adverb

Adverbs give extra meaning to a verb, an adjective, another adverb or a whole sentence:

> I <u>really enjoyed</u> the party. (adverb + verb)
> She's <u>really nice</u>. (adverb + adjective)
> He works <u>really slowly</u>. (adverb + adverb)
> <u>Really, he should do better</u>. (adverb + sentence)

Many adverbs are formed by adding *-ly* to an adjective, for example *quickly*, *dangerously*, *nicely*, but there are many adverbs which do <u>not</u> end in *-ly*. Note too that some *-ly* words are adjectives, not adverbs (eg *lovely*, *silly*, *friendly*).

In many cases, adverbs tell us:

> how (manner)   *slowly, happily, dangerously, carefully*
> where (place)   *here, there, away, home, outside*
> when (time)   *now, yesterday, later, soon*
> how often (frequency) *often, never, regularly*

Other adverbs show

> degree of intensity:
> <u>very</u> slow(ly) <u>fairly</u> dangerous(ly) <u>really</u> good/well

> the attitude of the speaker to what he or she is saying:
> *perhaps obviously fortunately*

> connections in meaning between sentences (see **connective**):
> *however furthermore finally*

An **adverbial phrase** is a group of words that functions in the same way as a single adverb. For example: *by car, to school, last week, three times a day, first of all, of course:*

> They left <u>*yesterday*</u>. (adverb)
> They left <u>*a few days ago*</u>.
> (adverbial phrase)

> She looked at me <u>*strangely*</u>. (adverb)
> She looked at me <u>*in a strange way*</u>.
> (adverbial phrase)

Similarly, an **adverbial clause** functions in the same way as an adverb. For example:

> *It was raining* <u>*yesterday*</u>. (adverb)
> *It was raining* <u>*when we went out*</u>. (adverbial clause).

affix

a **morpheme** which is not in itself a word, but is attached to a word. An affix can be a **prefix** (*<u>in</u>tolerant, <u>dis</u>like*) or a **suffix** (*kind<u>ness</u>, play<u>ing</u>*).

agreement (or concord)

In some cases the form of a verb changes according to its subject (so the verb and subject 'agree'). This happens with the verb *be:*

> *I am/he is/they are*
> *I was/you were*

and the third person singular (*he/she/it*) of the present tense:

> *I like/she likes*
> *I don't/he doesn't*

Note that singular collective **nouns** (eg *team, family, government*) can take a singular or plural verb form. For example:

> *The team (= it)* <u>*is*</u> *playing well.*
> *The team (= they)* <u>*are*</u> *playing well.*

There are a few cases where a **determiner** must agree with a noun according to whether it is singular or plural. For example:

> *this house*
> *much traffic*

> <u>*these*</u> *house<u>s</u>*
> <u>*many*</u> *car<u>s</u>*

alliteration

a phrase where adjacent or closely connected words begin with the same phoneme: *one wet wellington; free phone; several silent, slithering snakes.*

ambiguity

a phrase or statement which has more than one possible interpretation. This sometimes arises from unclear grammatical relationships. For example, in the phrase: *'police shot man with knife'*, it is not specified whether the man had the knife or the police used the knife to shoot the man. Both interpretations are possible, although only one is logical. In poetry, ambiguity may extend meanings beyond the literal.

The sentence: *'Walking dogs can be fun'* has two possible interpretations: *'it is fun to take dogs for walks'* or *'dogs which go walking are fun'*.

Ambiguity is often a source of humour. Ambiguity may be accidental or deliberate.

analogy

perception of similarity between two things; relating something known to something new; in spelling, using known spellings to spell unknown words: *night-knight-right-sight-light-fright;* in reading, using knowledge of words to attempt previously unseen words.

Emphasis on analogy encourages learners to generalise existing knowledge to new situations.

In their learning of grammar, pupils often apply **affixes** incorrectly by analogy: *goed, comed, mouses.* Analogy may also be used in literature to draw a parallel between two situations, for example using animal behaviour to draw attention to human behaviour.

anecdote

a brief written or spoken account of an amusing incident, often used to illustrate a point.

antonym

a word with a meaning opposite to another: *hot - cold, light - dark, light - heavy.* A word may have more than one word as an antonym: *cold - hot/warm; big - small/tiny/little/titchy.*

apostrophe (')

An apostrophe is a punctuation mark used to indicate either omitted letters or possession.

omitted letters

We use an apostrophe for the omitted letter(s) when a verb is contracted (= shortened). For example:

I'm (I am)	*who's (who is/has)*
they've (they have)	*he'd (he had/would)*
we're (we are)	*it's (it is/has)*
would've (would have	*she'll (she will)*

In contracted negative forms, *not* is contracted to *n't* and joined to the verb: *isn't, didn't, couldn't* etc.

In formal written style, it is more usual to use the full form.

There are a few other cases where an apostrophe is used to indicate letters that are in some sense 'omitted' in words other than verbs, eg *let's* (= *let us*), *o'clock* (= *of the clock*).

Note the difference between *its* (= 'belonging to it') and *it's* (= 'it is' or 'it has'):

> *The company is to close one of <u>its</u> factories.* (no apostrophe)
> *The factory employs 800 people. <u>It's</u> (= it is) the largest factory in the town.* (apostrophe necessary)

possession

We use an apostrophe + *s* for the possessive form:

> *my mother's* car
> *Joe and Fiona's* house
> *the cat's* tail
> *James's* ambition
> *a week's* holiday

With a plural 'possessor' already ending in *s* (eg *parents*), an apostrophe is added to the end of the word:

> *my parents'* car
> *the girls'* toilets

But irregular plurals (eg *men, children*) take an apostrophe + *s*:

> *children's* clothes

The regular plural form (-*s*) is often confused with possessive -*'s*:

> *I bought some apples.* (not *apple's*)

Note that the possessive words *yours*, *his*, *hers*, *ours*, *theirs*, and *its* are <u>not</u> written with an apostrophe.

---

appendix

a section added to a document which offers non-essential or illustrative information.

---

article

A, an and *the* are articles. *A* (*an* before a vowel sound) is the indefinite article; *the* is the definite article. Articles are a type of **determiner**.

---

ascender

In written or typed script, many letters have the same height: *a, c, e, m, n, o, r, s, u, v, w, x, z,* (although in some scripts, z has a **descender**). Some letters have parts which extend beyond this: *b, d, f, h, k, l, t*: These parts are called **ascenders**.

---

assonance

repetition of vowel sounds: *crying time; hop-scotch; great flakes; between trees; the kind knight rides by.*

---

asterisk (*)

An asterisk is a symbol used to refer the reader to footnotes below the text. It can also be used to replace letters in taboo words.

---

audience

the people addressed by a text. The term refers to listeners, readers of books, film/TV audiences and users of information technology.

autobiography

a life story of an individual written by that person. Generally written in the **first person**.

auxiliary verbs

These are verbs that are used together with other verbs. For example:

> we <u>are</u> going
> Lucy <u>has</u> arrived
> <u>can</u> you play

In these sentences, *going*, *arrived* and *play* are the main verbs. *Are*, *has* and *can* are auxiliary verbs, and add extra meaning to the main verb.

The most common auxiliary verbs are *be*, *have* and *do* (all of which can also be main verbs).

> *Be* is used in continuous forms (*be + -ing*) and in passive forms:
> We <u>are going</u> away. <u>Was</u> the car <u>damaged</u>?

> *Have* is used in perfect verb forms:
> Lucy <u>has arrived</u>. I <u>haven't finished</u>.

> *Do* is used to make questions and negatives in the simple present and past tenses:
> <u>Do</u> you <u>know</u> the answer? I <u>didn't see</u> anybody.

More than one auxiliary verb can be used together. For example:

> I <u>have been</u> waiting for ages. (*have* and *been* are auxiliary verbs)

The remaining auxiliary verbs are **modal verbs**, eg *can, will*.

ballad

a poem or song which tells a story. Characterised by short, regular verses with a rhyme scheme.

bibliography

a list of texts provided for readers. The list may contain:

a. texts consulted by a writer;
b. texts written on a particular subject;
c. texts written by a particular author.

biography

a life-story of an individual written by another author. Generally written in the **third person**.

blank verse

poetry written with rhythm and metre, but without rhyme. Especially linked with **iambic** pentameter (ten syllable line with unstressed/stressed syllable pattern) as in the work of Shakespeare.

blend

the process of combining phonemes into larger elements such as clusters, syllables and words. Also refers to a combination of two or more phonemes, particularly at the beginning and end of words, *st, str, nt, pl, nd.*

blurb

nformation about a book, designed to attract readers, usually printed on the back or inside flap of book jacket. Informs the prospective reader about genre, setting, etc

calligram

a poem in which the calligraphy, the formation of the letters or the font selected, represents an aspect of the poem's subject, as in: thin, ancient, gr*owth*. A poem about fear might be written in shaky letters to represent trembling.

character

an individual in a story, play or poem whose personality can be inferred from their actions and dialogue. Writers may also use physical description of the individual to give readers clues about a character.

chronological writing

writing organised in terms of sequences of events.

cinquain

a poem with a standard syllable pattern, like a haiku, invented by Adelaide Crapsey, an American poet. Five lines and a total of 22 syllables in the sequence: 2, 4, 6, 8, 2.

clause

A clause is a group of words that expresses an event (*she drank some water*) or a situation (*she was thirsty/she wanted a drink*). It usually contains a **subject** (*she* in the examples) and **verb** (*drank/was/wanted*)**.**

Note how a clause differs from a **phrase**:

a big dog	(a phrase - this refers to 'a big dog' but doesn't say what the dog did or what happened to it)
a big dog chased me	(a clause - the dog did something)

A sentence is made up of one or more clauses:

It was raining	(one clause)
<u>*It was raining*</u> and <u>*we were cold*</u>.	(two main clauses joined by *and*)
It was raining <u>*when we went out*</u>.	(main clause containing a subordinate clause - the subordinate clause is underlined)

A main clause is complete on its own and can form a complete sentence (eg *It was raining*.). A subordinate clause (*when we went out*) is part of the main clause and cannot exist on its own. In the following examples, the subordinate clauses are underlined:

You'll hurt yourself <u>if you're not careful</u>.
<u>*Although it was cold*</u>*, the weather was pleasant enough.*
Where are the biscuits <u>(that) I bought this morning</u>?
John, <u>who was very angry</u>, began shouting.
<u>*What you said*</u> *was not true.*

Although most clauses require a subject and verb, some subordinate clauses do not. In many such cases, the verb *be* can be understood. For example:

The weather, <u>although rather cold</u>, was pleasant enough.
   (= although it was rather cold)
<u>*When in Rome*</u>*, do as the Romans do.*
   (= when you are in Rome)
<u>*Glad to be home*</u>*, George sat down in his favourite armchair.*
   (= he was glad to be home)

see also **adverbial clause, noun clause, participle, phrase, relative clause, sentence**

---

clerihew

a four line comic verse with two rhyming couplets. Lines may be of any length. The first line is the name of the person about whom the rhyme is written:

Jeremiah Smith
Is boring to be with
The company he doth keep
Will send a person to sleep

Named after its inventor E. Clerihew Bentley who died in 1956.

---

cliché

an over-used phrase or opinion: *sick as a parrot; her eyes shone like stars; too many cooks spoil the broth.* May be **idiomatic**.

---

cloze

an exercise in which certain words are deleted from a text and a gap left. The learner's task is to supply the missing words. The teacher chooses which words to omit, depending on the learning task. Words can be deleted in a specific way, eg adjectives, conjunctions, or randomly (every nth word). Cloze procedure can be used to measure readability.

---

coherence and cohesion

An effective text needs to be coherent and cohesive.

The term **coherence** refers to the underlying logic and consistency of a text. The ideas expressed should be relevant to one another so that the reader can follow the meaning.

The term **cohesion** refers to the grammatical features in a text which enable the parts to fit together. One way of creating cohesion is the use of **connectives**:

I sat down and turned on the television. <u>Just then</u>, I heard a strange noise.

The phrase *'just then'* relates these events in time.

Cohesion is also achieved by the use of words (such as **pronouns**) that refer back to other parts of the text. In these examples, such words are underlined:

> There was a man waiting at the door. I had never seen <u>him</u> before.
> We haven't got a car. We used to have <u>one</u>, but we sold <u>it</u>.
> I wonder whether Sarah will pass her driving test. I hope <u>she does</u>. (= I hope Sarah passes her driving test)

colloquial

belonging to conversation/language used in familiar, informal contexts. Contrasted with formal or literary language.

colon (:)

A colon is a punctuation mark used to introduce a list or a following example (as in this glossary). It may also be used before a second clause that expands or illustrates the first:

> He was very cold: the temperature was below zero.

comma (,)

A comma is a punctuation mark used to help the reader by separating parts of a sentence. It sometimes corresponds to a pause in speech.

In particular we use commas:

> to separate items in a list (but not usually before *and*):
> My favourite sports are football, tennis, swimming and gymnastics.
> I got home, had a bath and went to bed.

> to mark off extra information:
> Jill, <u>my boss</u>, is 28 years old.

> after a subordinate **clause** which begins a sentence:
> <u>Although it was cold</u>, we didn't wear our coats.

> with many connecting **adverbs** (eg *however*, *on the other hand*, *anyway*, *for example*):
> <u>Anyway</u>, in the end I decided not to go.

commentary

a set of notes which explain, or give further detail or information on a text. For example, a commentary may explain imagery in a poem or section of prose; alternatively, it may draw viewers' attention to particular aspects of a piece of film. The purpose of a commentary is to deepen **comprehension**.

complement

In the sentences *Lisa is a fast runner* or *Lisa is very fit*, *'Lisa'* is the **subject** and *'is'* is the **verb**. Neither sentence has an **object**. The rest of the sentence (*a fast runner/very fit*) is called a complement. A complement usually tells you something about the subject of the sentence (especially after the verb *be* but also after other linking verbs such as *seem, look, get, become*). In the examples the complement is underlined:

These apples are <u>delicious</u>.   *Why did you become <u>a teacher</u>?*
You don't look <u>very well</u>.   *This is <u>John</u>. He's <u>a friend of mine</u>.*

A complement can also refer to the object of a sentence. For example:

I found the book <u>very interesting</u>. (*very interesting* refers to *the book*, which is the object of *found*)

compound word

a word made up of two other words: *football, headrest, broomstick*.

comprehension

the level of understanding of a text.

literal

the reader has access to the surface details of the text, and can recall details which have been directly related.

inferential

the reader can read meanings which are not directly explained. For example, the reader would be able to make inferences about the time of year from information given about temperature, weather, etc and from characters' behaviour and dialogue.

evaluative

the reader can offer an opinion on the effectiveness of the text for its purpose.

concrete poem

a poem in which the layout of the words represents an aspect of the subject. In some cases, these poems are presented as sculptures. Concrete poems blur the distinction between visual and linguistic art, as do other shape poems.

conditional

A conditional sentence is one in which one thing depends upon another. Conditional sentences often contain the **conjunction** *if*:

I'll help you if I can.
If the weather's bad, we might not go out.

Other conjunctions used in conditionals are *unless*, *providing*, *provided* and *as long as*.

A conditional sentence can refer to an imaginary situation. For example:

I would help you if I could. (but in fact I can't)
What would you do if you were in my position?
If the weather had been better, we could have gone to the beach.

The term 'conditional' is sometimes used to refer to the form *would* + verb: *would go*, *would help* etc.

see also **auxiliary verb**

conjunction

A word used to link **clauses** within a sentence. For example, in the following sentences, *but* and *if* are conjunctions:

It was raining <u>but</u> it wasn't cold.
We won't go out <u>if</u> the weather's bad.

There are two kinds of conjunction:

a. Co-ordinating conjunctions (*and*, *but*, *or* and *so*). These join (and are placed between) two clauses of equal weight.

Do you want to go now <u>or</u> shall we wait a bit longer?

And, *but* and *or* are also used to join words or phrases within a clause.

b. Subordinating conjunctions (eg *when*, *while*, *before*, *after*, *since*, *until*, *if*, *because*, *although*, *that*). These go at the beginning of a subordinate **clause**:

We were hungry <u>because</u> we hadn't eaten all day.
<u>Although</u> we'd had plenty to eat, we were still hungry.
We were hungry <u>when</u> we got home.

see also **clause, connective**

connective

A connective is a word or phrase that links clauses or sentences. Connectives can be **conjunctions** (eg *but*, *when*, *because*) or connecting adverbs (eg *however*, *then*, *therefore*).

Connecting adverbs (and adverbial phrases and clauses) maintain the **cohesion** of a text in several basic ways, including:

addition	*also, furthermore, moreover*
opposition	*however, nevertheless, on the other hand*
reinforcing	*besides, anyway, after all*
explaining	*for example, in other words, that is to say*
listing	*first(ly), first of all, finally*
indicating result	*therefore, consequently, as a result*
indicating time	*just then, meanwhile, later*

Commas are often used to mark off connecting adverbs or adverbial phrases or clauses:

First of all, I want to say …
I didn't think much of the film. Helen, on the other hand, enjoyed it.

Connecting adverbs and conjunctions function differently. Conjunctions (like *but* and *although*) join clauses <u>within a sentence</u>. Connecting adverbs (like *however*) connect ideas but the clauses remain <u>separate</u> sentences:

I was angry <u>but</u> I didn't say anything. (*but* is a conjunction - one sentence)
<u>Although</u> I was angry, I didn't say anything. (*although* is a conjunction - one sentence)
I was angry. <u>However,</u> I didn't say anything. (*however* is an adverb - two sentences)

consonant

A consonant is a speech sound which obstructs the flow of air through the vocal tract; for example, the flow of air is obstructed by the lips in *p* and by the tongue in *l*. The term also refers to those letters of the alphabet whose typical value is to represent such sounds, namely all except *a,e,i,o,u*. The letter *y* can represent a consonant sound (*yes*) or a vowel sound (*happy*).

contraction

see **apostrophe**

correspondence

matching of two separate types of information: for example, letters or letter strings with the phonemes they represent; matching one written with one spoken word.

couplet

two consecutive lines of poetry which are paired in length or rhyme.

cue

a source of information. In reading, children may use contextual, grammatical, graphic and phonological cues to work out unfamiliar words. Fluent readers orchestrate different cues and cross-check.

dash (—)

A dash is a punctuation mark used especially in informal writing (such as letters to friends, postcards or notes). Dashes may be used to replace other punctuation marks (**colons**, **semi-colons**, **commas**) or brackets:

It was a great day out — everybody enjoyed it.

declarative

see **sentence**.

decode

literally, this means to convert a message written/spoken in code into language which is easily understood. In reading, this refers to children's ability to read words - to translate the visual code of the letters into a word.

derivation

tracing the origin of a word or saying.

descender

In written or typed script, many letters have the same height: *a, c, e, m, n, o, r, s, u, v, w, x, z.* Some letters have parts which extend below this: *g, j, p, q, y.* These parts are called descenders. In some fonts, *f* and *z* have descenders.

determiner

Determiners include many of the most frequent English words, eg *the*, *a*, *my*, *this*. Determiners are used with nouns (*this book*, *my best friend*, *a new car*) and they limit (ie determine) the reference of the noun in some way.

Determiners include:

articles	*a/an*, *the*
demonstratives	*this/that*, *these/those*
possessives	*my/your/his/her/its/our/their*
quantifiers	*some*, *any*, *no*, *many*, *much*, *few*, *little*, *both*, *all*, *either*, *neither*, *each*, *every*, *enough*
numbers	*three*, *fifty*, *three thousand* etc
some question words	*which* (*which car?*), *what* (*what size?*), *whose* (*whose coat?*)

When these words are used as determiners, they are followed by a noun (though not necessarily immediately):

this book is yours
some new houses
which colour do you prefer?

Many determiners can also be used as **pronouns.** These include the demonstratives, question words, numbers and most of the quantifiers. When used as pronouns, these words are not followed by a noun - their reference *includes* the noun:

this is yours (= this book, this money, etc)
I've got some
which do you prefer?

dialect

A dialect is a variety of a language used in a particular area and which is distinguished by certain features of grammar or vocabulary. Examples of such features in some English dialects are:

non-standard subject + verb patterns, eg *I knows, you was, he like*
past tense forms, eg *I done, I seen*
various individual words and expressions, eg *owt/nowt* for *anything/nothing*

see also **double negative, standard English**

dialogue

a conversation between two parties. May be spoken or written.

digraph

two letters representing one phoneme: *bath*; *train*; *ch/ur/ch*.

diminutive

a term which implies smallness. This may reflect actual physical lack of stature; alternatively, it may be used as a term of endearment. The word may be a recognised word, eg Tiny Tim, Little Dorrit, or may be created by the addition of a suffix to a name or noun: *lambkin*, *starlet*, *kitchenette*.

direct speech and indirect speech

There are two ways of reporting what somebody says, direct speech and indirect speech.

In direct speech, we use the speaker's original words (as in a speech bubble). In text, speech marks ('…' or "…" — also called inverted commas or quotes) mark the beginning and end of direct speech:

Helen said, 'I'm going home'.
'What do you want?' I asked.

In indirect (or reported) speech, we report what was said but do not use the exact words of the original speaker. Typically we change pronouns and verb tenses, and speech marks are not used:

Helen said (that) she was going home.
I asked them what they wanted.

discrimination

Discrimination is the ability to perceive the difference between two things, for example **phonemes**. Some pairs of sounds are more difficult for children to discriminate between, for example *k/g, t/d,* and *p/b.*

discussion text

a text (written or spoken) which presents all sides of an issue. A discussion text typically begins by outlining the issues before making points for and against. These points are backed up with evidence. It often concludes by stating an opinion in favour of one particular side, or by asking the reader/listener to decide. An example of a discussion text would be presenting arguments for and against school uniform, or for and against a new runway at Manchester Airport.

double negative

In non-standard English, a double negative may be used. For example:

We did<u>n't</u> see <u>nobody</u>.
I <u>never</u> took <u>nothing</u>.

Such double negatives are not acceptable in **standard English.** The equivalent standard forms would be:

We didn't see <u>anybody</u>.
I didn't take <u>anything</u>.

draft

preliminary written form of document; a **text** may develop through a number of drafts before reaching final draft stage, at which time it may be published. The process of working on a document at the composition stage is called drafting.

edit

to modify written work, either own or another's, in preparation for publication. This process takes place after **drafting** (composition), **revising** (major restructuring) and before **proof-reading** (a final check for typographical, spelling errors, etc). It involves checking of facts, minor improvements to style at sentence level, and checking for **accuracy** and **agreement**.

elegy

a **poem** or song which is a lament, perhaps for someone or something which has died.

ellipsis

Ellipsis is the omission of words in order to avoid repetition. For example:

I don't think it will rain but it might. (= it might rain)
'Where were you born?' 'Bradford.' (= I was born in Bradford)

An ellipsis is also the term used for three dots *(…)* which show that something has been omitted or is incomplete.

empathy

identifying with another: a character in a story, or an historical figure; the ability to see situations from the other's point of view. Literally 'feeling with' or 'feeling in'.

epic

a poem or story relating the adventures of a heroic or legendary figure, often related to national identity, as Odysseus or Arthur.

epitaph

engraved wording on a tombstone. May be selected by the deceased or his/her family. Some will choose extracts from the Bible or from literature; others will compose their own epitaph.

etymology

the study of the origin and history of words.

eulogy

writing or speech, the purpose of which is praise of a named person or thing. In America, this refers specifically to funeral oration.

exclamation

An exclamation is an utterance expressing emotion (joy, wonder, anger, surprise, etc) and is usually followed in writing by an **exclamation mark (!)**. Exclamations can be **interjections**:

Oh dear!
Good grief!
Ow!

Some exclamations begin with *what* or *how*:

What a beautiful day!
How stupid (he is)!
What a quiet little girl.

Exclamations like these are a special type of **sentence** ('exclamative') and may have no verb.

see also **interjection, sentence**

exclamation mark (!)

An exclamation mark is used at the end of a **sentence** (which may be exclamative, imperative or declarative) or an **interjection** to indicate strong emotion:

> *What a pity!*
> *Get out!*
> *It's a goal!*
> *Oh dear!*

See also **exclamation, sentence**

exclamative

see **sentence**

explanation text

Explanation text is written to explain how or why something happens, eg how river valleys are formed or why the Romans built roads. Typically such text consists of a description of the phenomenon and an explanatory sequence. The writer will normally need to use **connectives** expressing cause and effect (eg *so, therefore, as a result*) and time (eg *later, meanwhile*).

The **passive** often occurs in writing of this kind. For example:

> *Roman roads <u>are considered</u> to be a miracle of engineering.*

fable

a short story which is devised and written to convey a useful moral lesson. Animals are often used as characters, as in Aesop's Fables.

See **parable**

fact

accepted, observable or demonstrable truth. What is accepted as truth may change over time, in the light of new evidence. Facts must be supported by evidence; if evidence is not available, they can only be given the status of opinion.

Fiction texts often make use of factual information, as in the case of historical fiction, or fiction which includes information about science or art, etc. In these texts, it is important that writers research the appropriate subject.

fairy tale

a story written for, or told to, children which includes elements of magic and magical folk, such as fairies, elves, goblins.

fiction

text which is invented by a writer or speaker. Characters, settings and events are created by the originator. In some cases, one of these elements may be factual: for example, the setting may be a named city or area; the text may be based on an historical event.

figurative language

use of metaphor or simile to create a particular impression or mood. A writer may develop an idea of a character's military approach to life by using phrases and words which are linked with the army, such as *he was something of a loose cannon* (**metaphor**); *he rifled through the papers; his arm shot out; he marched into the room; he paraded his knowledge.* To link a character with a bird, she/he may use: *he flew down the stairs; they twittered to each other; he perched on his chair; his feathers were definitely ruffled.*

flow chart

a diagrammatic representation of either:

    a. events in a story;
    b. a process; or
    c. an activity.

A flow chart illustrates sequences of events and explores possible consequences of decisions.

footnote

additional information which is printed at the bottom of the page rather than in the main body of the text.

format

the way in which a text is arranged or presented, for example as a book, leaflet, essay, video, audiotape. May also relate to the structure of the text, for example, the use of headings and sub-headings, diagrams/photographs with captions.

free verse

poetry which is not constrained by patterns of rhyme or rhythm.

generic structure

the way in which elements of a text are arranged to match its purpose. This structure can be observed by readers, and writers will use this knowledge to structure their writing, depending on their purpose.

See **discussion text, explanation text, instruction text, narrative text, recount text, report text**

genre

this term refers to different types of writing, each with its own specific characteristics which relate to origin (legend/folk tale) or reader interest area - the types of books individuals particularly choose to read: adventure, romance, science fiction.

Texts with these specific features - often related to story elements, patterns of language, structure, vocabulary - may be described as belonging to a particular genre. These attributes are useful in discussing text and in supporting development of writing skills.

Texts may operate at different levels, and so represent more than one genre; some will be combinations, for example historical romance.

glossary

part of a text, often an **appendix**, which defines terms the writer/editor considers may be unfamiliar to the intended audience.

grammar

the conventions which govern the relationships between words in any language. Includes the study of word order and changes in words: use of inflections, etc. Study of grammar is important, as it enhances both reading and writing skills; it supports effective communication.

grammatical boundary

A grammatical boundary is the edge of a grammatical unit (a sentence, clause or phrase) which, in writing, may be indicated by a punctuation mark such as a **comma**, full stop, **colon**, **semi-colon** or **dash**.

grapheme

written representation of a sound; may consist of one or more letters; for example the phoneme *s* can be represented by the graphemes *s, se, c, sc* and *ce* as in *sun, mouse, city, science*.

guided reading

a classroom activity in which pupils are taught in groups according to reading ability. The teacher works with each group on a text carefully selected to offer an appropriate level of challenge to the group. Usefully thought of as a 'mini lesson'. Challenge may be in terms of reading cues and strategies, language and vocabulary, or sophisticated aspects of grammar, inference, skimming and scanning.

Guided reading sessions have a similar format:

a. the teacher introduces the text, and sets the purpose for reading, for example reminding pupils of strategies and cues which will be useful, or asking them to gather particular information;
b. pupils read independently, solving problems as they read through the text. More fluent readers will read silently. The teacher is available to offer help when it is needed. S/he then guides pupils to appropriate cues, for example use of syntax, picture cues, initial letter;
c. the teacher discusses the text with the pupils, drawing attention to successful strategies and focusing on comprehension, referring back to the initial focus.

guided writing

a classroom activity in which pupils are grouped by writing ability. The teacher works with each group on a task carefully selected to offer an appropriate level of challenge to the group. Usefully thought of as a 'mini lesson'. Challenge may be in terms of spelling, letter formation, simple punctuation, language and vocabulary, or sophisticated aspects of generic structure, planning and editing, use of imagery and so on.

haiku

Japanese form. The poem has three lines and 17 syllables in total in the pattern 5, 7, 5:

Loving, faithful, fun
Trusting and loyal and true
Chocolate-brown Suki

half-rhyme

words which almost rhyme: *polish/relish; pun/man.*

homograph

words which have the same spelling as another, but different meaning: *the <u>calf</u> was eating/my <u>calf</u> was aching; the North <u>Pole</u>/totem <u>pole</u>; he is a <u>Pole</u>.* Pronunciation may be different: *a <u>lead</u> pencil/the dog's <u>lead</u>; furniture <u>polish</u>/<u>Polish</u> people.* A **homonym**.

homonym

words which have the same spelling or pronunciation as another, but different meaning or origin. May be a **homograph** or **homophone**.

homophone

words which have the same sound as another but different meaning or different spelling: *read/reed; pair/pear; right/write/rite.* A **homonym**.

hyphen (-)

A hyphen is sometimes used to join the two parts of a **compound** noun, as in *golf-ball* and *proof-read*. But it is much more usual for such compounds to be written as single words (eg *football, headache, bedroom*) or as separate words without a hyphen (*golf ball, stomach ache, dining room, city centre*).

However, hyphens are used in the following cases:

a. in compound adjectives and longer phrases used as modifiers before nouns:

a <u>foul-smelling</u> substance
a <u>well-known</u> painter
a <u>German-English</u> dictionary
a <u>one-in-a-million</u> chance
a <u>state-of-the-art</u> computer
a <u>ten-year-old</u> girl

b. in many compound nouns where the second part is a short word like *in, off, up* or *by*:

a break-in
a write-off
a mix-up
a passer-by

c.   in many words beginning with the prefixes *co-*, *non-* and *ex-*:

> *co-operate*
>
> *non-existent*
>
> *ex-husband*

Hyphens are also used to divide words at the end of a line of print.

idiom

An idiom is an expression which is not meant literally and whose meaning cannot be deduced from knowledge of the individual words. For example:

> *You look a bit <u>under the weather</u> this morning. Are you all right?*
>
> *Try and keep to the point of the discussion. You're always introducing <u>red herrings</u>.*
>
> *You and I have the same problems - we're <u>in the same boat</u>.*
>
> *That name <u>rings a bell</u>. I've heard it before somewhere.*

imagery

use of language to create a vivid sensory image - often visual. May include:

vocabulary	choice of synonym, for example *sprinted/ran/raced,* selection of adjectives and adverbs
simile	*he ran like the wind*
metaphor	*his feet had wings*

see **figurative language**

imperative

see **sentence**

indirect speech

see **direct speech**

infinitive

The infinitive is the base form of the verb without any additional endings. For example, *play* is an infinitive form (as opposed to *playing*, *played* or *plays*). The infinitive is used with many **auxiliary verbs**:

> *I will play*
>
> *he should play*
>
> *do you play?*

The infinitive is often used with *to* (*to play*, *to eat* etc):

> *I ought to play*
>
> *I want to play*
>
> *I'm going to play*
>
> *it would be nice to play*

The simple present tense (*I play, they play* etc) has the same form as the infinitive, except for the third **person** singular (*he/she/it plays*).

inflection

Inflection is a change to the ending of a word to indicate tense, number or other grammatical features. For example:

walk - walks/walked/walking
shoe - shoes
old - older/oldest

see also **suffix**

information text

text written to inform. Examples include **explanation**, **report**, **procedure** or **recount**.

innovation on text

a classroom strategy in which the teacher uses a familiar text as the model for a piece of new writing: *Georgina and the Dragon; The Very Hungry Kittens; Burglar Barry.*

instruction text

text written to help readers achieve certain goals. The text may consist of a statement of the intended outcome, the materials needed to achieve it and a sequence of actions in chronological order. Connectives will often be time-related; verbs may be imperative, and will often be placed at the beginning of sentences to form a series of commands. Examples of this type of text include recipes and instructions.

interjection

An interjection is a word like *Ouch!*, *Oh!* or *Damn!* expressing an emotion such as pain, surprise, anger, etc. An interjection is followed by an **exclamation mark (!)**.

see also **exclamation**

internal rhyme

placement of rhyming words within a line of poetry: *'Though the threat of snow was growing slowly...'*

see also **assonance** and **rhyme**

intonation

Intonation is the way in which changes in the musical pitch of the voice are used to structure speech and to contribute to meaning. Among other functions, intonation may distinguish questions from statements (as in 'Sure?' 'Sure!'), or indicate contrastive and emotive stress (as in 'I said *two*, not three', or 'I just *hate* that advertisement!').

jargon

language used by a particular profession or interest group. May include vocabulary unfamiliar to those outside the group, sometimes deliberately.

jingle

a short verse or line used to attract attention and be memorable. May be based on **alliteration** or **rhyme**. Often associated with advertising.

kenning

a compound expression used in Old English and Norse poetry, which named something without using its name, for example *mouse catcher = cat.* Anglo-Saxons often used kennings to name their swords: *death bringer.* A poem made of kennings would be a list of such expressions about one subject:

> *MY DOG*
> *ankle biter*
> *bone cruncher*
> *night howler*
> *rabbit catcher*
> *fur pillow.*

legend

a traditional story about heroic characters such as King Arthur, which may be based on truth, but which has been embellished over the years. Also refers to the wording on maps and charts which explains the symbols used.

letter string

a group of letters which together represent a **phoneme** or **morpheme**.

limerick

A five-line comic verse following the syllable pattern *8 8 6 6 8* with the rhyme scheme *a a b b a.* Early limericks, such as the nonsense verse of Edward Lear, repeat line 1 in line 5. However, recent verse does not always follow this model.

literacy

communication skill. The term *literacy* originally, and most often, applied to written communication; however, it can also be applied to other forms, as in *media literacy, computer literacy.*

logogram

a symbol or character which represents a **morpheme** or word. A logographic system contrasts with an alphabetic-phonetic system, such as English, in which symbols relate to sounds rather than meaning. There are a number of logograms which would be instantly recognisable to those using alphabetic systems, for example £, &, %.

metalanguage

the language we use when talking about language itself. It includes words like *sentence, noun, paragraph, preposition.* Those who understand these concepts are able to talk about language quite precisely; thus, acquisition of metalanguage is seen as a crucial step in developing awareness of and proficiency in communication, particularly written language.

metaphor

where the writer writes about something as if it were really something else. Fowler describes it as an 'imaginative substitution'. For example: *he is an ass; love's meteor. A poisoned apple passed along from generation to generation (McGough).*

mnemonic

a device to aid memory, for instance to learn particular spelling patterns or spellings: *I Go Home Tonight. There is a <u>rat</u> in sepa<u>rat</u>e.*

modal verb

The modal verbs are:

> *can/could*
> *will/would*
> *shall/should*
> *may/might*
> *must/ought*

These **auxiliary verbs** are used to express such ideas as possibility, willingness, prediction, speculation, deduction and necessity. They are all followed by the **infinitive**, and *ought* is followed by *to* + infinitive:

> *I <u>can help</u> you.*
> *We <u>might go</u> out tonight.*
> *You <u>ought to eat</u> something.*
> *Stephanie <u>will be</u> here soon.*
> *I <u>wouldn't do</u> that if I were you.*
> *I <u>must go</u> now.*

These verbs can occur with other auxiliary verbs (*be* and *have*):

> *I'<u>ll be</u> leaving at 11.30.*
> *You <u>should have</u> asked me.*
> *They <u>must have been</u> working.*

In this context *have* is unstressed and therefore identical in speech to unstressed *of*; this is why the misspelling *of* for standard *have* or *'ve* is not uncommon.

modelling

In literacy, this refers to demonstration of an aspect of reading or writing by an expert for learners. This would support direct instruction.

monologue

a text spoken by a lone speaker. In dramatic situations, this may be a 'one person show'; in other situations, it may refer to a speaker who monopolises the conversation.

morpheme

the smallest unit of meaning. A word may consist of one morpheme *(house)*, two morphemes *(house/s; hous/ing)* or three or more morphemes *(house/keep/ing; un/happi/ness)*. **Suffixes** and **prefixes** are morphemes.

myth

an ancient traditional story of gods or heroes which addresses a problem or concern of human existence. May include an explanation of some fact or phenomenon.

narrative poem

a poem which tells a story: *'Hiawatha', 'Charge of the Light Brigade'*. Often a ballad.

narrative text

text which re-tells events, often in chronological sequence. May be purely fictional, or include some information. May be in prose or poetic form.

non-chronological writing

writing organised without reference to time sequence. Typically, writing organised by characteristics and attributes, for example, a report on a town might be organised into population, situation, facilities.

noun

A noun is a word that denotes somebody or something. In the sentence *My younger sister won some money in a competition*, *'sister'*, *'money'* and *'competition'* are nouns.

Many nouns (countable nouns) can be **singular** (only one) or **plural** (more than one). For example *sister/sisters, problem/problems, party/parties*. Other nouns (mass nouns) do not normally occur in the plural. For example: *butter, cotton, electricity, money, happiness*.

A **collective noun** is a word that refers to a group. For example, *crowd, flock, team*. Although these are singular in form, we often think of them as plural in meaning and use them with a plural verb. For example, if we say *The team have* won all *their* games so far, we think of *'the team'* as *'they'* (rather than *'it'*).

Proper nouns are the names of people, places, organisations, etc. These normally begin with a capital letter: *Amanda, Birmingham, Microsoft, Islam, November*.

Noun phrase is a wider term than 'noun'. It can refer to a single noun *(money)*, a pronoun *(it)* or a group of words that functions in the same way as a noun in a sentence, for example:

> *a lot of money*
> *my younger sister*
> *a new car*
> *the best team in the world*

Similarly, a **noun clause** functions in the same way as a noun. For example:

> *The story was not true.* (noun)
> *What you said was not true.* (noun clause)

obituary

public notice of the death of an individual. May include an account of the life of the person.

object

see **subject**

ode

lyric poem usually addressed to the subject, so written in the **second person**. There is no fixed rhyme or rhythm pattern. Language may be unusual, perhaps self-consciously 'poetic': *Thou still unravish'd bride of quietness...* (Keats, 'On a Grecian Urn').

onomatopoeia

words which echo sounds associated with their meaning: *clang, hiss, crash, cuckoo.*

onset

the onset of a word or syllable is the initial consonant or consonant cluster: *<u>cl</u>ang; <u>tr</u>ike; <u>s</u>un.* Some words or syllables have no onset: *or; out; end; at; on; earth.*

see **rime**

opinion

a belief held by an individual or group of individuals for which there is insufficient evidence for it to be accepted as **fact**. May be presented as fact in writing.

palindrome

a word or phrase which is the same when read left-right or right-left: *madam; mum; dad; eve; pup; Madam, .'m Adam.*

parable

a short story told to illustrate a moral lesson or duty. Parables are often associated with the New Testament; however, many stories, including modern texts, may be classed as parables.

see **fable**

paragraph

a section of a piece of writing. A new paragraph marks a change of focus, a change of time, a change of place or a change of speaker in a passage of dialogue.

A new paragraph begins on a new line, usually with a one-line gap separating it from the previous paragraph. Some writers also indent the first line of a new paragraph.

Paragraphing helps writers to organise their thoughts, and helps readers to follow the story line, argument or dialogue

parenthesis

A parenthesis is a word or phrase inserted into a sentence to explain or elaborate. It may be placed in brackets or between **dashes** or **commas**:

Sam and Emma (his oldest children) are coming to visit him next weekend.
Margaret is generally happy — she sings in the mornings! — but responsibility weighs her down.
Sarah is, I believe, our best student.

The term parentheses can also refer to the brackets themselves.

parody

a literary caricature: a version of a story or poem which emphasises particular aspects of language or form to humorous effect.

part of speech

see **word class**

participle

Verbs have a present participle and a past participle.

present participle

The present participle ends in *-ing* (*working, reading, going* etc). Although it is called 'present', it is used in all continuous forms: *she <u>is</u> going, she <u>was</u> going, she <u>will be</u> going, she <u>would have been</u> going,* etc.

The *-ing* ending is also used for a verb functioning as a noun. For example: *I enjoy <u>reading</u>, <u>Reading</u> is important.* ('*Reading*' is used as a noun in these examples.) This *-ing* form is sometimes called a verbal noun or a gerund.

past participle

The past participle often ends in *-ed* (*worked, played*) but many common verbs are irregular and have other endings, eg *-t* (*kept*), *-n* (*flown*), and *-en* (*stolen*).

Past participles are used:

a. after *have* to make perfect forms: *I'<u>ve worked</u>, he <u>has fallen</u>, we should <u>have gone</u>*
b. after *be* (*is/was* etc) to make passive forms: *I <u>was asked</u>, they <u>are kept</u>, it has <u>been stolen</u>*

Here too, the name is misleading, because passive forms need not refer to the past: *A toast will be drunk.*

Participles (present and past) are sometimes used as adjectives: *the falling leaves, stolen goods.* They can also be used to introduce subordinate clauses, for example:

<u>*Being a student*</u>*, Tom doesn't have much money.*
<u>*Written in 1923*</u>*, the book has been translated into twenty-five languages.*

see also **active** and **passive**, **tense** and **verb**

passive

see **active**

person

In grammar, a distinction is made between first, second and third person.

One uses the first person when referring to oneself (*I/we*); the second person when referring to one's listener or reader (*you*); and the third person when referring to somebody or something else (*he/she/it/they/my friend/the books* etc).

In some cases the form of the verb changes according to person:

I/we/you/they <u>know</u>
I/we/you/they <u>have</u>
we/you/they <u>were</u>
he/she <u>knows</u>
he/she/it <u>has</u>
I/he/she/it <u>was</u>

see also **agreement**

personification

a form of **metaphor** in which language relating to human action, motivation and emotion is used to refer to non-human agents or objects or abstract concepts: *the weather is smiling on us today; Love is blind.*

persuasive text

text which aims to persuade the reader. A persuasive text typically consists of a statement of the viewpoint, arguments and evidence for this thesis, possibly some arguments and evidence supporting a different view, and a final summary or recommendation.

Connectives will be related to reasoning *(therefore, however)*.

An example of such a text would be an essay on banning fox-hunting or recycling, or whether Roald Dahl was the greatest writer in English. Advertisements are forms of persuasive text.

see also **discussion text**

phoneme

A phoneme is the smallest contrastive unit of sound in a word. There are approximately 44 phonemes in English (the number varies depending on the accent). A phoneme may have variant pronunciations in different positions; for example, the first and last sounds in the word 'little' are variants of the phoneme /l/. A phoneme may be represented by one, two, three or four letters. The following words end in the same phoneme (with the corresponding letters underlined):

t<u>o</u>
sh<u>oe</u>
thr<u>ough</u>

phonological awareness

awareness of sounds within words - demonstrated for example in the ability to generate rhyme and alliteration, and in segmenting and blending component sounds.

phrase

A phrase is a group of words that act as one unit. So *dog* is a word, but *the dog*, *a big dog* or *that dog over there* are all phrases. Strictly speaking, a phrase can also consist of just one word. For example, in the sentence *Dogs are nice*, *'dogs'* and *'nice'* are both one-word phrases.

A phrase can function as a noun, an adjective or an adverb:

a noun phrase	*a big dog, my last holiday*
an adjectival phrase	*(she's not) as old as you, (I'm) really hungry*
an adverbial phrase	*(they left) five minutes ago, (she walks) very slowly*

If a phrase begins with a **preposition** (like <u>*in* a hurry</u>, <u>*along* the lane</u>), it can be called a prepositional phrase. A prepositional phrase can be adjectival or adverbial in meaning:

adjectival	*(I'm) in a hurry, (the man) with long hair*
adverbial	*(they left) on Tuesday, (she lives) along the lane*

plural

see **singular**

poem

a text which uses features such as **rhythm, rhyme** or **syntax** and **vocabulary** to convey ideas in an intense way. Poets may also use **alliteration, figurative language** and other techniques. Prose may sometimes be poetic in effect.

portmanteau

a word made up from blending two others: *swurse = swear + curse; picture + dictionary = pictionary; smoke + fog = smog; breakfast + lunch = brunch.*

predicate

The predicate is that part of a sentence which is not the subject but which gives information about the subject. So, in the sentence *Clare went to school*, *'Clare'* is the subject and *'went to school'* is the predicate.

prefix

A prefix is a **morpheme** which can be added to the beginning of a word to change its meaning. For example:

<u>in</u>edible
<u>dis</u>appear
<u>super</u>market
<u>un</u>intentional

preposition

A preposition is a word like *at*, *over*, *by* and *with*. It is usually followed by a **noun phrase**. In the examples, the preposition and the following noun phrase are underlined:

> *We got home <u>at midnight</u>.*
> *Did you come here <u>by car</u>?*
> *Are you coming <u>with me</u>?*
> *They jumped <u>over a fence</u>.*
> *What's the name <u>of this street</u>?*
> *I fell asleep <u>during the film</u>.*

Prepositions often indicate time (<u>*at* midnight</u>/<u>*during* the film</u>/<u>*on* Friday</u>), position (<u>*at* the station</u>/<u>*in* a field</u>) or direction (<u>*to* the station</u>/<u>*over* a fence</u>). There are many other meanings, including possession (<u>*of* this street</u>), means (<u>*by* car</u>) and accompaniment (<u>*with* me</u>).

In questions and a few other structures, prepositions often occur at the end of the clause:

> *Who did you go out <u>with</u>?*
> *We haven't got enough money to live <u>on</u>.*
> *I found the book I was looking <u>for</u>.*

In formal style, the preposition can go before *whom* or *which* (*with whom*, *about which* etc):

> *<u>With whom</u> do you wish to speak?*

Many prepositions (eg *on*, *over*, *up*) can also be used as **adverbs** (without a following noun or pronoun):

> *We got on the bus.* (preposition - followed by a noun phrase)
> *The bus stopped and we got <u>on</u>.* (adverb - no following noun or pronoun)

procedural text

see **instruction text**

pronoun

There are several kinds of pronoun, including:

personal pronouns

> *I/me, you, he/him, she/her, we/us, they/them, it*
> *I like <u>him</u>. <u>They</u> don't want <u>it</u>.*

possessive pronouns

> *mine, yours, his, hers, ours, theirs, its*
> *Is this book <u>yours</u> or <u>mine</u>?*

reflexive pronouns

> *myself, herself, themselves etc*

I hurt <u>myself</u>. Enjoy <u>yourselves</u>!

indefinite pronouns

> *someone, anything, nobody, everything* etc
> *<u>Someone</u> wants to see you about <u>something</u>.*

interrogative pronouns

> *who/whom, whose, which, what*
> *<u>Who</u> did that? <u>What</u> happened?*

relative pronouns

> *who/whom, whose, which, that*
> *The person <u>who</u> did that … The thing <u>that</u> annoyed me was …*

Many **determiners** can also be used as pronouns, including *this/that/these/those* and the quantifiers (*some, much* etc). For example:
> *<u>These</u> are mine.*
> *Would you like <u>some</u>?*

Pronouns often 'replace' a noun or noun phrase and enable us to avoid repetition:

> *I saw your father but I didn't speak to <u>him</u>.* (= your father)
> *'We're going away for the weekend.' 'Oh, are you? <u>That</u>'s nice.'* (= the fact you're going away)

---

proof-read

to check a piece of work thoroughly before final publication.

---

prose

written language which does not follow poetic or dramatic forms.

---

proverb

a saying, which may have changed little over time, which states a belief about the world: *the early bird catches the worm; too many cooks spoil the broth; the grass is always greener on the other side.*

---

pun

a play on words; use of words with similar sounds but different meaning to humorous effect. For example, *grave* has two possible meanings, which Shakespeare used in 'Romeo and Juliet'. Mercutio's final words were: *'ask for me tomorrow And you shall find me a grave man'; red* and *read* sound the same, *so the book is never red/the book is never read; I'm on a seafood diet: I see food and I eat it.* Puns are often used in newspaper headlines.

---

punctuation

Punctuation is a way of marking text to help readers' understanding. The most commonly used marks in English are: **apostrophe, colon, comma, dash, ellipsis, exclamation mark**, full stop, **hyphen, semi-colon** and **speech marks** (inverted commas).

question mark (?)

A question mark is used at the end of an interrogative **sentence** (eg *Who was that?*) or one whose function is a question (eg *You're leaving already?*)

rap

a form of oral poetry which has a very strong rhythm and rapid pace. Associated with Caribbean and Afro-Caribbean cultures, has now been assimilated into other literary traditions. Rap is often used in modern music.

recount text

a text written to retell for information or entertainment. A fictional narrative recount may consist of scene-setting, a starting point, a problem, account and a conclusion. The language is descriptive, and there may be dialogue. Characters are defined and often named.

A non-fiction recount may begin with a scene-setting introduction, and then retell events in chronological order. An example of this type of text would include writing about visits, newspaper accounts of an event or a biography.

reference text

an information text organised in a clearly defined way, for example alphabetically, and used for study purposes.

relative clause

A relative clause is one that defines or gives information about somebody or something. Relative clauses typically begin with relative pronouns *(who/whom/whose/which/that):*

> *Do you know the people <u>who live in the house on the corner</u>?* (defines *'the people'*)
> *The biscuits <u>(that) Tom bought this morning</u> have all gone.* (defines *'the biscuits'*)
> *Our hotel, <u>which was only two minutes from the beach</u>, was very nice.* (gives more information about the hotel)

renga

a series of **haiku**, each linked to the next by two seven-syllable lines, sometimes written by different poets in turn, and forming a series of complete poems.

report text

a non-chronological text written to describe or classify. The text often begins with a general classification, moving to a description of particular characteristics with a final summary. It is often written in the continuous present tense with generalised participants *(people, cats, buildings).* An example of this sort of text would include a report on dinosaurs or Roman housing, a guide-book or a description of a scene.

rhetorical expression

an utterance in which the meaning intended by the speaker/writer is an expression different from that which might be inferred by a listener who is unaware of the conventions of the language; for example *Do you know his name?* is a question which seems to require a yes/no response: in fact, the speaker is asking *What is his name?* Rhetorical expressions are often questions disguising imperatives: *Would you like to get out your English books?* usually means *Get out your English books.*

rhyme

A rhyme occurs when words share the same stressed vowel phoneme, eg *she/tea, way/delay* and subsequent consonant(s) eg *sheet/treat, made/lemonade* and final unstressed vowel eg *laughter/after*.

rhythm

Rhythm is the more or less regular alternation of light beats and heavy beats (stresses) in speech or music. Some poetry uses very regular rhythm patterns.

riddle

a question or statement, sometimes in rhyme, which forms a puzzle to be solved by the reader/listener.

rime

that part of a syllable which contains the vowel and final consonant or consonant cluster if there is one: *at* in c*at*; *orn* in h*orn*; *ow* in c*ow*. Some words consist of rime only: *or, ate, eel*.

see **onset**

root word

a word to which **prefixes** and **suffixes** may be added to make other words; for example in *unclear, clearly, cleared*, the root word is *clear*.

scan

this word has two relevant meanings:

    a. to look over a text very quickly, trying to locate information by locating a key word;
    b. a line of poetry which conforms to the rhythm (metre) of the rest of the poem is said to scan.

segment

to break a word or part of a word down into its component phonemes, for example: *c-a-t; ch-a-t; ch-ar-t; g-r-ou-n-d; s-k-i-n*.

semi-colon (;)

A semi-colon can be used to separate two main **clauses** in a sentence:

    I liked the book; it was a pleasure to read.

This could also be written as two separate sentences:

    I liked the book. It was a pleasure to read.

However, where the two clauses are closely related in meaning (as in the above example), a writer may prefer to use a semi-colon rather than two separate sentences.

Semi-colons can also be used to separate items in a list if these items consist of longer phrases. For example:

I need large, juicy tomatoes; half a pound of unsalted butter; a kilo of fresh pasta, preferably tagliatelle; and a jar of black olives.

In a simple list, **commas** are used.

sentence

A sentence can be simple, compound or complex.

A simple sentence consists of one **clause**:

It was late.

A compound sentence has two or more clauses joined by *and*, *or*, *but* or *so*. The clauses are of equal weight (they are both main clauses):

<u>It was late</u> but <u>I wasn't tired</u>.

A complex sentence consists of a main clause which itself includes one or more subordinate clauses:
<u>Although it was late</u>, I wasn't tired. (subordinate clause beginning with *although* underlined)

Simple sentences can also be grouped as follows according to their structure:

declarative (for statements, suggestions, etc):

The class yelled in triumph. Maybe we could eat afterwards.

interrogative (for questions, requests, etc):

Is your sister here? Could you show me how?

imperative (for commands, instructions, etc):

Hold this! Take the second left.

exclamative (for exclamations):

How peaceful she looks. What a pity!

In writing, we mark sentences by using a capital letter at the beginning, and a full stop (or question mark or exclamation mark) at the end.

shape poem

a poem in which the layout of the words reflects an aspect of the subject. There is a huge variety of shape poems.

see **calligrams, concrete poems**

shared reading

in shared reading the teacher, as an expert reader, models the reading process by reading the text to the learners. The text chosen may be at a level which would be too difficult for the readers to read independently. The teacher demonstrates use of cues and strategies such as syntax, initial letter, re-reading. Learners have opportunities to join in with the reading, singly or chorally, and are later encouraged to re-read part or all of the text.

shared writing

a classroom process where the teacher models the writing process for children: free from the physical difficulties of writing, children can observe, and subsequently be involved in, planning, composition, redrafting, editing and publishing through the medium of the teacher. Shared writing is interactive in nature and is appropriate for teaching all forms and genres.

simile

the writer creates an image in readers' minds by comparing a subject to something else: *as happy as a lark; as strong as an ox*. Many similes are **idiomatic**: *he smokes like a chimney*.

singular and plural

Singular forms are used to refer to one thing, person etc. For example: *tree, student, party*.

Many nouns (countable nouns) can be **singular** (only one) or **plural** (more than one). The plural is usually marked by the ending -*s*: *tree*s, *student*s, *partie*s.

Some plural forms are irregular. For example: *children, teeth, mice*.

Other nouns (mass nouns) do not normally occur in the plural. For example: *butter, cotton, electricity, money, happiness*.

Verbs, **pronouns**, and **determiners** sometimes have different singular and plural forms:

> *He was late*   *They were late*
> *Where is the key? Have you seen it?*   *Where are the keys? Have you seen them?*
> *Do you like this hat?*   *Do you like these shoes?*

Note that *they/them/their* (plural words) are sometimes used to refer back to singular words that don't designate a specific person, such as *anyone* or *somebody*. In such cases, *they* usually means 'he or she':

> *If anyone wants to ask a question, they can ask me later.* (= he or she can ask me)
> *Did everybody do their homework?*
> *Work with a partner. Ask them their name.*

See also **agreement, pronoun**

skim

read to get an initial overview of the subject matter and main ideas of a passage.

slang

words and phrases which are used in informal context, often linked with certain regions or used by people identifying with particular groups. May differentiate that group from others.

sonnet

a poem of 14 lines. May follow any rhyme scheme. Two examples of rhyme schemes:

    a. Petrarchan rhyme: *a b b a a b b a* followed by two or three other rhymes in remaining six lines;
    b. Elizabethan rhyme: *a b a b c d c d e f e f g g*

speech, speech marks

see **direct speech** and **indirect speech**

spelling log

a personal, ongoing record of words which are being learnt. Pupils would decide, with the teacher's guidance, words to be learnt. These words would be kept in a folder so the pupil can work on them during the week with a partner or teacher, or at home. Once learnt, the words can be added to the pupil's record.

standard English

Standard English is the variety of English used in public communication, particularly in writing. It is the form taught in schools and used by educated speakers. It is not limited to a particular region and can be spoken with any accent.

There are differences in vocabulary and grammar between standard English and other varieties. For example, *we were robbed* and *look at those trees* are standard English; *we was robbed* and *look at them trees* are non-standard.

To communicate effectively in a range of situations - written and oral - it is necessary to be able to use standard English, and to recognise when it is appropriate to use it in preference to any other variety.

Note that standard British English is not the only standard variety; other English-speaking countries, such as the United States and Australia, have their own standard forms.

see also **agreement**, **dialect**, **double negative**

stanza

a verse or set of lines of poetry, the pattern of which is repeated throughout the poem.

story board

a plan for a visual text (video, film, etc) which demonstrates the plot and critical events through a sequence of pictures. Children may do a story board after reading to demonstrate comprehension; story-boarding may also be used to plan a piece of writing.

subject and object

In the sentence *John kicked the ball*, the subject is *'John'*, and the object is *'the ball'*.

The subject is the person or thing about which something is said. In sentences with a subject and an object, the subject typically carries out an action, while the object is the person or thing affected by the action. In declarative sentences (statements), the subject normally goes before the verb; the object goes after the verb.

Some verbs (eg *give*, *show*, *buy*) can have two objects, indirect and direct. For example:

She gave the man some money.

Here, *'some money'* is the direct object (= what she gave). *'The man'* is the indirect object (= the person who receives the direct object).

When a verb has an object, it is transitive, eg <u>find</u> a job, <u>like</u> chocolate, <u>lay</u> the table. If it has no object, it is intransitive (eg *go, talk, lie*).

see also **active** and **passive, complement**

suffix

A suffix is a **morpheme** which is added to the end of a word. There are two main categories:
  a. An **inflectional** suffix changes the tense or grammatical status of a word, eg from present to past *(work<u>ed</u>)* or from singular to plural *(accident<u>s</u>)*.
  b. A **derivational** suffix changes the word class, eg from verb to noun *(work<u>er</u>)* or from noun to adjective *(accident<u>al</u>)*.

syllable

Each beat in a word is a syllable. Words with only one beat *(cat, fright, jail)* are called **monosyllabic**; words with more than one beat *(super, coward, superficiality)* are **polysyllabic**.

synonym

words which have the same meaning as another word, or very similar: *wet/damp.* Avoids overuse of any word; adds variety.

synopsis

a brief summary or outline of a paragraph, chapter or book.

syntax

Syntax is the study of **sentence** structure, ie how words are used together in a sentence.

tanka

Japanese poem based on the **haiku** but with two additional lines giving a complete picture of an event or mood. Traditionally, when a member of the Japanese court wrote a haiku for a friend, the receiver would add two lines and return it, giving a total of five lines with 31 syllables in the pattern *5 7 5 7 7.*

tautology

use of an extra word in a phrase or sentence which unnecessarily repeats an idea: *this <u>annual</u> event is staged <u>yearly</u>, this <u>unacceptably poor</u> work is of a <u>low standard</u>.*

tense

A tense is a verb form that most often indicates time. English verbs have two basic tenses, present and past, and each of these can be simple or continuous. For example:

present
I play (simple)
I am playing (continuous)

past
I played (simple)
I was playing (continuous)

Additionally, all these forms can be perfect (with *have*):

present perfect
I have played (perfect)
I have been playing (perfect continuous)

past perfect
I had played (perfect)
I had been playing (perfect continuous)

English has no specific future tense. Future time can be expressed in a number of ways using *will* or present tenses. For example:

John <u>will arrive</u> tomorrow.
John <u>will be arriving</u> tomorrow.
John <u>is going to arrive</u> tomorrow.
John <u>is arriving</u> tomorrow.
John <u>arrives</u> tomorrow.

see also **verb**

text

language organised to communicate. Includes written, spoken and electronic forms.

text type

this term describes texts which share a purpose: to inform/persuade/describe. Whole texts or parts of texts with specific features - patterns of language, structure, vocabulary - which help them achieve this purpose may be described as belonging to a particular text type. These attributes are not obligatory, but are useful in discussing text and in supporting development of a range of writing skills.

Texts may consist of mixed genres: for example, a guide-book may contain procedural text (the path or route) and report (information about exhibits).

theme

the subject of a piece of writing. This may not be explicitly stated, but can be deduced by the reader. For example, many traditional stories have similar themes: the triumph of good over evil, cunning over strength, kindness over beauty.

thesaurus

a reference text which groups words by meaning. A thesaurus can help writers to select words, consider the full range of alternatives and vary words which are used frequently: *said, went, nice.*

trigraph

three letters representing one phoneme: <u>*high*</u>; *fu<u>dge</u>*.

verb

A verb is a word that expresses an action, a happening, a process or a state. It can be thought of as a 'doing' or 'being' word. In the sentence *Mark is tired and wants to go to bed*, *'is'*, *'wants'* and *'go'* are verbs. Sometimes two or more words make up a verb phrase, such as *are going, didn't want, has been waiting*.

Most verbs (except modal verbs, such as *can* or *will*) have four or five different forms. For example:

base form or infinitive	+ -s	+ -ing (present participle)	simple past	past participle
wait	*waits*	*waiting*		*waited*
make	*makes*	*making*		*made*
drive	*drives*	*driving*	*drove*	*driven*

A verb can be present or past:

> *I wait/she waits* (present)
> *I waited/she waited* (past)

Most verbs can occur in simple or continuous forms (*be + -ing*):

> *I make* (simple present)/*I'm making* (present continuous)
> *she drove* (simple past)/*she was driving* (past continuous)

A verb can also be perfect (with *have*):

> *I have made/I have been making* (present perfect)
> *he had driven/he had been driving* (past perfect)

If a verb is regular, the simple past and the past participle are the same, and end in *-ed*. For example:

> *wanted*
> *played*
> *answered*

Verbs that do not follow this pattern are irregular. For example:

> *make/made*
> *catch/caught*
> *see/saw/seen*
> *come/came/come*

see also **active** and **passive**, **auxiliary verbs**, **infinitive**, **modal verbs**, **participle**, **person**, **tense**

voice

see **active and passive**

vowel

a phoneme produced without audible friction or closure. Every syllable contains a vowel. A vowel phoneme may be represented by one or more letters. These may be vowels (*m<u>ai</u>d*, or a combination of vowels and consonants (*st<u>ar</u>t*; *c<u>oul</u>d*).

word class

The main word classes are **verb**, **noun**, **adjective**, **adverb**, **pronoun**, **determiner**, **preposition** and **conjunction**. These are all dealt with separately in this glossary.

Note that a word can belong to more than one class. For example:

play	verb (*I play*) or noun (*a play*)
fit	noun (*a fit*), verb (*they fit*) or adjective (*I'm fit*)
until	preposition (*until Monday*) or conjunction (*until I come back*)
like	verb (*I like*) or preposition (*do it like this*)
hard	adjective (*it's hard work*) or adverb (*I work hard*)
that	determiner (*that book*) or pronoun (*who did that?*) or conjunction (*he said that he …*)

writing frame

a structured prompt to support writing. A writing frame often takes the form of opening phrases of paragraphs, and may include suggested vocabulary. It often provides a template for a particular text type.

Further reading

The Linguistics Association maintain a page of further information at
http://www.art.man.ac.uk/english/staff/dd/reading.htm

Grammatical subject index

Grammatical feature	Teaching units			
	Y3	Y4	Y5	Y6
Adjectives	10	26		44
Adverbs		23	39	44
Apostrophes		27		
Audience			35, 41	53
Capitalisation	4, 6, 12			
Commas	7, 19	24, 28	40	
Complex sentences	17	28	34, 40, 43	47
Compound sentences	17	28		
Conditionals				51
Conjunctions	17	32	34	47
Connectives	18			46
Direct speech	4, 16		36	
Exclamation marks	3			
Formal language			35	49
Full stops	6			
Grammatical agreement	14, 15	20		
Imperative			37	
Negatives		31		
Note taking	13			50
Nouns	7, 11		39	44
Paragraphing	8, 9	25, 28	38	52
Passive				45, 48
Pluralisation	11	30		
Preposition			42	44
Presentation	5			
Pronouns	15		39	
Punctuation			34, 41, 43	46
Purpose			35, 41	53
Question marks	3			
Questions		31		
Reported speech			36	
Simple sentences	6	20, 28		
Speech marks	4, 16		36	
Standard English			33	54
Subordinate clauses		28	34, 40, 43	
Verbs	1, 2, 7, 14	22, 30	37	